CONTENTS

A Brief History

In 1929, Rollin Turner deduced that ketone bodies were produced by the liver if one ate a low-carb, moderate-protein and high-fat diet. He was exploring the interrelationship between diabetics and diet plans, trying to figure out the ideal food plan that lowered insulin levels in the blood. Later, Dr. Russel Wilder introduced the world to ketogenic diet which was previously used to treat children with epilepsy.

How Does the Keto Diet Work?

The keto diet plan is actually based around one key fact: The body can derive a large amount of acetoacetate, acetone, β-hydroxybutyrate and other ketone bodies from a fat-rich diet. These ketones can then be used to harness energy. Usually, the largest component of our food is made of carbohydrates. These carbs, in turn, break down into glucose which is the main energy source for most of the cells in our body. But it so happens that increased levels of glucose in the bloodstream also elevate the blood insulin levels which can cause diabetes and weight gain. Therefore, the ketogenic diet is influential and gaining popularity over the years. Such a diet helps the body gain energy from lipids (commonly called fats) rather than carbohydrates. It can help reduce weight fast and has also been found to alleviate diabetes.

What is ketosis?

Consuming a diet replete with fats initiates a process within the healthy human body that, in biochemical terms, is called ketosis. Ketosis is a normal metabolic condition of the body in which the fats make up the greatest energy reserve. These fats are broken down into ketones and ketone bodies. Ketone bodies include acetone, acetoacetate (AcAc) and 3-beta-hydroxybutyrate (3HB). These acidic chemicals are efficient generators of energy and power for the cells. This method of obtaining energy is unconventional as it varies from the customary utilization of carbohydrates for energy.

A person can easily induce ketosis by consuming a high-fat, low-carb diet (the standard being between twenty and fifty grams of carbohydrates per day). When we eat meals that have minimum carbohydrates, the levels of sugar (and hence insulin) in the bloodstream go down and the body starts burning fat and releasing fatty acids in the blood. Most of these fatty acids find their way to the liver where they are oxidized and turned into ketones. Ketosis also occurs by itself during fasting, starvation, pregnancy, and infancy.

Other than rapid weight loss (as the fats are burned), there are uncountable advantages associated with initiating and maintaining ketosis within the body. This has led to the drift towards eating a ketogenic diet within the general population. Some of these merits are:

- Contrary to popular belief, ketones can cross the blood-brain barrier and provide energy to the cells in the brain.
- A ketogenic diet helps reduce seizures in epileptic patients, mainly young children who don't respond to conventional treatment. The diet has clear benefits for epileptic kids that fail to get better with drug therapy.
- A ketogenic diet is also linked to enhanced cardiovascular function. Reducing the

- intake of carbs sets ketosis into motion which reduces the risk of heart disease. chiefly HDL Cholesterol and atherosclerosis.
- The consumption of a fat-rich diet ameliorates the condition of most diabetics especially those suffering from Type II diabetes. It enhances insulin sensitivity and improves glycemic control. Research has even shown that taking the keto route when it comes to your dietary choices reduces your risk of getting diabetes even if you don't have it yet.
- Scientists have explored the effects of a ketogenic diet on patients of Alzheimer's and Parkinson's disease and the results are promising.
- Adopting a ketogenic diet is also considered a therapeutic approach in the treatment of cancer. The logic that doctors imply is that if one feeds on a lesser amount of sugar, the cancer cells may starve and ultimately wilt.

What are the symptoms of ketosis?

The ketogenic diet is a sought-after and popular plan for health enthusiasts. The main goal of a keto diet plan is to achieve ketosis. But how can you be sure that you have succeeded in inducing ketosis after you start eating low-carb meals? Here's how. Listed below are the indicators that your body is in a state of ketosis:

1. **Rapid weight loss**
   The visible sign of ketosis is a rapid and significant fall in body weight. When you are on low carbs and overall caloric intake is minimal, the body starts burning fat for energy. But you lose weight initially because the body releases the water held within the fat cells. As a result, the greatest decrease in body mass occurs within the first few weeks of a keto diet. As you continue down this path, the loss in your weight becomes steady and consistent.

2. **Thirst and dry mouth**
   Another indicator that your keto plan is working is an increase in thirst. You may feel thirstier than normal as the water is released from your fat cells. People have also complained of a dry mouth while on the keto diet. Dehydration can result from raised levels of ketones in the body. Electrolyte imbalance can also arise at the same time which can lead to complications.
   Furthermore, dehydration can also cause an increased incidence of kidney stones. This was illustrated in research conducted on athletes. While on a keto diet, make sure to stay well hydrated by drinking plenty of water and other drinks. It is also very important to consult a doctor if symptoms of dehydration (persistent dark-colored urine and extreme thirst) continue for a long time.

3. **Muscle cramps and spasms**
   Muscle cramps result because of electrolyte imbalance and dehydration. You feel a sudden painful contraction and a hard lump of muscle tissue beneath your skin. This is most common in the thighs and can last for hours to days.
   Electrolytes are responsible for the conduction of nerve impulses and flawless functioning of the skeletal muscles. If the ketogenic diet that you follow doesn't contain enough electrolytes (sodium, potassium, calcium, and magnesium mainly), then your body can't perform muscular activity efficiently. You should take precautions and make sure you are getting the requisite amount of electrolytes from your ketogenic routine.

4. **Bad breath**

   The most unpleasant sign of ketosis is bad breath, the fancy scientific term for which is halitosis. A lot of people who have achieved full ketosis report bad breath as the ultimate sign. It results because one of the ketones involved in ketosis has a fruity smell. The said ketone is acetone. It leaves the body via the urine and the oral respiratory route (mouth). You may have a bad breath mostly after you wake up. Having a foul smell emanating from your mouth can have a negative effect on your social interactions. You can easily solve this issue by chewing sugar-free gum or brushing your teeth multiple times during the day.

5. **Elevated levels of ketones in the bloodstream**

   In addition to ketones in your breath and urine, you would also have elevated levels of ketones in your blood. This corresponds with the high ratio of fats in your diet that degrades to give ketones. The blood sugar levels go down.

6. **Fatigue and weakness**

   People who follow a keto plan report feeling extremely tired in the starting days. This is called the "keto flu" or the "low carb flu." This is because your body is still getting used to the switch between carbs and fats. Also, carbs tend to spike your energy level. Fats don't provide the same burst of energy. But within weeks of your ketosis diet, you would feel energized and revitalized instead of exhausted. If you don't experience rejuvenation within a month, then it means you are making a critical mistake in your diet plan.

7. **Loss of appetite**

   Keto aficionados often report having a feeling of satiety despite eating low-calorie foods. This is credited to the body's use of fat stores to derive energy. Also, the level of Ghrelin (the hunger hormone) falls in the body. The person feels that he is full due to fluctuations in his hunger hormones. Some scientists also think that ketones themselves suppress the hunger-inducing mechanisms of the brain. The bottom line is if you feel your appetite is suppressed despite having small portions of food, it is a clear sign that your body is in ketosis.

8. **Increased brain function**

   Long-term followers of a keto diet report increased mental focus and cerebral function. This is because ketones are a powerful energy source for the brain cells and are even considered to be therapeutic for neurological illnesses such as Parkinson's. Lower levels of blood glucose also reset your brain and reduce brain fog.

Who should not follow a keto diet?

The ketogenic diet is not appropriate for the following people:

- **Diabetic patients**

  If you have diabetes, be it type I or type II, you must consult your physician before starting a keto routine. This diet may or may not be helpful for you which is exactly why you require medical supervision to experiment with this. It is not at all prudent to go keto if you are diabetic. However, if you have no other choice, it is wiser to follow a moderate keto diet rather than a strict one. Also, make sure that you keep a daily check on your blood sugar levels. In addition to blood glucose, you must also keep an eye on the level of ketones in the bloodstream. An elevated number of ketones in the blood can lead to diabetic ketoacidosis (DKA) and come in rare cases.

The acceptable range of blood ketones is less than 0.6mmol/L. The ADA (American Diabetes Association) recommends monitoring your ketone levels if your blood sugar surpasses 240mg/dL.

- **Patients of rare conditions such as muscular dystrophy**

  Several diseases may be aggravated if you change the internal energy-deriving mechanisms of the body all of a sudden. One such illness is Muscular Dystrophy and having gallstones. If you are on lifetime medication for asthma or arthritis, then going keto may further complicate and distress your internal systems.

- **Pregnant ladies especially those with gestational diabetes and nursing women**

  If you are an expecting woman then you must not try to sway your metabolism toward ketosis. This is because, during pregnancy, the bioenergetic mechanism of the body can naturally go into a state of ketosis. Therefore, it is better to avoid hurdles by not considering a keto diet. It is also considered inappropriate for nursing women or those suffering from gestational diabetes. It is not safe for a breastfeeding woman to switch to a keto diet as it may affect the nutrition of the baby. It is advisable to drink enough water in order to avoid dehydration for better milk production.

- **People who suffer from an eating disorder**

  If you already have an eating disorder such as bulimia nervosa, anorexia nervosa, binge eating disorder or pica, then you may attract further problems by going keto. Eating disorders are irregular eating habits that stem from hereditary causes or concerns about bodyweight. These are serious mental issues that must not be taken lightly. Therefore, consult your nutritionist before switching diets.

What are the basic constituents of a keto diet?

Anybody who is on a ketogenic diet has meals that are high in fats but low in carbs such as seafood and low-carb vegetables. These meals usually encompass four components:

- a low-carbohydrate fruit or vegetable
- fat such as butter, olive oil or coconut oil
- whipping cream
- a protein-rich item such as meat or fish

<u>Guidelines for Proper Implementation of the Ketogenic Diet</u>

After learning about the features and flaws of the ketogenic lifestyle, it is now up to you to decide whether it is the ideal diet plan for you. If you decide in the affirmative, then you need a well-structured and detailed plan for your meals and snacks. We will lay out the basic framework that you should keep in mind as you set out on this new path.

Introduce fat-rich edibles into your diet

Since the purpose of a KD is to supply the body with a surplus amount of fats, it is sensible to consume a great deal of them. Nutritionists recommend anywhere between 80-85% of fats. While on the keto diet, fats act as the constant fuel both for the body and the brain. They are broken down into fatty acids that are oxidized into ketones in the liver. The process is called Beta Oxidation. If you still feel hungry it means you need to augment your lipid intake.

Restriction of Carbohydrates

As we already know, half of the typical human diet is made up of carbohydrates. But in the KD, we manipulate the usage of macronutrients in such a manner that fats become the chief energy source. Fats constitute over 75% of the dietary intake in the keto diet. Therefore, a high-fat, low-carb regime restricts the daily use of carbs to 20-50 g.

Adequate intake of dietary fiber

It is notable, however, that dietary fiber must be taken in adequate amounts and is excluded from the digestible carbs. Dietary fiber is an essential part of the diet as it has a host of benefits. In addition to lowering blood pressure and inflammation, it maintains body weight and improves gut mobility.

Moderate consumption of proteins

A well-planned low-carb diet must have an average amount of protein. Mostly, it happens that people who eat a low-carb diet end up consuming a lot of lean meats. Consequently, their body starts converting this excess protein into amino acids and subsequently glucose. This process is termed as gluconeogenesis. Its drawback is that it prevents the body from going into full-fledged ketosis. This is a very common mistake and can be prevented by following the following ratios of macronutrients.

Macronutrient	Percentage(rough estimate)
Carbohydrates	<5% of total calories
Fats	85% of the total calories
Protein	0.8-1.2g/kg body weight or 10%of total calories

Micronutrients on a keto diet

The micronutrients that are most important for the bodily systems are sodium, potassium, magnesium, and calcium. Lowering the intake of carbohydrates can also diminish the consumption of micronutrient-rich nutriments (i.e. fruits and green vegetables). These ions act as electrolytes. Sodium is particularly involved in nerve impulse conduction and muscular contraction. It also regulates acid-base balance, water balance, extracellular fluid composition, and cell membrane potential. Potassium is the chief cation in the intracellular fluid. It maintains cell membrane potential across all cells of the body specifically the cardiomyocytes. Similarly, magnesium helps to conserve normal muscle and nerve function. It boosts the immune system and helps the bones stay strong. Calcium is involved in bone health and it controls dental health. The levels of these electrolytes can fall at the beginning of a keto routine due to their excretion in the urine. But as the body adapts and sets its pace within the keto diet, these deficiencies subside. The functions and food sources of these ions are provided below:

Electrolyte	Function	Food source
Sodium	nerve-muscle conduction and muscular contraction	Shrimp, cottage cheese, table salt, vegetable juice
Potassium	present in ICF maintains cell membrane potential	Nuts, avocados, dark green vegetables
Magnesium	Improved bone health, heart health, calcium absorption, and muscle contractions	Spinach, whole grain, cashew, almonds, dark chocolate, avocado, black beans, cultured yogurt
Calcium	activates oocytes, provides strength to teeth and bones, involved in blood clotting and nerve impulse transmission	Milk, cheese, tofu, soybeans, spinach, bread, cabbage, okra, sardines

Micronutrients also include vitamins in addition to minerals. These vitamins that are vital to life and must be incorporated into the KD are Vitamin D, Vitamin B Complex and Vitamin K.

Vitamin K

Vitamin K plays a significant role in blood clotting and bone metabolism. It produces prothrombin which is a protein needed for blood clotting. It also sustains normal levels of blood clotting. Vitamin K can be added in the diet by eating leafy vegetables such as kale, cabbage, broccoli, and spinach.

Vitamin D

This vitamin absorbs calcium and promotes the health of your bones. If Vitamin D becomes deficient, kids can get a disease called rickets that is characterized by fragile, malformed bones. In the case of adults, the condition is called Osteomalacia (softening of the bones and weakness of the joints). Food sources of this micronutrient include Cod liver oil, Salmon, Tuna, Sardines, margarine, orange juice, egg yolk, cereal, and milk. You should also catch some sunlight during the daytime as its rays are enriched with this vitamin.

Vitamin B Complex

This complex comprises all the B vitamins that perform a multitude of functions from antioxidation on one extreme to cellular signaling on the other. The complex is critical for DNA production, amino acid metabolism, and cell growth. It has many other functions as well that are reflective of its significance. Its sources are sunflower seeds, tuna, mushrooms, fish, chickpeas, yogurt, cheese, and leafy greens. You can also buy a supplement that combines all eight vitamins into one solid pill.

Kitchen Equipment You Will Need

A lot of people who are new to the world of the keto diet are unaware of the nitty-gritty involved in cooking and consuming low-carb foods. We throw some light on a few must-have kitchen utensils that you should own for your carb-free ride. Here we go!

Slow cooker

When you are cooking a natural, organic meal, you need to spend long hours in the kitchen. In today's haphazard and busy world, that is very tough to do. Therefore, it is wise to invest your money into a slow cooker that you can use without the fear of overheating or spoiling your food.

Hand Immersion Blender

You need this product to prepare cauliflower mash, low carb smoothies, and butter coffee. You can also make various cream soups and mayonnaise yourself. Making it a great addition to your keto journey, and because it is portable, you can easily carry it with you on vacation. Also, a stick blender is a must-have to grind and blend ingredients in a keto kitchen. These can be purchased on Amazon at a reasonable price.

Digital weighing scale

A scale is simply a balance to measure ingredients that would grace your dining table. It is crucial to measure the masses of all the ingredients and constituent items be it the course meal or a snack. Only then can we work out the calories we are taking and ensuring our energy requirements are being met. It is a sure way to confirm that we are taking the right quantities of macronutrients i.e. fats, carbs and protein.

Lunch box

Meals that fit the requirements of an ideal keto diet are largely unavailable in the market, so while going out with friends or embarking on a work trip, you must pack yourself some low-carb eatables. For this purpose, buy a high quality, durable lunch box on your next visit to the grocery store. Try to avoid buying a plastic one as it is a strong carcinogen. Maybe, with a little bit of hunting, you could find a stainless steel one.

Measuring cups and spoons

Because all the ingredients can't be quantified with a weighing scale, you would also need measuring cups and spoons making it easy to calculate liquids and other small food items. You don't have to measure all the food items but do try to be as accurate as possible for your own good. These cups, spoons and other related measuring utensils are a great investment as they would help you measure the serving sizes every time you are fixing a meal.

Silicone molds and bakeware

Using traditional tin molds for your baked items can be somewhat of a hurdle. This is because low-carb baked products are usually soft and may disintegrate when warm. It is a great idea to use the flexible silicone molds for these freshly baked, hot bakery items. These items are often made with nut flour or coconut flour that lacks gluten and increase their vulnerability to falling apart. The next time you bake a nut butter bomb, having silicone molds at hand will make it much easier.

Spiralizer

Surprisingly, a spiralizer can convert your vegetables into noodle-like helices and coils. This change is exciting and tasteful. It would bring a spice of change to your carb-free existence. You can buy either an electronic or a handheld spiralizer to rev up your culinary adventures.

Food processor

A food processor is an indispensable device in any lady's cooking quarters. It can chop your onions for you (no more teary-eyed mornings), knead your dough for you and peel off and slice vegetables for you. Just one instrument with many versatile functions. It really is a fundamental and central part of one's kitchen.

Good non-stick frying pan

Since the ketogenic diet really centers and builds on fat, we often find ourselves bent over a sizzling crepes dish or green curry. For this, don't be deceived by buying steel or some other frying pan as they will stick and burn and will eventually be disposed of. Make the healthy choice and get yourself a non-stick frying pan or skillet as soon as possible.

Waffle maker and a coffee maker

These efficient tools would make your kitchen experience so much smoother. You can make keto waffles using sugar and wheat and add a wholesome snack to your keto regime. The coffee maker is, of course, helpful in fixing yourself a nice cup of warm coffee when stressed.

In addition to the above-mentioned items, there is a vast range of kitchen utensils that can help you cook luscious and tasty keto meals. These include storage containers, food prep bowls, glass containers, egg cooker, mortar and pestle, knives of various sizes, cutting boards, baking mats and last but not the least, a keto-specific cookbook. The cookbook would have all the recipes for ketogenic dishes and guide your path with its well-balanced ingredients and tips.

Keto Diet-Food List

As a beginner, it may be hard to figure out what to eat and what to avoid. In order to successfully light the keto spark, make sure to feed on fat-rich fruits, vegetables, and bakery items. Some of these items are listed below:

Fat component

This is the largest part of our ketogenic diet. It constitutes three-fourths of our entire caloric intake. Most popular food items that fall under this category are:

- Natural fat sauces
- Meat
- Sunflower oil
- Safflower oil
- Butterfat
- Vegetables that grow above the ground
- Coconut fat
- Bearnaise sauce
- Olive oil
- Avocado oil
- Heavy cream
- Garlic butter
- Nuts and berries

High-fat dairy such as high-fat yogurt, cheese and butter can be ingested every now and then. **Regular milk is not recommended** because it has way too much sugar. An average glass of milk contains 18 g of carbs. If you really like milk, you can use it to flavor your coffee.

Dietitians also suggest a moderate intake of both nuts and berries. Nuts have a lot of lipids in addition to minerals. Always prefer macadamia or pecan nuts over cashews as the latter have a relatively higher concentration of carbs. You can add flavor to your berries with a whipping cream which is popular among keto aficionados.

Vegetables that grow above the ground are a good source of fat. They add more color and variety to your otherwise bland keto meals. Such vegetables are cabbage, avocado, Brussels sprouts, cucumber, cauliflower, zucchini, spinach, asparagus, celery, kale, broccoli, mint leaves, ivy leaves, and lettuce. You can sauté these veggies in olive oil or butter and pour them on your salad.

Protein portion

The protein part of a KD is provided by lean meat, eggs, fish and seafood. Try to get unprocessed and organic meats as fresh as possible. Grass-fed beef is a superb option. You can have dark meat chicken which is often carb. Avoid eating a surplus amount of protein because your body will turn it into glucose by a process called gluconeogenesis and you will not go into ketosis. So just devour your regular portion of protein. Also, steer clear of processed sausages, cold cuts and frozen meat as it carries added carbs. Basically, don't buy any processed meat that has over 5% carbs. If you can get your meat from freshly slaughtered, farm-raised animals then that is probably the best.

In the case of fish, the most common fish used in keto meals is salmon. It has high protein, low carbs and those very critical, must-have Omega 3 fatty acids. You can bake a salmon cake, have it with creamy dill sauce or simply stuff it inside an avocado. Tuna and cod are also great sources of fats. Cod liver oil is a great alternative. Prefer wild-caught fish over those that are commercially bred.

Eggs contain protein as well as TAGs. You can eat them as you like - boiled, scrambled or fried in butter. Some other edibles that will help you fulfill your requisite protein are:

- Skinless chicken breast
- Shrimp
- Bacon

Minimal carbohydrate component

On a keto diet, you must eat only foods that meet the very low requirement of carbs. These are the high-fat foods already mentioned. You can have a Lettuce wrapped Burger, a Chipotle salad or Buffalo wings. Always take coffee without sugar.

Drinks

You can have water, coffee (without sugar), tea and bone broth. Don't drink milk as it contains an unreasonably large quantity of carbs. Just add it to your coffee if you really wish to. Other low-carb options are already mentioned. Stay hydrated with clean mineral water, coffee, green, black, mint, herbal, Orange Pekoe and other types of teas. Bone broth is a delicious and satisfying drink that goes very well with your keto meals. It is also very easy to brew.

Fruits

Fruits are like God's gift to man. They stem and arise from flower buds. This is reasoning enough for you to relish their taste and succulent juices. Some foods that work best with the keto lifestyle are avocados, raspberries, strawberries, and blackberries. You can also add lemon to your salad dressings or simply make yourself a glass of lemonade.

Keto Diet-Foods That Hinder Ketosis

We have talked about the food items that stimulate ketosis. Let's talk about the food essentials that stop or slow down ketosis. Some of these items are listed below to help you avoid making any costly mistakes.

Carbs to avoid on a ketogenic diet

These are the high-carb items that you should avoid while on a keto diet:

- kidney beans
- yams
- sweet potatoes
- wheat
- rice
- oats
- barley
- Amarnath
- Sprouted Grains
- millet
- Lima beans
- green peas
- corn
- carrots
- raw sugar
- honey
- maple syrup
- cane sugar

Protein foods to avoid on a low-carb diet

- milk
- shredded cheese
- evaporated skim milk
- low-fat cream cheese
- hot dogs
- salami
- beef jerky
- smoked meat
- chicken nuggets
- fish sticks

Unhealthy oils

- Canola oil
- Sesame oil
- peanut oil
- grapeseed oil
- corn oil

Drinks to avoid on KD diet

- sweetened milk products
- diet sodas
- cocktails
- wines
- flavored liquors
- flavored milk such as Milo
- beers
- raw milk

Dietary experts also discourage the use of processed and packaged foods as much as possible. This may be fast food, margarine, candies, artificial sweeteners, ice cream, gluten, and soda.

What Essentials Do You Need to Stock a Keto Pantry?

No pantry is stocked within a week or two. It takes months to choose and buy polished cutlery, fresh vegetables, bakery goods, and exceptional, high-grade crockery. On the other hand, you may already have many of the items you need.

The three most important requirements to shine on a keto diet are:

- organic protein food
- fat-rich nutriment
- a keto snack for travel and workplace

If you are ready to take control of your dietary choices and have the perseverance to stick to a diet plan, you would need to stock your pantry. Here, we would enlist the essentials that your pantry must be equipped with. For ease of organization, we divide all must-have items into six broad categories:

- Vegetables and fruits
- Fats and oils
- Lean meats and fish
- Dairy products
- Keto snacks on-the-go
- Baking essentials for your ketogenic pantry

Vegetables and fruits

- cauliflower
- cabbage
- zucchini
- eggplants
- asparagus
- blueberries
- raspberries

Fats and oils

- Avocado oil
- Extra virgin olive oil
- Coconut oil
- Hazelnut oil
- walnut oil
- coconut butter

Lean meats and fish

- turkey
- ground beef
- lamb
- salmon
- cod
- clams
- oyster
- canned tuna

Dairy products

- almond milk
- cream cheese
- coffee and tea
- eggs
- Nut butter
- coconut butter

Keto snacks on-the-go

- grain-free granola bars
- Macadamia nuts
- Lily's dark chocolate
- Canned tuna
- Low-carb Salmon Patties
- Tomato paste
- Bearnaise sauce
- Mini frittatas
- Keto sushi rolls
- Cajun-style shrimp

Baking essentials for your ketogenic pantry

- coconut flour
- almond flour
- Psyllium Husk
- Shredded coconut
- oat fiber
- finely grated Parmesan

For crockery and other technological devices, see the utensil listed above.

Smoothies Recipes

Chocolate Peanut Butter Smoothie

Serves: 2/Prep Time: 5 mins

Ingredients

- ¼ cup creamy peanut butter
- 2 tablespoons cocoa powder
- 2 scoops stevia
- 1 cup heavy cream
- 1 cup almond milk, unsweetened

Directions

1. Put all the ingredients in a blender and blend until smooth.
2. Pour into two glasses and serve immediately.

Nutrition Amount per serving

Calories 429	Cholesterol 82mg 27%	Dietary Fiber 4.2g 15%
Total Fat 40.9g 52%	Sodium 262mg 11%	Total Sugars 3.2g
Saturated Fat 17.8g 89%	Total Carbs 12g 4%	Protein 10.9g

Keto Berry Smoothie

Serves: 4/Prep Time: 10 mins

Ingredients

- ¾ cup frozen strawberries
- ¾ cup spinach
- ¾ cup frozen blackberries
- 1½ cups coconut milk
- 1 cup heavy cream

Directions

1. Put all the ingredients in a blender and blend until smooth.
2. Pour into 4 glasses and serve instantly.

Nutrition Amount per serving

Calories 333	Cholesterol 41mg 14%	Dietary Fiber 4.1g 15%
Total Fat 32.7g 42%	Sodium 30mg 1%	Total Sugars 6.1g
Saturated Fat 25.9g 130%	Total Carbs 11.1g 4%	Protein 3.2g

Avocado Berry Smoothie

Serves: 3/Prep Time: 15 mins

Ingredients

- 1 teaspoon Erythritol
- 1½ cups coconut milk
- ¼ avocado
- 1 teaspoon almond butter
- ¼ cup blackberries

Directions

1. Put all the ingredients in a blender and blend until smooth.
2. Pour into 3 glasses and immediately serve.

Nutrition Amount per serving

Calories 348	Cholesterol 0mg 0%	Dietary Fiber 4.9g 18%
Total Fat 34.9g 45%	Sodium 19mg 1%	Total Sugars 4.9g
Saturated Fat 26.3g 131%	Total Carbs 11.6g 4%	Protein 4.4g

Vanilla Cinnamon Smoothie

Serves: 2/Prep Time: 10 mins
Ingredients
- 1 cup coconut milk
- ½ cup vanilla whey protein
- 1 cup water + few ice cubes
- 1 teaspoon cinnamon
- 2 tablespoons MCT oil

Directions
1. Pour all the ingredients in a blender and blend until smooth.
2. Pour into two glasses and immediately serve.

Nutrition Amount per serving

Calories 406	Cholesterol 10mg 3%	Dietary Fiber 3.3g 12%
Total Fat 43g 55%	Sodium 31mg 1%	Total Sugars 4.3g
Saturated Fat 39.6g 198%	Total Carbs 7.8g 3%	Protein 8.3g

Citrus Keto Green Smoothie

Serves: 4/Prep Time: 20 mins
Ingredients
- 2 scoops green tea powder
- 16 oz coconut milk
- 2 tablespoons MCT oil
- ¼ cup spinach
- 4 teaspoons orange zest

Directions
1. Put spinach with all other ingredients in a blender and blend until smooth.
2. Pour into 4 glasses and immediately serve.

Nutrition Amount per serving

Calories 315	Cholesterol 0mg 0%	Dietary Fiber 3.2g 12%
Total Fat 34g 44%	Sodium 19mg 1%	Total Sugars 3.8g
Saturated Fat 31g 155%	Total Carbs 6.9g 2%	Protein 3.2g

Ginger and Turmeric Smoothie

Serves: 1/Prep Time: 12 mins
Ingredients
- ¾ cup full-fat coconut milk
- ¼ teaspoon turmeric
- ¼ avocado
- ½ teaspoon ginger, freshly grated
- ½ teaspoon Erythritol

Directions
1. Put all the ingredients in a blender and blend until smooth.
2. Ladle out into a glass and immediately serve.

Nutrition Amount per serving

Calories 164	Cholesterol 0mg 0%	Dietary Fiber 3.5g 12%
Total Fat 14.9g 19%	Sodium 13mg 1%	Total Sugars 4.7g
Saturated Fat 9.4g 47%	Total Carbs 9.5g 3%	Protein 2.2g

Vanilla Coconut Keto Smoothie

Serves: 2/Prep Time: 10 mins
Ingredients
- 1½ cups full-fat organic coconut milk
- 4 scoops collagen protein
- ½ tablespoon vanilla essence
- 10 drops liquid coconut Stevia
- 8 ice cubes

Directions
1. Put all the ingredients in a blender and blend until smooth.
2. Pour into 2 glasses and serve immediately.

Nutrition Amount per serving

Calories 212	Cholesterol 0mg 0%	Dietary Fiber 0g 0%
Total Fat 8.3g 11%	Sodium 28mg 1%	Total Sugars 0.4g
Saturated Fat 8.3g 41%	Total Carbs 1.2g 0%	Protein 30.8g

Avocado Matcha Smoothie

Serves: 3/Prep Time: 15 mins
Ingredients
- 8 oz coconut milk
- ½ medium avocado
- 1 scoop Matcha powder
- 1 scoop vanilla whey protein
- 3 scoops Stevia

Directions
1. Put avocado with rest of the ingredients in a blender and blend until smooth.
2. Pour into 3 glasses and serve immediately.

Nutrition Amount per serving

Calories 399	Cholesterol 13mg 4%	Dietary Fiber 2.6g 9%
Total Fat 36.4g 47%	Sodium 45mg 2%	Total Sugars 0.5g
Saturated Fat 31g 155%	Total Carbs 5.9g 2%	Protein 11g

Cinnamon Dolce Latte Breakfast Smoothie

Serves: 1/Prep Time: 10 mins
Ingredients
- 6 ounces cold brewed coffee
- ½ cup unsweetened almond milk
- ½ tablespoon chia seeds
- 1 tablespoon MCT oil
- ½ teaspoon Ceylon cinnamon

Directions
1. Put all the ingredients in a blender and blend until smooth.
2. Pour into a glass and serve immediately.

Nutrition Amount per serving

Calories 173	Cholesterol 0mg 0%	Dietary Fiber 4.6g 16%
Total Fat 18.9g 24%	Sodium 95mg 4%	Total Sugars 0g
Saturated Fat 14.5g 72%	Total Carbs 6.1g 2%	Protein 2.4g

Acai Almond Butter Smoothie

Serves: 4/Prep Time: 10 mins
Ingredients
- 3 cups unsweetened almond milk
- 4 (100g) pack unsweetened acai puree
- 2 avocados
- 4 tablespoons almond butter
- 4 tablespoons matcha powder

Directions
1. Put all the ingredients in a blender and blend until smooth.
2. Pour into 4 glasses and serve instantly.

Nutrition Amount per serving

Calories 304	Cholesterol 0mg 0%	Dietary Fiber 8.7g 31%
Total Fat 26.4g 34%	Sodium 149mg 6%	Total Sugars 3g
Saturated Fat 4.5g 22%	Total Carbs 12.8g 5%	Protein 7.1g

Keto Iced Coffee Smoothie

Serves: 2/Prep Time: 5 mins
Ingredients
- ½ cup black coffee
- 1 cup almond milk, unsweetened
- 4 tablespoons coconut cream
- 1 scoop matcha green tea powder
- 1½ cups ice cubes

Directions
1. Put all the ingredients in a blender and blend until smooth.
2. Pour into 2 glasses and serve immediately.

Nutrition Amount per serving

Calories 91	Cholesterol 0mg 0%	Dietary Fiber 1.7g 6%
Total Fat 8.9g 11%	Sodium 96mg 4%	Total Sugars 1g
Saturated Fat 6.5g 32%	Total Carbs 2.7g 1%	Protein 1.8g

Chocolate Tahini Smoothie

Serves: 3/Prep Time: 10 mins
Ingredients
- ½ cup coconut cream
- 1 tablespoon tahini
- 3 tablespoons cocoa powder, unsweetened
- 10 drops Stevia
- 12 ounces water

Directions
1. Put all the ingredients in a blender and blend until smooth.
2. Pour into 3 glasses and instantly serve.

Nutrition Amount per serving

Calories 134	Cholesterol 0mg 0%	Dietary Fiber 3.1g 11%
Total Fat 13g 17%	Sodium 16mg 1%	Total Sugars 1.5g
Saturated Fat 9.3g 46%	Total Carbs 6.2g 2%	Protein 2.8g

Energizing Keto Sm

Serves: 1/Prep Time: 15 mins
Ingredients
- 1 tablespoon MCT Oil
- 1 cup unsweetened cashew milk
- 1 tablespoon almond butter

Directions
1. Put maca powder with all other ingredients in
2. Pour into a glass and immediately serve.

Nutrition Amount per serving

Calories 236	Cholesterol 0m
Total Fat 25g 32%	Sodium 161mg 7%
Saturated Fat 14.7g 74%	Total Carbs 6g 2%

Collagen Chocolate Smoothie

Serves: 2/Prep Time: 15 mins
Ingredients
- 1 scoop chocolate collagen
- ½ medium avocado
- 1 tablespoon chia seeds, soaked in 1 cup water for 15 minutes
- ¾ cup heavy whipping cream
- 1 tablespoon almond butter

Directions
1. Put all the ingredients in a blender and blend until smooth.
2. Pour into 2 glasses and serve immediately.

Nutrition Amount per serving

Calories 393	Cholesterol 65mg 22%	Dietary Fiber 7g 25%
Total Fat 32.7g 42%	Sodium 143mg 6%	Total Sugars 0.7g
Saturated Fat 13.1g 66%	Total Carbs 10.3g 4%	Protein 19.4g

Peanut Butter Strawberry Spinach Smoothie

Serves: 2/Prep Time: 12 mins
Ingredients
- 3 large frozen strawberries
- 10 oz unsweetened almond milk
- 1 scoop vanilla protein powder
- ¼ cup baby spinach
- 2 tablespoons creamy peanut butter

Directions
1. Put all the ingredients in a blender and blend until smooth.
2. Pour into 2 glasses and serve instantly.

Nutrition Amount per serving

Calories 176	Cholesterol 5mg 2%	Dietary Fiber 2.1g 8%
Total Fat 10.4g 13%	Sodium 209mg 9%	Total Sugars 3.3g
Saturated Fat 1.9g 9%	Total Carbs 7.5g 3%	Protein 16.4g

Keto Mint Chocolate Matcha Smoothie

Prep Time: 10 mins

- ...spoons coconut cream
- ...unsweetened almond milk
- ...teaspoon mint extract
- 1 scoop Matcha powder
- 1 tablespoon cacao nibs

Directions
1. Put coconut cream with all other ingredients in a blender and blend until smooth.
2. Pour into a glass and serve immediately.

Nutrition Amount per serving

Calories 225	Cholesterol 0mg 0%	Dietary Fiber 5.1g 18%
Total Fat 20.7g 26%	Sodium 187mg 8%	Total Sugars 1.6g
Saturated Fat 13.7g 68%	Total Carbs 7.6g 3%	Protein 4.3g

Strawberry Avocado Keto Smoothie

Serves: 6/Prep Time: 25 mins

Ingredients
- 2 cups almond milk, unsweetened
- ½ pound frozen strawberries
- 1 avocado
- 2 cups ice cubes
- 1 tablespoon Erythritol

Directions
1. Put strawberries with all other ingredients in a blender and blend until smooth.
2. Pour into 6 glasses and immediately serve.

Nutrition Amount per serving

Calories 265	Cholesterol 0mg 0%	Dietary Fiber 4.8g 17%
Total Fat 25.6g 33%	Sodium 14mg 1%	Total Sugars 7.6g
Saturated Fat 18.3g 91%	Total Carbs 13.1g 5%	Protein 2.5g

Chocolate Fat Bomb Smoothie

Serves: 2/Prep Time: 10 mins

Ingredients
- 1 scoop chocolate collagen
- ½ cup avocado, frozen pieces
- 1 tablespoon cacao powder
- 1 cup Ice
- 1 cup almond milk

Directions
1. Put all the ingredients in a blender and blend until smooth.
2. Pour into 2 glasses and serve immediately.

Nutrition Amount per serving

Calories 413	Cholesterol 4mg 1%	Dietary Fiber 7.7g 28%
Total Fat 35.1g 45%	Sodium 141mg 6%	Total Sugars 5.4g
Saturated Fat 27g 135%	Total Carbs 13.5g 5%	Protein 19.5g

Low Carb Ginger Smoothie

Serves:2/Prep Time: 10 mins
Ingredients
- 2/3 cup water
- 2 teaspoons fresh ginger, grated
- ½ cup coconut milk, full-fat and organic
- 2 tablespoons lime juice
- 1 oz. frozen spinach

Directions
1. Put all the ingredients in a blender and blend until smooth.
2. Pour into 2 glasses and serve immediately.

Nutrition Amount per serving

Calories 149	Cholesterol 0mg 0%	Dietary Fiber 1.9g 7%
Total Fat 14.5g 19%	Sodium 23mg 1%	Total Sugars 2.2g
Saturated Fat 12.7g 64%	Total Carbs 5.5g 2%	Protein 2g

Cucumber Green Tea Detox Smoothie

Serves: 4/Prep Time: 5 mins
Ingredients
- 4 teaspoons Matcha green tea powder
- 2 teaspoons lemon liquid Stevia
- 16 ounces water
- 2 cups cucumber, sliced
- 4 ounces ripe avocado

Directions
1. Put cucumber with all other ingredients in a blender and blend until smooth.
2. Pour into 4 glasses and serve immediately.

Nutrition Amount per serving

Calories 72	Cholesterol 0mg 0%	Dietary Fiber 4.2g 15%
Total Fat 5.6g 7%	Sodium 3mg 0%	Total Sugars 1g
Saturated Fat 1.2g 6%	Total Carbs 4.3g 2%	Protein 2.9g

Blueberry Coconut Chia Smoothie

Serves: 3/Prep Time: 10 mins
Ingredients
- 1 cup coconut cream
- 2 scoops Stevia
- ½ cup frozen blueberries
- 1 cup unsweetened cashew milk
- 2 tablespoons ground chia seeds

Directions
1. Put all the ingredients in a blender and blend until smooth.
2. Pour into 3 glasses and immediately serve.

Nutrition Amount per serving

Calories 219	Cholesterol 0mg 0%	Dietary Fiber 3.4g 12%
Total Fat 20.7g 27%	Sodium 66mg 3%	Total Sugars 5.1g
Saturated Fat 17g 85%	Total Carbs 9.4g 3%	Protein 2.4g

Keto Flu Smoothie

Serves: 2/Prep Time: 10 mins
Ingredients
- ½ cup kale
- 50 grams avocado
- ½ cup cucumber
- 1 cup almond milk, unsweetened
- 1 scoop Stevia

Directions
1. Put all the ingredients in a blender and blend until smooth.
2. Pour into 2 glasses and immediately serve.

Nutrition Amount per serving

Calories 83	Cholesterol 0mg 0%	Dietary Fiber 2.6g 9%
Total Fat 6.7g 9%	Sodium 99mg 4%	Total Sugars 0.6g
Saturated Fat 1.2g 6%	Total Carbs 5.8g 2%	Protein 1.7g

Salted Caramel Keto Smoothie

Serves: 1/Prep Time: 5 mins
Ingredients
- 1 cup almond milk, unsweetened
- 1 bag salted caramel tea, steeped in 6 oz. water
- 2 tablespoons whipping cream
- ½ teaspoon Stevia
- 1 tablespoon MCT oil

Directions
1. Combine steeped salted caramel tea with the remaining ingredients in a blender.
2. Blend until smooth and pour into a glass to serve.

Nutrition Amount per serving

Calories 237	Cholesterol 33mg 11%	Dietary Fiber 1g 4%
Total Fat 26.9g 35%	Sodium 193mg 8%	Total Sugars 1.4g
Saturated Fat 20.3g 101%	Total Carbs 4.4g 2%	Protein 1.8g

Keto Milkshake Smoothie with Raspberries

Serves: 3/Prep Time: 12 mins
Ingredients
- 1 cup crushed ice
- 1 cup almond milk, unsweetened
- ¼ cup heavy whipping cream
- ½ ounce cream cheese
- ¼ cup fresh raspberries

Directions
1. Put the cream cheese in a small bowl and transfer into a microwave oven.
2. Microwave for about 5 seconds and transfer into a blender.
3. Blend until smooth and pour into 3 glasses to serve.

Nutrition Amount per serving

Calories 240	Cholesterol 19mg 6%	Dietary Fiber 2.4g 9%
Total Fat 24.5g 31%	Sodium 30mg 1%	Total Sugars 3.1g
Saturated Fat 20.3g 101%	Total Carbs 6.1g 2%	Protein 2.5g

Coconut Milk Strawberry Smoothie

Serves: 3/Prep Time: 10 mins
Ingredients
- 1¼ cups unsweetened coconut milk
- ¾ cup strawberries, frozen
- 2 tablespoons smooth almond butter
- 1 cup ice cubes
- 2 packets Stevia

Directions
1. Put all the ingredients in a blender and blend until smooth.
2. Pour into 3 glasses and serve immediately.

Nutrition Amount per serving

Calories 305	Cholesterol 0mg 0%	Dietary Fiber 3.9g 14%
Total Fat 29.6g 38%	Sodium 15mg 1%	Total Sugars 5.8g
Saturated Fat 21.6g 108%	Total Carbs 11.6g 4%	Protein 4.5g

Vanilla Almond Keto Protein Smoothie

Serves: 3/Prep Time: 25 mins
Ingredients
- 2 tablespoons almond butter
- 1 cup frozen cauliflower
- 1 cup avocados
- 1 tablespoon Stevia
- 1 cup almond milk, full-fat and organic

Directions
1. Put all the ingredients in a blender and blend until smooth.
2. Pour into a glass and serve immediately.

Nutrition Amount per serving

Calories 202	Cholesterol 0mg 0%	Dietary Fiber 6.2g 22%
Total Fat 17.4g 22%	Sodium 16mg 1%	Total Sugars 3.1g
Saturated Fat 5.6g 28%	Total Carbs 10.1g 4%	Protein 5g

Keto Chow Shamrock Smoothie

Serves: 3/Prep Time: 10 mins
Ingredients
- 1 tablespoon fresh mint
- ¼ teaspoon vanilla extract
- ½ square 85% dark chocolate
- 1½ cups coconut milk, full-fat and organic
- 3 tablespoons whipped cream

Directions
1. Put all other ingredients along with dark chocolate in a blender and blend until smooth.
2. Pour into 3 glasses and serve immediately.

Nutrition Amount per serving

Calories 310	Cholesterol 2mg 1%	Dietary Fiber 3.2g 12%
Total Fat 31.4g 40%	Sodium 22mg 1%	Total Sugars 4.7g
Saturated Fat 27.1g 136%	Total Carbs 7.8g 3%	Protein 3.3g

Blackberry Coconut Yogurt Smoothie

Serves: 3/Prep Time: 10 mins
Ingredients
- 1 pot (120 ml) of coconut yogurt
- ½ cup blackberries
- 1½ cups coconut milk
- ½ teaspoon vanilla extract
- 1 scoop Stevia

Directions
1. Put all the ingredients in a blender and blend until smooth.
2. Pour into 3 glasses and serve instantly.

Nutrition Amount per serving

Calories 111	Cholesterol 0mg 0%	Dietary Fiber 1.3g 5%
Total Fat 7.2g 9%	Sodium 5mg 0%	Total Sugars 6.5g
Saturated Fat 6.5g 33%	Total Carbs 8.4g 3%	Protein 2.4g

Mocha Smoothie

Serves: 3/Prep Time: 15 mins
Ingredients
- 2 scoops Stevia
- 3 tablespoons cocoa powder, unsweetened
- 2 cups coconut milk
- 2 teaspoons instant coffee crystals
- 1 cup avocado, cut in half with pit removed

Directions
1. Put avocado with all other ingredients in a blender and blend until smooth.
2. Pour into 3 glasses and serve immediately.

Nutrition Amount per serving

Calories 185	Cholesterol 0mg 0%	Dietary Fiber 5.1g 18%
Total Fat 17.6g 23%	Sodium 11mg 0%	Total Sugars 0.3g
Saturated Fat 9.8g 49%	Total Carbs 7.8g 3%	Protein 2.7g

Chocolate and Chia Seeds Smoothie

Serves: 1/Prep Time: 10 mins
Ingredients
- ¼ cup coconut milk, full-fat and organic
- 2 tablespoons 100% cocoa dark chocolate
- 2 tablespoons chia seeds, soaked in 1 cup water
- 1/3 cup full-fat Greek yogurt
- 10 drops liquid Stevia

Directions
1. Put all the ingredients in a blender and blend until smooth.
2. Pour into a glass and immediately serve.

Nutrition Amount per serving

Calories 310	Cholesterol 10mg 3%	Dietary Fiber 5.8g 21%
Total Fat 25g 32%	Sodium 45mg 2%	Total Sugars 5.5g
Saturated Fat 15.9g 80%	Total Carbs 12.5g 5%	Protein 11.2g

Breakfast Recipes

Cheesy Ham Souffle

Serves: 4
Prep Time: 30 mins
Ingredients

- 1 cup cheddar cheese, shredded
- ½ cup heavy cream
- 6 large eggs
- 6 ounces ham, diced
- Salt and black pepper, to taste

Directions

1. Preheat the oven to 350°F and grease 4 ramekins gently.
2. Whisk together eggs in a medium bowl and add all other ingredients.
3. Mix well and pour the mixture into the ramekins.
4. Transfer into the ramekins and bake for about 18 minutes.
5. Remove from the oven and allow to slightly cool and serve.

Nutrition Amount per serving

Calories 342	Cholesterol 353mg 118%	Dietary Fiber 0.6g 2%
Total Fat 26g 33%	Sodium 841mg 37%	Total Sugars 0.8g
Saturated Fat 13g 65%	Total Carbs 3g 1%	Protein 23.8g

Browned Butter Pumpkin Latte

Serves: 2
Prep Time: 10 mins
Ingredients

- 2 shots espresso
- 2 tablespoons butter
- 2 scoops Stevia
- 2 cups hot almond milk
- 4 tablespoons pumpkin puree

Directions

1. Heat butter on low heat in a small pan and allow to lightly brown.
2. Brew two shots of espresso and stir in the Stevia.
3. Add browned butter along with pumpkin puree and hot almond milk.
4. Blend for about 10 seconds on high and pour into 2 cups to serve.

Nutrition Amount per serving

Calories 227	Cholesterol 31mg 10%	Dietary Fiber 0.9g 3%
Total Fat 22.6g 29%	Sodium 93mg 4%	Total Sugars 1g
Saturated Fat 18.3g 92%	Total Carbs 4.5g 2%	Protein 1.5g

Cauliflower Toast with Avocado

Serves: 2/Prep Time: 20 mins
Ingredients

- 1 large egg
- 1 small head cauliflower, grated
- 1 medium avocado, pitted and chopped
- ¾ cup mozzarella cheese, shredded
- Salt and black pepper, to taste

Directions
1. Preheat the oven to 420°F and line a baking sheet with parchment.
2. Place the cauliflower in a microwave safe bowl and microwave for about 7 minutes on high.
3. Spread on paper towels to drain after the cauliflower has completely cooled and press with a clean towel to remove excess moisture.
4. Put the cauliflower back in the bowl and stir in the mozzarella cheese and egg.
5. Season with salt and black pepper and stir until well combined.
6. Spoon the mixture onto the baking sheet in two rounded squares, as evenly as possible.
7. Bake for about 20 minutes until golden brown on the edges.
8. Mash the avocado with a pinch of salt and black pepper.
9. Spread the avocado onto the cauliflower toast and serve.

Nutrition Amount per serving

Calories 127	Cholesterol 99mg 33%	Dietary Fiber 4.8g 17%
Total Fat 7g 9%	Sodium 139mg 6%	Total Sugars 3.4g
Saturated Fat 2.4g 12%	Total Carbs 9.1g 3%	Protein 9.3g

Breakfast Cheesy Sausage

Serves: 1/Prep Time: 20 mins
Ingredients
- 1 pork sausage link, cut open and casing discarded
- Sea salt and black pepper, to taste
- ¼ teaspoon thyme
- ¼ teaspoon sage
- ½ cup mozzarella cheese, shredded

Directions
1. Mix sausage meat with thyme, sage, mozzarella cheese, sea salt and black pepper.
2. Shape the mixture into a patty and transfer to a hot pan.
3. Cook for about 5 minutes per side and dish out to serve.

Nutrition Amount per serving

Calories 91	Cholesterol 17mg 6%	Dietary Fiber 0.2g 1%
Total Fat 7.1g 9%	Sodium 218mg 9%	Total Sugars 0.2g
Saturated Fat 3g 15%	Total Carbs 1.1g 0%	Protein 6g

Keto Avocado Toast

Serves: 2/Prep Time: 20 mins
Ingredients
- 2 tablespoons sunflower oil
- ½ cup parmesan cheese, shredded
- 1 medium avocado, sliced
- Sea salt, to taste
- 4 slices cauliflower bread

Directions
1. Heat oil in a pan and cook cauliflower bread slices for about 2 minutes per side.
2. Season avocado with sea salt and place on the cauliflower bread.
3. Top with parmesan cheese and microwave for about 2 minutes.

Nutrition Amount per serving

Calories 141	Cholesterol 20mg 7%	Dietary Fiber 2.4g 9%
Total Fat 10g 13%	Sodium 385mg 17%	Total Sugars 0.7g
Saturated Fat 4.6g 23%	Total Carbs 4.5g 2%	Protein 10.6g

Cream Cheese and Chive Fold-Overs

Serves: 2/Prep Time: 15 mins

Ingredients

- 6 tablespoons cream cheese
- 1 teaspoon lemon juice
- 4 coconut flour tortillas
- 3 tablespoons fresh chives, chopped
- 4 teaspoons olive oil

Directions

1. Whisk cream cheese thoroughly in a bowl and stir in chives and lemon juice.
2. Spread the cream cheese mixture evenly over the tortillas and fold into half-moon shapes.
3. Heat quarter of oil over medium high heat in a skillet and add a tortilla.
4. Cook until browned on both sides and repeat with the remaining tortillas.
5. Serve warm.

Nutrition Amount per serving

Calories 158	Cholesterol 17mg 6%	Dietary Fiber 6.5g 23%
Total Fat 11.5g 15%	Sodium 45mg 2%	Total Sugars 0.1g
Saturated Fat 5g 25%	Total Carbs 11.2g 4%	Protein 3.4g

Chocolate Chip Waffles

Serves: 2/Prep Time: 30 mins

Ingredients

- 2 scoops vanilla protein powder
- 1 pinch pink Himalayan sea salt
- 50 grams sugar free chocolate chips
- 2 large eggs, separated
- 2 tablespoons butter, melted

Directions

1. Mix together egg yolks, vanilla protein powder and butter in a bowl.
2. Whisk together egg whites thoroughly in another bowl and transfer to the egg yolks mixture.
3. Add the sugar free chocolate chips and a pinch of pink salt.
4. Transfer this mixture in the waffle maker and cook according to manufacturer's instructions.

Nutrition Amount per serving

Calories 301	Cholesterol 229mg 76%	Dietary Fiber 1.3g 4%
Total Fat 18.8g 24%	Sodium 242mg 11%	Total Sugars 1.4g
Saturated Fat 9.7g 49%	Total Carbs 6.9g 3%	Protein 29.9g

Low Carb Cereal

Serves: 2/Prep Time: 25 mins

Ingredients

- 2 tablespoons flaxseeds
- ¼ cup almonds, slivered
- 1 tablespoon chia seeds
- 1½ cups almond milk, unsweetened
- 10 grams cocoa nibs

Directions

1. Mix together flaxseeds, almonds, chia seeds and cocoa nibs in a bowl.
2. Top with the almond milk and serve.

Nutrition Amount per serving

Calories 244	Cholesterol 0mg 0%	Dietary Fiber 6.5g 23%
Total Fat 20.6g 26%	Sodium 11mg 0%	Total Sugars 1.9g
Saturated Fat 10.4g 52%	Total Carbs 9.8g 4%	Protein 6.5g

Low Carb Detox Tea

Serves: 1/Prep Time: 10 mins
Ingredients
- 2 tablespoons apple cider vinegar
- 1 scoop Stevia
- 1 cup water
- 2 tablespoons lemon juice
- 1 teaspoon cinnamon

Directions
1. Boil water and add remaining ingredients.
2. Pour into a cup and serve hot.

Nutrition Amount per serving

Calories 19	Cholesterol 0mg 0%	Dietary Fiber 1.3g 5%
Total Fat 0.3g 0%	Sodium 15mg 1%	Total Sugars 0.8g
Saturated Fat 0.3g 1%	Total Carbs 2.8g 1%	Protein 0.3g

Iced Matcha Latte

Serves: 1/Prep Time: 10 mins
Ingredients
- 1 tablespoon coconut oil
- 1 cup unsweetened cashew milk
- 1 teaspoon matcha powder
- 2 ice cubes
- 1/8 teaspoon vanilla bean

Directions
1. Mix together all the ingredients in a blender and blend until smooth.
2. Pour into a glass to serve.

Nutrition Amount per serving

Calories 161	Cholesterol 3mg 1%	Dietary Fiber 2g 7%
Total Fat 16g 21%	Sodium 166mg 7%	Total Sugars 1.4g
Saturated Fat 12g 60%	Total Carbs 2.9g 1%	Protein 2.4g

Low Carb Strawberry Jam

Serves: 8/Prep Time: 1 hour 20 mins
Ingredients
- 1 tablespoon organic lemon juice
- 1 cup fresh organic strawberries, chopped
- ½ tablespoon grass fed gelatin
- 1 teaspoon Xylitol
- 1 tablespoon gelatin, dissolved in 1 tablespoon water

Directions
1. Put strawberries in a small saucepan over medium heat and add lemon juice and Xylitol.
2. Mix well and cook for about 15 minutes, stirring occasionally.
3. Mash the strawberries with a fork and stir in the gelatin mixture.
4. Remove from heat and pour into a mason jar.

5. Allow to cool and refrigerate for 1 hour until jelly-like.

Nutrition Amount per serving

Calories 8	Cholesterol 0mg 0%	Dietary Fiber 0.4g 1%
Total Fat 0.1g 0%	Sodium 2mg 0%	Total Sugars 0.9g
Saturated Fat 0g 0%	Total Carbs 1.5g 1%	Protein 0.5g

Keto Iced Matcha Latte

Serves: 1/Prep Time: 10 mins

Ingredients
- 1 teaspoon matcha powder, high quality
- 1 cup water
- ½ tablespoon coconut oil
- ½ teaspoon Stevia powder
- 1 cup organic coconut milk, frozen into ice cubes

Directions
1. Put all the ingredients except collagen powder in a high powered blender.
2. Pulse until completely smooth and pour into a glass to serve.

Nutrition Amount per serving

Calories 175	Cholesterol 0mg 0%	Dietary Fiber 2g 7%
Total Fat 17.8g 23%	Sodium 10mg 0%	Total Sugars 0g
Saturated Fat 16.9g 84%	Total Carbs 1g 0%	Protein 3g

Keto Breakfast Wrap

Serves: 1/Prep Time: 20 mins

Ingredients
- 1 organic nori sheet
- 1½ avocado, sliced
- 3 pastured eggs
- ¼ teaspoon salt
- ½ tablespoon butter

Directions
1. Whisk eggs and salt in a bowl until combined.
2. Heat butter on medium heat in a frying pan and stir in whisked eggs.
3. Cook for about 3 minutes on both sides and dish out.
4. Place the omelet on top of the nori sheet and top with avocado slices.
5. Roll up the breakfast wrap and slice in half to serve.

Nutrition Amount per serving

Calories 476	Cholesterol 660mg 220%	Dietary Fiber 7.7g 28%
Total Fat 38.8g 50%	Sodium 788mg 34%	Total Sugars 0.5g
Saturated Fat 12.2g 61%	Total Carbs 11.7g 4%	Protein 21g

Egg Crepes with Avocados

Serves: 2/Prep Time: 15 mins

Ingredients
- 4 eggs
- ¾ avocado, thinly sliced
- 2 teaspoons olive oil
- ½ cup alfalfa sprouts
- 4 slices turkey breast cold cuts, shredded

Directions

1. Heat olive oil over medium heat in a pan and crack in the eggs.
2. Spread the eggs lightly with the spatula and cook for about 3 minutes on both sides.
3. Dish out the egg crepe and top with turkey breast, alfalfa sprouts and avocado.
4. Roll up tightly and serve warm.

Nutrition Amount per serving

Calories 372	Cholesterol 364mg 121%	Dietary Fiber 4.4g 16%
Total Fat 25.9g 33%	Sodium 1000mg 43%	Total Sugars 4g
Saturated Fat 6g 30%	Total Carbs 9.3g 3%	Protein 27.2g

Breakfast Bacon Muffins

Serves: 6/Prep Time: 30 mins

Ingredients

- 1 cup bacon bits
- 3 cups almond flour, organic
- ½ cup ghee, melted
- 1 teaspoon baking soda
- 4 eggs

Directions

1. Preheat the oven to 350°F and line muffin tins with muffin liners.
2. Melt ghee in a bowl and stir in the almond flour and baking soda.
3. Mix well and add the bacon bits and eggs.
4. Divide the mixture into the muffin tins and transfer into the oven.
5. Bake for about 20 minutes and remove from the oven to serve.

Nutrition Amount per serving

Calories 485	Cholesterol 156mg 52%	Dietary Fiber 2.6g 9%
Total Fat 49.8g 64%	Sodium 343mg 15%	Total Sugars 4.2g
Saturated Fat 37.3g 186%	Total Carbs 6.9g 3%	Protein 7.7g

Keto Non-Oatmeal Breakfast

Serves: 2/Prep Time: 25 mins

Ingredients

- 1 cup organic coconut milk, full-fat
- 1 cup cauliflower, riced
- 1/3 cup fresh organic raspberries
- 3 drops liquid Stevia
- 3 tablespoons unsweetened coconut, shredded

Directions

1. Mix together cauliflower and coconut milk and pour in a pot.
2. Cook over medium heat until cauliflower warms up and add raspberries.
3. Mash the raspberries and stir in coconut and Stevia.
4. Cover the lid and cook for about 10 minutes.
5. Dish into a bowl and serve warm.

Nutrition Amount per serving

Calories 326	Cholesterol 0mg 0%	Dietary Fiber 5.9g 21%
Total Fat 31.3g 40%	Sodium 35mg 2%	Total Sugars 6.6g
Saturated Fat 27.6g 138%	Total Carbs 12.9g 5%	Protein 4.3g

Spaghetti Squash Hash Browns

Serves: 3/Prep Time: 25 mins
Ingredients
- Sea salt and black pepper, to taste
- 1½ cups spaghetti squash
- 3 tablespoons avocado oil, for frying
- ½ cup sour cream
- ½ cup green onions

Directions
1. Season the spaghetti squash with sea salt and black pepper.
2. Add green onions and sour cream and form into patties.
3. Heat avocado oil in a skillet over medium heat and add patties.
4. Fry until golden brown from both sides and dish out to serve.

Nutrition Amount per serving

Calories 122	Cholesterol 17mg 6%	Dietary Fiber 1g 4%
Total Fat 10.1g 13%	Sodium 32mg 1%	Total Sugars 0.5g
Saturated Fat 5.4g 27%	Total Carbs 7.1g 3%	Protein 2g

Mini Bacon Guacamole Cups

Serves: 4/Prep Time: 40 mins
Ingredients
- 1 ripe avocado
- 9 bacon slices, 6 slices halved, and 3 slices quartered
- 2 tablespoons onion, minced
- Kosher salt and black pepper, to taste
- 1 small jalapeno, seeded and minced

Directions
1. Preheat the oven to 400°F and turn 4 mini-muffin pans upside down on a baking sheet.
2. Spray the tops of the overturned muffin tins and place the quarter of the slice on top.
3. Wrap the sides of the mini-muffin pans with the longer portions of bacon and secure with a toothpick.
4. Bake for about 25 minutes and remove carefully from the mini muffin cups.
5. Meanwhile, mash avocado with a fork in a medium bowl and stir in the jalapeno, onions, salt and black pepper.
6. Put the guacamole in the bacon cups and serve warm.

Nutrition Amount per serving

Calories 337	Cholesterol 47mg 16%	Dietary Fiber 3.6g 13%
Total Fat 27.7g 36%	Sodium 991mg 43%	Total Sugars 0.6g
Saturated Fat 7.9g 40%	Total Carbs 5.6g 2%	Protein 16.9g

Coconut Macadamia Bars

Serves: 6/Prep Time: 10 mins
Ingredients
- ¼ cup coconut oil
- 10 drops Stevia drops
- 60 grams macadamia nuts, crushed
- ½ cup almond butter
- 6 tablespoons unsweetened coconut, shredded

Directions
1. Mix together coconut oil, almond butter and coconut in a bowl.
2. Stir in Stevia and macadamia nuts and mix well.

3. Pour this mixture into a baking dish and refrigerate overnight.
4. Slice and serve chilled.

Nutrition Amount per serving

Calories 176	Cholesterol 0mg 0%	Dietary Fiber 1.4g 5%
Total Fat 19.1g 24%	Sodium 2mg 0%	Total Sugars 0.8g
Saturated Fat 10.6g 53%	Total Carbs 2.4g 1%	Protein 1.2g

Fried Radish, Bacon and Cauliflower Hash Browns

Serves: 4/Prep Time: 30 mins
Ingredients
- 3 cups cauliflower, riced
- 1 pound radishes, shredded
- Paprika, sea salt and black pepper, to taste
- 6 strips bacon, cooked crisp and crumbled
- 3 tablespoons olive oil

Directions
1. Mix together cauliflower, radishes, paprika, sea salt and black pepper in a large bowl.
2. Heat olive oil over medium high heat in a large skillet and pour the mixture in a thin even layer.
3. Add bacon strips and fry for about 20 minutes, stirring and flipping occasionally.
4. Dish out and season with more sea salt and black pepper to serve.

Nutrition Amount per serving

Calories 281	Cholesterol 31mg 10%	Dietary Fiber 3.7g 13%
Total Fat 22.6g 29%	Sodium 725mg 32%	Total Sugars 3.9g
Saturated Fat 5.5g 27%	Total Carbs 8.3g 3%	Protein 12.8g

Cinnamon Bun Fat Bomb Bars

Serves: 2/Prep Time: 30 mins
Ingredients
- ¼ teaspoon ground cinnamon
- 1 cup creamed coconut, cut into chunks
- ½ teaspoon ground cinnamon
- 1 tablespoon extra-virgin coconut oil
- 1½ tablespoons almond butter

Directions
1. Line 2 muffin pans with liners and keep aside.
2. Meanwhile, mix together creamed coconut and ground cinnamon in a bowl.
3. Pour this mixture into the muffin pans.
4. Whisk together coconut oil, almond butter and cinnamon in another bowl.
5. Divide this icing mixture into the muffin pans and place in the freezer for about 10 minutes.
6. Remove from the freezer after 5 minutes and serve.

Nutrition Amount per serving

Calories 410	Cholesterol 0mg 0%	Dietary Fiber 4.3g 15%
Total Fat 42.2g 54%	Sodium 19mg 1%	Total Sugars 4.6g
Saturated Fat 31.8g 159%	Total Carbs 9.6g 3%	Protein 5.3g

Keto Zucchini Breakfast Hash

Serves: 2/Prep Time: 30 mins
Ingredients
- 1 medium zucchini, diced
- 2 bacon slices
- 1 tablespoon ghee
- ¼ teaspoon pink Himalayan salt
- 1 large egg, fried

Directions
1. Heat ghee in a pan over medium heat and add bacon.
2. Cook for about 3 minutes until lightly browned and stir in the zucchini and pink salt.
3. Cook for about 15 minutes and dish out in a plate.
4. Top with a fried egg and serve to enjoy.

Nutrition Amount per serving

Calories 210	Cholesterol 130mg 43%	Dietary Fiber 1.1g 4%
Total Fat 17g 22%	Sodium 864mg 38%	Total Sugars 1.9g
Saturated Fat 7.4g 37%	Total Carbs 3.7g 1%	

Bulletproof Breakfast Bowl

Serves: 2/Prep Time: 45 mins
Ingredients
- 2 Paleo sausages, precooked
- 2 pastured eggs, poached
- 1 cup cauliflower rice
- 2 handfuls organic leafy greens, lightly steamed
- 3 tablespoons grass fed ghee for cooking

Directions
1. Divide the leafy greens into 2 plates.
2. Heat ghee in a pan over medium heat and add cauliflower rice.
3. Cook for about 4 minutes and transfer it to the plates alongside the leafy greens.
4. Top with the poached eggs and keep aside.
5. Meanwhile, put the sausages to the same pan and cook until done.
6. Transfer the sausages to the plate and serve.

Nutrition Amount per serving

Calories 386	Cholesterol 302mg 101%	Dietary Fiber 2.5g 9%
Total Fat 31.3g 40%	Sodium 745mg 32%	Total Sugars 4.8g
Saturated Fat 16.8g 84%	Total Carbs 9g 3%	Protein 18.4g

Spaghetti Squash Patties with Avocado and Poached Egg

Serves: 4/Prep Time: 55 mins
Ingredients
- 1 medium spaghetti squash, seeds removed
- 1 pasture raised egg
- ½ avocado
- 1 tablespoon avocado oil
- 2 teaspoons sea salt

Directions
1. Preheat the oven to 320°F and cut the spaghetti squash into a circular shape with biscuit cutter.
2. Season the squash with sea salt and drizzle with avocado oil.
3. Transfer into the oven and bake for about 45 minutes.

4. Boil water and crack the egg in it.
5. Cook for about 3 minutes and remove the egg to a plate.
6. Remove the squash patties from the oven and transfer onto the plate.
7. Mash the avocado and place it alongside the squash and poached egg.

Nutrition Amount per serving

Calories 96	Cholesterol 54mg 18%	Dietary Fiber 1.3g 5%
Total Fat 8.5g 11%	Sodium 959mg 42%	Total Sugars 0.1g
Saturated Fat 1.7g 8%	Total Carbs 4.1g 1%	Protein 2.1g

Ham and Cheese Pockets

Serves: 2/Prep Time: 30 mins

Ingredients
- 1 oz cream cheese
- ¾ cup mozzarella cheese, shredded
- 4 tablespoons flax meal
- 3 oz provolone cheese slices
- 3 oz ham

Directions
1. Preheat the oven to 400°F and line a baking sheet with parchment paper.
2. Microwave mozzarella cheese and cream cheese for about 1 minute.
3. Stir in the flax meal and combine well to make the dough.
4. Roll the dough and add provolone cheese slices and ham.
5. Fold the dough like an envelope, seal it and poke some holes in it.
6. Place on the baking sheet and transfer into the oven.
7. Bake for about 20 minutes until golden brown and remove from the oven.
8. Allow it to cool and cut in half while still hot to serve.

Nutrition Amount per serving

Calories 361	Cholesterol 83mg 28%	Dietary Fiber 4.6g 16%
Total Fat 27.6g 35%	Sodium 835mg 36%	Total Sugars 0g
Saturated Fat 13.1g 65%	Total Carbs 7.9g 3%	Protein 24.8g

Tomato Parmesan Mini Quiches

Serves: 8/Prep Time: 35 mins

Ingredients
- 2½ cups Roma tomatoes, seeded and chopped
- 24 (4 inch) round ham, cooked and thinly sliced
- Salt and black pepper, to taste
- 6 eggs, lightly beaten
- 1½ cups parmesan cheese, finely shredded

Directions
1. Preheat the oven to 350°F and grease the muffin cups.
2. Place ham at the bottom of the muffin cups and top with tomatoes.
3. Pour beaten eggs over tomato and season with salt and black pepper.
4. Top with parmesan cheese and transfer into the oven.
5. Bake for about 20 minutes and then remove from the muffin cups.
6. Serve warm.

Nutrition Amount per serving

Calories 305	Cholesterol 213mg 71%	Dietary Fiber 0.7g 2%
Total Fat 10.9g 14%	Sodium 1624mg 71%	Total Sugars 7.7g
Saturated Fat 4g 20%	Total Carbs 9.2g 3%	Protein 41.4g

Avocado and Smoked Salmon Omelet

Serves: 2/Prep Time: 15 mins

Ingredients

- 4 large eggs
- 3 teaspoons extra virgin olive oil, divided
- 2 ounce smoked salmon
- Pinch of salt
- ½ avocado, sliced

Directions

1. Whisk together eggs and salt in a bowl.
2. Heat 2 teaspoons of oil over medium heat in a skillet and stir in the egg mixture.
3. Cook for about 2 minutes until the center is still a bit runny and the bottom is set.
4. Flip the omelet and cook for about 30 seconds.
5. Transfer to a plate and top with smoked salmon and avocado
6. Sprinkle with the remaining olive oil and serve.

Nutrition Amount per serving

Calories 339	Cholesterol 379mg 126%	Dietary Fiber 3.4g 12%
Total Fat 28g 36%	Sodium 865mg 38%	Total Sugars 1g
Saturated Fat 6.4g 32%	Total Carbs 5.1g 2%	Protein 18.7g

Cauliflower Bagels

Serves: 4/Prep Time: 45 mins

Ingredients

- ½ cup sharp cheddar cheese, shredded
- 6 cups cauliflower florets, finely chopped
- ½ cup mozzarella cheese, shredded
- 2½ teaspoons everything bagel seasoning
- 1 large egg, lightly beaten

Directions

1. Preheat the oven to 425°F and line a baking sheet with parchment paper.
2. Transfer the cauliflower to a microwave oven and microwave for about 3 minutes.
3. Allow it to cool slightly and transfer into a bowl.
4. Stir in the egg and sharp cheddar cheese until well combined.
5. Divide the mixture into 8 equal parts and transfer on the prepared baking sheet.
6. Flatten into 3½ inch circles and make a hole in the center of each circle with a 1 inch biscuit cutter.
7. Top with mozzarella cheese and sprinkle with bagel seasoning.
8. Bake for about 25 minutes until browned around the edges and serve warm.

Nutrition Amount per serving

Calories 125	Cholesterol 63mg 21%	Dietary Fiber 3.9g 14%
Total Fat 6.8g 9%	Sodium 172mg 7%	Total Sugars 3.8g
Saturated Fat 3.8g 19%	Total Carbs 9g 3%	Protein 9.2g

Banana Pancakes

Serves: 4/Prep Time: 25 mins
Ingredients
- 1 medium banana
- 2 large eggs
- 2 tablespoons butter
- 1 tablespoon sugar free maple syrup
- 4 tablespoons ricotta cheese

Directions
1. Put the banana and eggs in a blender and blend until smooth.
2. Heat ½ tablespoon of butter over medium heat in a large nonstick pan and pour 2 tablespoons of the batter.
3. Cook for about 2 minutes until bubbles appear on the surface.
4. Flip the pancakes gently with a spatula and cook for 2 more minutes.
5. Dish out the pancakes to a plate and repeat with the remaining batter.

Nutrition Amount per serving

Calories 147	Cholesterol 113mg 38%	Dietary Fiber 0.8g 3%
Total Fat 9.6g 12%	Sodium 96mg 4%	Total Sugars 6.8g
Saturated Fat 5.2g 26%	Total Carbs 11.1g 4%	Protein 5.3g

Clementine and Pistachio Ricotta

Serves: 1/Prep Time: 10 mins
Ingredients
- 2 teaspoons pistachios, chopped
- ⅓ cup ricotta
- 2 strawberries
- 1 tablespoon butter, melted
- 1 clementine, peeled and segmented

Directions
1. Put the ricotta into a serving bowl.
2. Top with clementine segments, strawberries, pistachios and butter to serve.

Nutrition Amount per serving

Calories 311	Cholesterol 71mg 24%	Dietary Fiber 1.2g 4%
Total Fat 25.1g 32%	Sodium 243mg 11%	Total Sugars 7.1g
Saturated Fat 15.1g 76%	Total Carbs 12.7g 5%	Protein 10.7g

Salads Recipes

Cottage Cheese with Berries and Nuts

Serves: 3/Prep Time: 10 mins
Ingredients
- ¼ cup blueberries
- ¾ cup cottage cheese
- ¼ cup blackberries
- 1 tablespoon almonds, chopped
- 1 tablespoon walnuts, chopped

Directions
1. Put the blueberries and blackberries in a bowl followed by cottage cheese.
2. Top with almonds and walnuts to serve.

Nutrition Amount per serving

Calories 90

Total Fat 3.7g 5%

Saturated Fat 0.9g 4%

Cholesterol 5mg 2%

Sodium 230mg 10%

Total Carbs 5.6g 2%

Dietary Fiber 1.4g 5%

Total Sugars 2.1g

Protein 9.1g

Keto Salami and Brie Cheese Salad

Serves: 4/Prep Time: 10 mins

Ingredients

- 6 oz. salami
- 2 oz. lettuce
- ¼ cup olive oil
- 7 oz. Brie cheese
- ½ cup macadamia nuts

Directions

1. Put Brie cheese, lettuce, salami and macadamia nuts in a plate.
2. Sprinkle with olive oil and immediately serve.

Nutrition Amount per serving

Calories 507

Total Fat 48.5g 62%

Saturated Fat 16.7g 83%

Cholesterol 80mg 27%

Sodium 798mg 35%

Total Carbs 3.8g 1%

Dietary Fiber 1.5g 5%

Total Sugars 1.8g

Protein 17g

Keto Turkey Salad

Serves: 5/Prep Time: 10 mins

Ingredients

- 6 oz. deli turkey
- 3 oz. cream cheese
- 2 avocados
- ¼ cup olive oil
- Salt and black pepper, to taste

Directions

1. Season the turkey with salt and black pepper.
2. Place the seasoned turkey on a plate and top with sliced avocados and cream cheese.
3. Drizzle with olive oil and serve immediately.

Nutrition Amount per serving

Calories 348

Total Fat 32.7g 42%

Saturated Fat 8.5g 43%

Cholesterol 37mg 12%

Sodium 463mg 20%

Total Carbs 10g 4%

Dietary Fiber 5.5g 20%

Total Sugars 1.8g

Protein 7.4g

Salad in a Jar

Serves: 2/Prep Time: 20 mins

Ingredients

- 1/6 oz. cherry tomatoes
- 4 oz. smoked salmon
- 1/6 oz. cucumber
- 4 tablespoons olive oil
- ½ scallion, chopped

Directions

1. Put cucumber, scallions and cherry tomatoes in a jar.
2. Top with smoked salmon and drizzle with olive oil to serve.

Nutrition Amount per serving

Calories 308

Total Fat 30.5g 39%

Saturated Fat 4.5g 23%

Cholesterol 13mg 4%

Sodium 1135mg 49%

Total Carbs 0.5g 0%

Dietary Fiber 0.1g 1%

Total Sugars 0.2g

Protein 10.5g

Tuna Salad with Capers

Serves: 4/Prep Time: 10 mins
Ingredients
- ½ cup mayonnaise
- 4 oz. tuna in olive oil, drained
- 2 tablespoons crème fraiche
- Salt, black pepper and chili flakes, to taste
- 1 tablespoon capers

Directions
1. Mix together tuna, capers, mayonnaise and crème fraiche in a bowl.
2. Season with salt, black pepper and chili flakes to serve.

Nutrition Amount per serving

Calories 375	Cholesterol 8mg 3%	Dietary Fiber 0.1g 0%
Total Fat 35.5g 46%	Sodium 273mg 12%	Total Sugars 1.9g
Saturated Fat 1.5g 7%	Total Carbs 7.1g 3%	Protein 7.6g

Roasted Fennel and Snow Pea Salad

Serves: 4/Prep Time: 35 mins
Ingredients
- 3 tablespoons olive oil
- 2 tablespoons pumpkin seeds, toasted
- 1 pound fresh fennel, cut into small wedges
- Sea salt and black pepper, to taste
- 5 1/3 oz. snow peas

Directions
1. Preheat the oven to 425°F and lightly grease a baking dish.
2. Arrange the fennel wedges in a baking dish and sprinkle with olive oil, sea salt and black pepper.
3. Transfer to the oven and bake for about 25 minutes until the fennel is golden in color.
4. Meanwhile, put the pumpkin seeds in a pan and toast for about 2 minutes over medium heat.
5. Mix the roasted fennel, snow peas and pumpkin seeds in a bowl and serve.

Nutrition Amount per serving

Calories 164	Cholesterol 0mg 0%	Dietary Fiber 4.8g 17%
Total Fat 12.8g 16%	Sodium 61mg 3%	Total Sugars 1.6g
Saturated Fat 1.9g 9%	Total Carbs 11.7g 4%	Protein 3.7g

Cauliflower Slaw

Serves: 5/Prep Time: 10 mins
Ingredients
- 1 cup sour cream
- 1 tablespoon Dijon mustard
- 1 pound cauliflower, chopped
- ½ cup mayonnaise
- Salt, black pepper and garlic powder

Directions
1. Season the cauliflower with salt, black pepper and garlic powder.
2. Place the seasoned turkey in a bowl and stir in sour cream, Dijon mustard and mayonnaise.
3. Mix well and immediately serve.

Nutrition Amount per serving

Calories 217	Cholesterol 26mg 9%	Dietary Fiber 2.4g 9%
Total Fat 17.7g 23%	Sodium 254mg 11%	Total Sugars 3.9g
Saturated Fat 7.2g 36%	Total Carbs 12.9g 5%	Protein 3.7g

Cottage Cheese with Bacon, Avocado and Hot Pepper Salad

Serves: 2/Prep Time: 15 mins

Ingredients

- 1 cup cottage cheese
- 2 bacon slices, crumbled
- 3 avocado slices
- Crushed red pepper, to taste
- 1 pinch salt

Directions

1. Put the bacon and avocado slices in a bowl followed by cottage cheese.
2. Season with salt and crushed red pepper to serve.

Nutrition Amount per serving

Calories 205	Cholesterol 30mg 10%	Dietary Fiber 0g 0%
Total Fat 10.1g 13%	Sodium 975mg 42%	Total Sugars 0.4g
Saturated Fat 4g 20%	Total Carbs 4.4g 2%	Protein 22.6g

Swedish Shrimp Dill Salad

Serves: 6/Prep Time: 10 mins

Ingredients

- 1 cup mayonnaise
- 10 oz. shrimp, peeled and cooked
- ¼ cup crème fraiche
- 2 tablespoons fresh dill
- Salt and black pepper, to taste

Directions

1. Mix together mayonnaise and crème fraiche in a bowl.
2. Stir in the shrimp and dill and season with salt and black pepper to serve.

Nutrition Amount per serving

Calories 232	Cholesterol 114mg 38%	Dietary Fiber 0.2g 1%
Total Fat 15.9g 20%	Sodium 401mg 17%	Total Sugars 2.5g
Saturated Fat 3.4g 17%	Total Carbs 11.1g 4%	Protein 11.6g

Spinach Salad

Serves: 8/Prep Time: 10 mins

Ingredients

- 4 oz. bacon, chopped
- 4 hardboiled eggs, chopped
- 2/3 cup parmesan cheese, finely grated
- 12 cups fresh spinach
- ½ cup olive oil

Directions

1. Divide the spinach into 8 salad plates evenly and add eggs and bacon.
2. Sprinkle with parmesan cheese and drizzle with olive oil to serve.

Nutrition Amount per serving

Calories 260	Cholesterol 105mg 35%	Dietary Fiber 1g 4%
Total Fat 23.1g 30%	Sodium 491mg 21%	Total Sugars 0.4g
Saturated Fat 6g 30%	Total Carbs 2.4g 1%	Protein 12.7g

Keto Chicken Salad

Serves: 6/Prep Time: 15 mins
Ingredients
- 6 thin cut slices bacon, baked
- 2 boneless chicken breasts, cooked
- 1 large avocado, sliced
- 2 tablespoons ranch dressing
- 4 cups mixed leafy greens

Directions
1. Put the leafy greens in a bowl and top with bacon, chicken breasts, avocado and ranch dressing.
2. Serve immediately.

Nutrition Amount per serving

Calories 285	Cholesterol 64mg 21%	Dietary Fiber 4.9g 18%
Total Fat 18.1g 23%	Sodium 644mg 28%	Total Sugars 1.6g
Saturated Fat 5g 25%	Total Carbs 6.1g 2%	Protein 24.5g

Chicken Pecan Salad

Serves: 6/Prep Time: 10 mins
Ingredients
- 3 ribs celery, diced
- 1½ pounds chicken breast, cooked
- ½ cup mayonnaise
- ¼ cup pecans, salted and chopped
- 2 teaspoons brown mustard

Directions
1. Toss the chicken with celery and pecans in a bowl.
2. Stir in the mayonnaise and brown mustard.
3. Transfer to refrigerator and serve chilled.

Nutrition Amount per serving

Calories 225	Cholesterol 78mg 26%	Dietary Fiber 0.6g 2%
Total Fat 11.1g 14%	Sodium 253mg 11%	Total Sugars 1.6g
Saturated Fat 1.1g 6%	Total Carbs 5.6g 2%	Protein 24.6g

/Turkey BLT Salad

Serves: 4/Prep Time: 20 mins
Ingredients
- 1 oz. salted butter
- 1 pound boneless turkey, shredded
- 10 oz. Romaine lettuce
- ½ tablespoon garlic powder
- ¾ cup mayonnaise

Directions
1. Mix together mayonnaise and garlic powder in a bowl.
2. Divide lettuce in 4 plates and top with shredded turkey, salted butter and garlic mayonnaise to serve.

Nutrition Amount per serving

Calories 330	Cholesterol 126mg 42%	Dietary Fiber 0.6g 2%
Total Fat 23.3g 30%	Sodium 428mg 19%	Total Sugars 2.9g
Saturated Fat 7g 35%	Total Carbs 6.6g 2%	Protein 24g

Sunflower Seed Salad

Serves: 6/Prep Time: 20 mins
Ingredients
- ½ cup low carb Greek yogurt
- ½ cup sunflower seeds
- Salt and black pepper, to taste
- 2 cups fish, cooked and shredded
- ½ cup celery, minced

Directions
1. Place fish in a bowl and season with salt and black pepper.
2. Toss in rest of the ingredients and serve to enjoy.

Nutrition Amount per serving

Calories 78	Cholesterol 8mg 3%	Dietary Fiber 0.6g 2%
Total Fat 4.8g 6%	Sodium 129mg 6%	Total Sugars 0.3g
Saturated Fat 0.8g 4%	Total Carbs 5g 2%	Protein 4.3g

Citrus Cheesy Brussels Sprout Salad

Serves: 8/Prep Time: 12 mins
Ingredients
- 1¼ cups walnuts
- 1¼ pounds Brussels sprouts
- ¼ cup EVOO
- 1¼ cups parmesan cheese, freshly grated
- 1 lemon, juiced

Directions
1. Put walnuts and Brussels sprouts in a food processor and process until chopped.
2. Transfer into a bowl and drizzle with EVOO and lemon juice.
3. Top with parmesan cheese and serve immediately.

Nutrition Amount per serving

Calories 225	Cholesterol 13mg 4%	Dietary Fiber 4.2g 15%
Total Fat 17.3g 22%	Sodium 183mg 8%	Total Sugars 1.9g
Saturated Fat 3.5g 18%	Total Carbs 9.7g 4%	Protein 12.9g

Caesar Dressing Beef Salad

Serves: 2/Prep Time: 10 mins
Ingredients
- 1 large avocado, cubed
- 2 cups beef, cooked and cubed
- ¾ cup cheddar cheese, shredded
- Salt and black pepper, to taste
- ¼ cup Caesar dressing

Directions
1. Put avocado and beef in a bowl and season with salt and black pepper.
2. Top with cheese and Caesar dressing and refrigerate to serve chilled.

Nutrition Amount per serving

Calories 279	Cholesterol 51mg 17%	Dietary Fiber 3.6g 13%
Total Fat 20.8g 27%	Sodium 283mg 12%	Total Sugars 3g
Saturated Fat 7.4g 37%	Total Carbs 8g 3%	Protein 16g

Cottage Cheese with Pineapple and Macadamia Nut Salad

Serves: 2/Prep Time: 25 mins
Ingredients
- ½ cup pineapples, diced
- ½ cup cottage cheese
- 1 tablespoon macadamia nuts, chopped
- Salt and black pepper, to taste
- ¼ cup heavy whipping cream

Directions
1. Put the pineapples and macadamia nuts in a bowl followed by cottage cheese.
2. Top with heavy whipping cream and season with salt and black pepper to serve.

Nutrition Amount per serving

Calories 153	Cholesterol 25mg 8%	Dietary Fiber 0.9g 3%
Total Fat 9.9g 13%	Sodium 236mg 10%	Total Sugars 4.5g
Saturated Fat 4.7g 23%	Total Carbs 8.5g 3%	Protein 8.6g

Keto Strawberry Spinach Salad

Serves: 4/Prep Time: 15 mins
Ingredients
- 200 g strawberries, sliced
- 200 g baby spinach
- 60 g pecans, lightly toasted and roughly chopped
- Salt and black pepper, to taste
- 40 g feta cheese

Directions
1. Mix together strawberries, baby spinach and pecans in a bowl.
2. Season with salt and black pepper and top with feta cheese to serve.

Nutrition Amount per serving

Calories 158	Cholesterol 9mg 3%	Dietary Fiber 3.7g 13%
Total Fat 13.2g 17%	Sodium 152mg 7%	Total Sugars 3.6g
Saturated Fat 2.6g 13%	Total Carbs 8.2g 3%	Protein 4.8g

Greek Keto Salad

Serves: 4/Prep Time: 10 mins
Ingredients
- ½ cucumber, diced
- 12 olives
- 4 medium tomatoes, chopped
- 140 g feta cheese, crumbled
- 1 small green bell pepper, diced

Directions
1. Put the tomatoes, cucumber, feta cheese and bell pepper in a bowl.
2. Top with olives and serve to enjoy.

Nutrition Amount per serving

Calories 140	Cholesterol 31mg 10%	Dietary Fiber 2.5g 9%
Total Fat 9.2g 12%	Sodium 513mg 22%	Total Sugars 5.8g
Saturated Fat 5.5g 27%	Total Carbs 9.5g 3%	Protein 6.6g

Mixed Green Spring Salad

Serves: 3/Prep Time: 15 mins
Ingredients
- 2 tablespoons parmesan cheese, shaved
- 2 ounces mixed greens
- 3 tablespoons pine nuts, roasted
- Salt and black pepper, to taste
- 2 bacon slices, crispy and crumbled

Directions
1. Put the bacon along with rest of the ingredients in a bowl.
2. Serve and enjoy.

Nutrition Amount per serving

Calories 169	Cholesterol 21mg 7%	Dietary Fiber 1.2g 4%
Total Fat 13.2g 17%	Sodium 386mg 17%	Total Sugars 0.9g
Saturated Fat 3.5g 18%	Total Carbs 4.1g 1%	Protein 9.4g

Keto Cobb Salad

Serves: 2/Prep Time: 10 mins
Ingredients
- 2 hardboiled eggs
- 8 cherry tomatoes
- 4 cups mixed green salad
- 4 oz. feta cheese, crumbled
- 4 oz. chicken breast, shredded

Directions
1. Place the mixed green salad, eggs and tomatoes into a large bowl.
2. Add chicken breast and top with feta cheese to serve.

Nutrition Amount per serving

Calories 160	Cholesterol 125mg 42%	Dietary Fiber 2g 7%
Total Fat 9.1g 12%	Sodium 376mg 16%	Total Sugars 3.6g
Saturated Fat 4.9g 25%	Total Carbs 6.1g 2%	Protein 14g

Strawberry Cheesecake Salad

Serves: 4/Prep Time: 15 mins
Ingredients
- ½ cup heavy cream
- ¼ cup almond flour
- 9 oz. fresh strawberries, hulled and chopped
- 8 oz. cream cheese
- 2 scoops Stevia

Directions
1. Whisk together heavy cream and cream cheese in a bowl until combined.
2. Stir in rest of the ingredients until well mixed.
3. Transfer into a serving dish and refrigerate until required.
4. Serve chilled.

Nutrition Amount per serving

Calories 312	Cholesterol 83mg 28%	Dietary Fiber 2g 7%
Total Fat 28.8g 37%	Sodium 177mg 8%	Total Sugars 3.3g
Saturated Fat 16.2g 81%	Total Carbs 8.3g 3%	Protein 6.5g

Lobster Roll Salad

Serves: 4/Prep Time: 10 mins

Ingredients

- 1½ cups cauliflower florets, cooked until tender and chilled
- 2 cups lobster meat, cooked and chopped into bite sized pieces
- ½ cup mayonnaise
- ½ cup bacon, cooked and chopped
- 1 teaspoon fresh tarragon leaves, chopped

Directions

1. Mix together cooked lobster, bacon and cauliflower in a bowl.
2. Stir in mayonnaise and serve topped with fresh tarragon leaves.

Nutrition Amount per serving

Calories 275	Cholesterol 131mg 44%	Dietary Fiber 1g 3%
Total Fat 17.1g 22%	Sodium 939mg 41%	Total Sugars 2.8g
Saturated Fat 3.8g 19%	Total Carbs 9.3g 3%	Protein 20.7g

Steak Salad

Serves: 3/Prep Time: 12 mins

Ingredients

- 6 cups mixed green lettuce
- 1 cup feta cheese, crumbled
- 1 pound flank steak
- 2 avocados, sliced
- Salt and black pepper, to taste

Directions

1. Preheat a grill pan to medium high heat.
2. Season flank steak with salt and black pepper on both sides and transfer to the grill.
3. Cook for about 4 minutes per side and remove to a bowl.
4. Add mixed green lettuce and avocados and mix well.
5. Top with feta cheese and immediately serve.

Nutrition Amount per serving

Calories 357	Cholesterol 64mg 21%	Dietary Fiber 4.8g 17%
Total Fat 24.8g 32%	Sodium 328mg 14%	Total Sugars 1.9g
Saturated Fat 9.1g 46%	Total Carbs 8.4g 3%	Protein 26.1g

Broccoli Cauliflower Salad

Serves: 6/Prep Time: 40 mins

Ingredients

- 8 oz broccoli florets, cut into bite sized pieces
- 4 oz cheddar cheese, cubed
- 2 tablespoons purple onion
- 8 oz cauliflower florets, cut into bite sized pieces
- 1/3 pound bacon, cooked crisp and crumbled

Directions

1. Mix together broccoli, onion, cauliflower and bacon in a bowl.
2. Top with cheddar cheese and serve instantly.

Nutrition Amount per serving

Calories 236	Cholesterol 48mg 16%	Dietary Fiber 2g 7%
Total Fat 17g 22%	Sodium 723mg 31%	Total Sugars 1.8g
Saturated Fat 7.5g 37%	Total Carbs 5.4g 2%	Protein 15.9g

Italian Sub Salad

Serves: 6/Prep Time: 30 mins
Ingredients

- ¼ cup pickled banana peppers, sliced
- 1 cup mixed Italian olives, pitted
- 6 cups Romaine lettuce, shredded
- 1 tablespoon Italian seasoning
- 6 ounces pepperoni, diced

Directions

1. Mix together pickled banana peppers, Italian olives, Romaine lettuce and pepperoni in a bowl.
2. Sprinkle with Italian seasoning and serve instantly.

Nutrition Amount per serving

Calories 196	Cholesterol 31mg 10%	Dietary Fiber 0.4g 1%
Total Fat 17.9g 23%	Sodium 509mg 22%	Total Sugars 0.8g
Saturated Fat 5g 25%	Total Carbs 1.9g 1%	Protein 6.7g

Israeli Salad

Serves: 4/Prep Time: 10 mins
Ingredients

- 4 organic ripe tomatoes, finely chopped
- 3 large organic cucumbers, finely chopped
- 1/3 cup fresh Italian parsley, finely chopped
- Himalayan sea salt and black pepper, to taste
- 3 tablespoons extra-virgin olive oil

Directions

1. Mix together tomatoes, cucumbers and parsley in a medium bowl.
2. Season with sea salt and black pepper and drizzle with olive oil.
3. Cover and refrigerate to serve chilled.

Nutrition Amount per serving

Calories 120	Cholesterol 0mg 0%	Dietary Fiber 1.9g 7%
Total Fat 10.8g 14%	Sodium 10mg 0%	Total Sugars 3.9g
Saturated Fat 1.6g 8%	Total Carbs 6.5g 2%	Protein 1.5g

Iceberg Wedge Salad

Serves: 4/Prep Time: 15 mins
Ingredients

- 1/3 cup bacon, cooked and crumbled
- 1 Iceberg lettuce, cut into fourths
- 4 hardboiled eggs, chopped into pieces
- 4 tablespoons extra blue cheese, crumbled
- 4 grape tomatoes, sliced in half

Directions

1. Divide iceberg lettuce into 4 plates and top with bacon, eggs, tomatoes and blue cheese.
2. Serve and enjoy.

Nutrition Amount per serving

Calories 194	Cholesterol 184mg 61%	Dietary Fiber 2g 7%
Total Fat 12.4g 16%	Sodium 479mg 21%	Total Sugars 4.4g
Saturated Fat 4.7g 23%	Total Carbs 7.9g 3%	Protein 13.4g

Green Bean Summer Salad

Serves: 6/Prep Time: 25 mins

Ingredients
- 1 pound green beans
- 2 cups cherry tomatoes, cut in half
- Salt and black pepper, to taste
- 1 cup fresh basil, thinly sliced
- 3 tablespoons olive oil

Directions
1. Steam green beans for 5 minutes in a boiling water and transfer in a bowl of ice water.
2. Drain well and place in a serving bowl.
3. Add cherry tomatoes and basil and mix well.
4. Season with salt and black pepper and drizzle with olive oil to serve.

Nutrition Amount per serving

Calories 95	Cholesterol 0mg 0%	Dietary Fiber 3.4g 12%
Total Fat 7.2g 9%	Sodium 8mg 0%	Total Sugars 2.7g
Saturated Fat 1g 5%	Total Carbs 7.8g 3%	Protein 2g

Cottage Cheese with Cherry Tomatoes and Basil Salad

Serves: 1/Prep Time: 10 mins

Ingredients
- ¼ cup cherry tomatoes, quartered
- ½ cup cottage cheese
- 1 tablespoon basil, chopped
- Ground black pepper, to taste
- 2 tablespoons sour cream

Directions
1. Put the cherry tomatoes and basil in a bowl followed by cottage cheese.
2. Top with sour cream and season with black pepper to serve.

Nutrition Amount per serving

Calories 162	Cholesterol 20mg 7%	Dietary Fiber 0.6g 2%
Total Fat 7.3g 9%	Sodium 474mg 21%	Total Sugars 1.6g
Saturated Fat 4.5g 23%	Total Carbs 7g 3%	Protein 16.8g

Poultry Recipes

Turkey with Cream Cheese Sauce

Serves: 4/Prep Time: 30 mins

Ingredients
- 20 oz. turkey breast
- 2 tablespoons butter
- 2 cups heavy whipping cream
- Salt and black pepper, to taste
- 7 oz. cream cheese

Directions
1. Season the turkey generously with salt and black pepper.
2. Heat butter in a skillet over medium heat and cook turkey for about 5 minutes on each side.
3. Stir in the heavy whipping cream and cream cheese.
4. Cover the skillet and cook for about 15 minutes on medium low heat.
5. Dish out to serve hot.

Nutrition Amount per serving

Calories 386	Cholesterol 142mg 47%	Dietary Fiber 0.5g 2%
Total Fat 31.7g 41%	Sodium 1100mg 48%	Total Sugars 3.4g
Saturated Fat 19.2g 96%	Total Carbs 6g 2%	Protein 19.5g

Keto Pesto Chicken Casserole

Serves: 3/Prep Time: 45 mins
Ingredients
- 1½ pounds boneless chicken thighs, cut into bite sized pieces
- Salt and black pepper, to taste
- 2 tablespoons butter
- 3 oz. green pesto
- 5 oz. feta cheese, diced

Directions
1. Preheat the oven to 400 F and grease a baking dish.
2. Season the chicken with salt and black pepper.
3. Heat butter in a skillet over medium heat and cook chicken for about 5 minutes on each side. Dish out in the greased baking dish and add feta cheese and pesto.
4. Transfer the baking dish to the oven and bake for about 30 minutes.
5. Remove from the oven and serve hot.

Nutrition Amount per serving

Calories 438	Cholesterol 190mg 63%	Dietary Fiber 0g 0%
Total Fat 30.4g 39%	Sodium 587mg 26%	Total Sugars 1.5g
Saturated Fat 11g 55%	Total Carbs 1.7g 1%	Protein 39.3g

Italian Turkey

Serves: 6/Prep Time: 25 mins
Ingredients
- 1½ cups Italian dressing
- Salt and black pepper, to taste
- 2 tablespoons butter
- 1 (2 pound) bone-in turkey breast
- 2 garlic cloves, minced

Directions
1. Preheat the oven to 350°F and grease a baking dish with butter.
2. Mix together minced garlic cloves, salt and black pepper and rub the turkey breast with this mixture. Arrange turkey breast in the baking dish and top evenly with Italian dressing.
3. Bake for about 2 hours, coating with pan juices occasionally.
4. Dish out and serve immediately.

Nutrition Amount per serving

Calories 464	Cholesterol 144mg 48%	Dietary Fiber 0g 0%
Total Fat 31.3g 40%	Sodium 234mg 10%	Total Sugars 4.9g
Saturated Fat 7.8g 39%	Total Carbs 6.5g 2%	Protein 32.7g

Caprese Chicken

Serves: 4/Prep Time: 30 mins
Ingredients
- 1 pound chicken breasts, boneless and skinless
- ¼ cup balsamic vinegar
- 1 tablespoon extra-virgin olive oil
- Kosher salt and black pepper, to taste
- 4 mozzarella cheese slices

Directions
1. Season the chicken with salt and black pepper.
2. Heat olive oil in a skillet over medium heat and cook chicken for about 5 minutes on each side. Stir in the balsamic vinegar and cook for about 2 minutes.
3. Add mozzarella cheese slices and cook for about 2 minutes until melted.
4. Dish out in a plate and serve hot.

Nutrition Amount per serving

Calories 329	Cholesterol 116mg 39%	Dietary Fiber 0g 0%
Total Fat 16.9g 22%	Sodium 268mg 12%	Total Sugars 0.1g
Saturated Fat 5.8g 29%	Total Carbs 1.1g 0%	Protein 40.8g

Roasted Chicken with Herbed Butter

Serves: 6/Prep Time: 30 mins

Ingredients

- 1 tablespoon garlic paste
- 6 chicken legs
- 4 cups water
- Salt, to taste
- 4 tablespoons herbed butter

Directions

1. Season the chicken legs with salt and mix with garlic paste.
2. Put a rack in an electric pressure cooker and add water.
3. Place the marinated pieces of chicken on the rack and lock the lid.
4. Cook on high pressure for about 15 minutes.
5. Naturally release the pressure and dish out in a platter.
6. Spread herbed butter on the chicken legs and serve.

Nutrition Amount per serving

Calories 304	Cholesterol 137mg 46%	Dietary Fiber 0g 0%
Total Fat 12.7g 16%	Sodium 177mg 8%	Total Sugars 0.1g
Saturated Fat 3.8g 19%	Total Carbs 0.7g 0%	Protein 44g

Chicken Enchiladas

Serves: 2/Prep Time: 25 mins

Ingredients

- 2 ounces chicken, shredded
- ½ tablespoon olive oil
- 2 ounces shiitake mushrooms, chopped
- Sea salt and black pepper, to taste
- ½ teaspoon apple cider vinegar

Directions

1. Heat olive oil in a skillet and add mushrooms.
2. Sauté for about 30 seconds and stir in chicken.
3. Cook for about 2 minutes and pour in apple cider vinegar.
4. Season with sea salt and black pepper and cover the lid.
5. Cook for about 20 minutes on medium low heat. Dish out and serve hot.

Nutrition Amount per serving

Calories 88	Cholesterol 22mg 7%	Dietary Fiber 0.6g 2%
Total Fat 4.4g 6%	Sodium 86mg 4%	Total Sugars 1g
Saturated Fat 0.8g 4%	Total Carbs 3.9g 1%	Protein 8.7g

Turkey Balls

Serves: 6/Prep Time: 35 mins

Ingredients

- 1 cup broccoli, chopped
- 1 pound turkey, boiled and chopped
- 2 teaspoons ginger-garlic paste
- Salt and lemon pepper seasoning, to taste
- ½ cup olive oil

Directions

1. Preheat the oven to 360°F and grease a baking tray.
2. Mix together turkey, olive oil, broccoli, ginger-garlic paste, salt and lemon pepper seasoning in a bowl.
3. Make small balls out of this mixture and arrange on the baking tray.
4. Transfer to the oven and bake for about 20 minutes.
5. Remove from the oven and serve with the dip of your choice.

Nutrition Amount per serving

Calories 275	Cholesterol 58mg 19%	Dietary Fiber 0.4g 1%
Total Fat 20.1g 26%	Sodium 53mg 2%	Total Sugars 0.3g
Saturated Fat 3g 15%	Total Carbs 1.5g 1%	Protein 22.4g

Chicken Zucchini Cutlets

Serves: 6/Prep Time: 20 mins

Ingredients

- 3 zucchinis, boiled and mashed
- 3 tablespoons lemon pepper seasoning
- ½ pound chicken, boiled and chopped
- ½ cup avocado oil
- Salt and black pepper, to taste

Directions

1. Mix together chicken, zucchinis, lemon pepper seasoning, salt and black pepper in a bowl.
2. Make cutlets out of this mixture and set aside.
3. Heat avocado oil in a pan and put the cutlets in it.
4. Fry for about 2-3 minutes on each side and dish out to serve.

Nutrition Amount per serving

Calories 106	Cholesterol 29mg 10%	Dietary Fiber 2.8g 10%
Total Fat 3.8g 5%	Sodium 36mg 2%	Total Sugars 1.8g
Saturated Fat 0.9g 4%	Total Carbs 6.4g 2%	Protein 12.7g

Sour Grilled Turkey Breasts

Serves: 3/Prep Time: 40 mins

Ingredients

- ½ onion, chopped
- 2 garlic cloves, minced
- 1 pound pastured turkey breasts
- ½ cup sour cream
- Salt and black pepper, to taste

Directions

1. Preheat the grill to medium high heat.
2. Mix together sour cream, onion, garlic, salt and black pepper in a bowl.
3. Add turkey breasts to this mixture and marinate for about an hour.
4. Transfer the marinated turkey breasts to the grill.
5. Grill for about 25 minutes and transfer to a plate to serve.

Nutrition Amount per serving

Calories 380	Cholesterol 151mg 50%	Dietary Fiber 0.4g 2%
Total Fat 19.3g 25%	Sodium 151mg 7%	Total Sugars 0.9g
Saturated Fat 8.1g 40%	Total Carbs 4g 1%	Protein 45.3g

Cheesy Chicken Tenders

Serves: 6/Prep Time: 35 mins

Ingredients

- 1 cup cream
- 4 tablespoons butter
- 2 pounds chicken tenders
- Salt and black pepper, to taste
- 1 cup feta cheese

Directions

1. Preheat the oven to 350°F and grease a baking dish.
2. Season chicken tenders with salt and black pepper.
3. Heat butter in a skillet and add chicken tenders.
4. Cook for about 3 minutes on each side and transfer to the baking dish.
5. Top with cream and feta cheese and place in the oven.
6. Bake for about 25 minutes and remove from the oven to serve.

Nutrition Amount per serving

Calories 447	Sodium 477mg 21%	Protein 47.7g
Total Fat 26.4g 34%	Total Carbs 2.3g 1%	
Saturated Fat 13.1g 65%	Dietary Fiber 0g 0%	
Cholesterol 185mg 62%	Total Sugars 1.8g	

Air Fried Chicken

Serves: 2/Prep Time: 20 mins
Ingredients
- 1 tablespoon olive oil
- 4 skinless, boneless chicken tenderloins
- 1 egg
- Salt and black pepper, to taste
- ½ teaspoon turmeric powder

Directions
1. Preheat the air fryer to 370°F and coat the fryer basket with olive oil.
2. Beat the egg and dip the chicken tenderloins in it.
3. Mix together turmeric powder, salt and black pepper in a bowl and dredge chicken tenderloins.
4. Arrange the chicken tenderloins in the fryer basket and cook for about 10 minutes.
5. Dish out on a platter and serve with salsa.

Nutrition Amount per serving

Calories 304	Cholesterol 179mg 60%	Dietary Fiber 0.1g 0%
Total Fat 15.2g 20%	Sodium 91mg 4%	Total Sugars 0.2g
Saturated Fat 4g 20%	Total Carbs 0.6g 0%	Protein 40.3g

Ham Wrapped Turkey Rolls

Serves: 4/Prep Time: 40 mins
Ingredients
- 2 tablespoons fresh sage leaves
- Salt and black pepper, to taste
- 4 ham slices
- 4 (6 ounce) turkey cutlets
- 1 tablespoon butter, melted

Directions
1. Preheat the oven to 350°F and grease a baking dish.
2. Season the turkey cutlets with salt and black pepper.
3. Roll the turkey cutlets and tightly wrap with ham slices.
4. Coat each roll with butter and sprinkle evenly with the sage leaves.
5. Arrange the rolls on the baking dish and transfer to the oven.
6. Bake for about 25 minutes, flipping halfway in between.
7. Remove from the oven and serve immediately.

Nutrition Amount per serving

Calories 363	Cholesterol 152mg 51%	Dietary Fiber 0.8g 3%
Total Fat 13.9g 18%	Sodium 505mg 22%	Total Sugars 0g
Saturated Fat 5.5g 28%	Total Carbs 1.7g 1%	Protein 54.6g

Stuffed Whole Chicken

Serves: 6/Prep Time: 1 hour 15 mins
Ingredients
- 1 cup mozzarella cheese
- 4 garlic cloves, peeled
- 1 (2 pound) whole chicken, cleaned, pat dried
- Salt and black pepper, to taste
- 2 tablespoons fresh lemon juice

Directions
1. Preheat the oven to 360°F and grease a baking dish.
2. Season the chicken with salt and black pepper.
3. Stuff the chicken cavity with garlic cloves and mozzarella cheese.
4. Transfer the chicken to oven on the baking dish and drizzle with lemon juice.
5. Bake for about 1 hour and remove from the oven to serve.

Nutrition Amount per serving

Calories 305	Cholesterol 137mg 46%	Dietary Fiber 0.1g 0%
Total Fat 12.1g 15%	Sodium 160mg 7%	Total Sugars 0.1g
Saturated Fat 3.6g 18%	Total Carbs 1g 0%	Protein 45.2g

Turkey with Mozzarella and Tomatoes

Serves: 2/Prep Time: 1 hour 30 mins

Ingredients
- 1 tablespoon butter
- 2 large turkey breasts
- ½ cup fresh mozzarella cheese, thinly sliced
- Salt and black pepper, to taste
- 1 large Roma tomato, thinly sliced

Directions
1. Preheat the oven to 375°F and grease the baking tray with butter.
2. Make some deep slits in the turkey breasts and season with salt and black pepper.
3. Stuff the mozzarella cheese slices and tomatoes in the turkey slits.
4. Put the stuffed turkey breasts on the baking tray and transfer to the oven.
5. Bake for about 1 hour 15 minutes and dish out to serve warm.

Nutrition Amount per serving

Calories 104	Cholesterol 25mg 8%	Dietary Fiber 1g 4%
Total Fat 7.4g 9%	Sodium 256mg 11%	Total Sugars 2.6g
Saturated Fat 4.4g 22%	Total Carbs 5.1g 2%	Protein 5.7g

Boursin Stuffed Chicken

Serves: 4/Prep Time: 50 mins

Ingredients
- 4 chicken breasts, boneless and skinless
- 4 oz. Boursin cheese
- 4 prosciutto slices
- Kosher salt and black pepper, to taste
- ½ cup mozzarella cheese, shredded

Directions
1. Preheat the oven to 400°F and grease a baking dish.
2. Season the chicken with salt and black pepper and top with Boursin and mozzarella cheese.
3. Wrap chicken breasts with prosciutto slices and transfer into a baking dish.
4. Place in the oven and bake for about 35 minutes.
5. Remove from the oven and serve hot.

Nutrition Amount per serving

Calories 462	Cholesterol 187mg 62%	Dietary Fiber 0g 0%
Total Fat 26.1g 33%	Sodium 828mg 36%	Total Sugars 0.9g
Saturated Fat 12.6g 63%	Total Carbs 1.7g 1%	Protein 54g

Mediterranean Turkey Cutlets

Serves: 6/Prep Time: 45 mins

Ingredients
- 2 teaspoons Greek seasoning
- 2 pounds turkey cutlets
- 4 tablespoons olive oil
- 2 teaspoons turmeric powder
- 1 cup almond flour

Directions
1. Mix together almond flour, Greek seasoning and turmeric powder in a bowl.
2. Dredge the turkey cutlets and set aside for about 15 minutes.
3. Heat olive oil in a skillet and transfer half of the turkey cutlets.
4. Cover the lid and cook on medium low heat for about 20 minutes.
5. Dish out in a serving platter and repeat with the remaining batch.

Nutrition Amount per serving
Calories   454
Total Fat 25.9g   33%
Saturated Fat 4.5g   23%
Cholesterol 114mg   38%
Sodium 165mg   7%
Total Carbs 5g   2%
Dietary Fiber 2.2g   8%
Total Sugars 0g
Protein 48.4g

Cheesy Bacon Ranch Chicken

Serves: 4/Prep Time: 35 mins
Ingredients
- 4 boneless skinless chicken breasts
- 4 slices thick cut bacon, cooked and crisped
- Kosher salt and black pepper, to taste
- 1½ cups mozzarella cheese, shredded
- 2 teaspoons ranch seasoning

Directions
1. Preheat the oven to 390°F and grease a baking dish.
2. Season the chicken breasts with kosher salt and black pepper.
3. Cook chicken breasts in a nonstick skillet for about 5 minutes per side.
4. Top the chicken with mozzarella cheese and ranch seasoning and transfer to the oven.
5. Bake for about 15 minutes and dish out on a platter.
6. Crumble the crispy bacon and sprinkle over the chicken to serve.

Nutrition Amount per serving
Calories   415
Total Fat 20.6g   26%
Saturated Fat 6.7g   34%
Cholesterol 156mg   52%
Sodium 740mg   32%
Total Carbs 0.7g   0%
Dietary Fiber 0g   0%
Total Sugars 0g
Protein 52.3g

Keto Garlic Turkey Breasts

Serves: 4/Prep Time: 35 mins
Ingredients
- ½ teaspoon garlic powder
- 4 tablespoons butter
- ½ teaspoon dried oregano
- Salt and black pepper, to taste
- 1 pound turkey breasts, boneless

Directions
1. Preheat the oven to 450°F and grease a baking dish.
2. Sprinkle garlic powder, dried oregano, salt and black pepper on both sides of the turkey.
3. Heat butter in a skillet and add seasoned turkey.
4. Cook for about 5 minutes on each side and dish out.
5. Arrange the turkey on the baking dish and transfer to the oven.
6. Bake for about 15 minutes and dish out in a platter.

Nutrition Amount per serving
Calories   222
Total Fat 13.4g   17%
Saturated Fat 7.7g   38%
Cholesterol 79mg   26%
Sodium 1233mg   54%
Total Carbs 5.2g   2%
Dietary Fiber 0.7g   2%
Total Sugars 4.1g
Protein 19.6g

Grilled Chicken Breast

Serves: 4/Prep Time: 45 mins
Ingredients
- 3 tablespoon extra-virgin olive oil
- ¼ cup balsamic vinegar
- 2 teaspoons dried rosemary and thyme
- Kosher salt and black pepper, to taste
- 4 chicken breasts

Directions
1. Preheat grill to medium high heat.
2. Whisk together balsamic vinegar, olive oil, dried rosemary, dried thyme, kosher salt and black pepper in a bowl.
3. Reserve about one fourth of the marinade and add chicken breasts in the marinade.
4. Mix well and allow it to marinate for about 30 minutes.
5. Transfer chicken to the grill and cook for about 6 minutes on each side, basting with reserved marinade.
6. Remove from the grill and serve on a platter.

Nutrition Amount per serving

Calories 373	Cholesterol 130mg 43%	Dietary Fiber 0.3g 1%
Total Fat 21.4g 27%	Sodium 127mg 6%	Total Sugars 0.1g
Saturated Fat 4.5g 23%	Total Carbs 0.5g 0%	Protein 42.3g

Buffalo Skillet Turkey

Serves: 4/Prep Time: 25 mins
Ingredients
- 4 boneless skinless turkey breasts
- 3 tablespoons butter
- 8 slices muenster cheese
- Garlic powder, cayenne pepper, kosher salt and black pepper
- 1 cup buffalo sauce

Directions
1. Heat half of the butter over medium heat in a large skillet and add turkey.
2. Season with garlic powder, kosher salt and black pepper.
3. Cook for about 5 minutes on each side until golden and dish out on a plate.
4. Heat the rest of the butter in the same skillet and add cayenne pepper and buffalo sauce.
5. Return the turkey to the skillet and top with 2 slices of muenster cheese on each breast.
6. Cover with a lid and cook for about 3 minutes until the cheese is melted.
7. Dish out and serve warm.

Nutrition Amount per serving

Calories 389	Cholesterol 77mg 26%	Dietary Fiber 0.3g 1%
Total Fat 26g 33%	Sodium 653mg 28%	Total Sugars 0.8g
Saturated Fat 16.2g 81%	Total Carbs 1.5g 1%	Protein 37.3g

Low Carb Chicken Nuggets

Serves: 6/Prep Time: 25 mins
Ingredients
- ¼ cup mayonnaise
- 2 medium chicken breasts
- 1 cup blanched almond flour
- 2 tablespoons olive oil
- Sea salt and black pepper, to taste

Directions
1. Put the chicken in the salted water for about 10 minutes.
2. Drain it and cut the chicken into nugget sized pieces.
3. Put mayonnaise in one bowl and mix almond flour, sea salt and black pepper in another bowl.
4. Coat each chicken nugget with mayonnaise and dredge in the almond flour mixture.
5. Heat oil over medium high heat in a skillet and add chicken nuggets in a single layer.
6. Cook for about 3 minutes per side until golden and dish out to serve.

Nutrition Amount per serving

Calories 283	Cholesterol 46mg 15%	Dietary Fiber 2g 7%
Total Fat 20.4g 26%	Sodium 118mg 5%	Total Sugars 0.6g
Saturated Fat 2.8g 14%	Total Carbs 6.3g 2%	Protein 18.2g

Keto Turkey with Cream Cheese Sauce

Serves: 8/Prep Time: 35 mins

Ingredients

- 20 oz. turkey breast
- Salt and black pepper, to taste
- 2 tablespoons butter
- 3 cups cream cheese
- 1 tablespoon tamari soy sauce

Directions

1. Season the turkey generously with salt and black pepper.
2. Heat butter in a large pan over medium heat and add turkey breasts.
3. Cook for about 6 minutes on each side and stir in cream cheese and tamari soy sauce.
4. Cook for about 15 minutes on medium low heat and dish out to serve hot.

Nutrition Amount per serving

Calories 404	Cholesterol 134mg 45%	Dietary Fiber 0.4g 1%
Total Fat 34.4g 44%	Sodium 1123mg 49%	Total Sugars 2.7g
Saturated Fat 21.2g 106%	Total Carbs 5.4g 2%	Protein 18.9g

Chicken Spinach Coconut Curry

Serves: 6/Prep Time: 5 hours 10 mins

Ingredients

- 2 tablespoons curry paste
- 1 onion, finely sliced
- 1 pound chicken, cubed
- 800 g fresh spinach, chopped
- 400 ml coconut cream

Directions

1. Put all the ingredients in a slow cooker and stir well.
2. Lock the lid and cook on High Pressure for about 5 hours.
3. Dish out in a serving bowl and serve hot.

Nutrition Amount per serving

Calories 341	Cholesterol 58mg 19%	Dietary Fiber 4.8g 17%
Total Fat 21.9g 28%	Sodium 164mg 7%	Total Sugars 3.6g
Saturated Fat 15g 75%	Total Carbs 11.7g 4%	Protein 27.7g

Turkey Garlic Mushroom Sauté

Serves: 4/Prep Time: 30 mins

Ingredients

- 1 cup mushrooms, sliced
- 3 tablespoons butter, divided in half
- 1½ pounds turkey thighs, skinless and boneless
- Sea salt and black pepper, to taste
- 3 garlic cloves, minced

Directions

1. Season the turkey with sea salt and black pepper.
2. Heat half of butter over medium high heat in a large skillet and add turkey.
3. Cook for about 6 minutes on each side and dish out on a plate.
4. Heat the rest of the butter in the skillet and add garlic and mushrooms.
5. Sauté for about 5 minutes and stir in the cooked turkey.
6. Sauté for about 3 minutes and dish out to serve.

Nutrition Amount per serving

Calories 357	Cholesterol 84mg 28%	Dietary Fiber 0.2g 1%
Total Fat 23.9g 31%	Sodium 184mg 8%	Total Sugars 0.3g
Saturated Fat 5.5g 27%	Total Carbs 1.3g 0%	Protein 32.7g

Smokey Mountain Chicken

Serves: 8/Prep Time: 30 mins
Ingredients

- 1 cup low carb Barbecue sauce
- 1½ cups provolone cheese, sliced
- 2 pounds chicken breast, boneless and skinless
- ½ pound bacon, cooked
- ½ cup mozzarella cheese, shredded

Directions

1. Preheat the grill to medium high heat.
2. Grill chicken for about 8 minutes over medium heat.
3. Drizzle with barbecue sauce and flip the chicken.
4. Baste the other side with the barbecue sauce and layer with bacon strips, mozzarella and provolone cheese slices.
5. Cover the grill and cook for about 2 more minutes until the cheese is melted.
6. Remove from the grill and serve hot.

Nutrition Amount per serving

Calories 421	Cholesterol 122mg 41%	Dietary Fiber 0.2g 1%
Total Fat 21.7g 28%	Sodium 1290mg 56%	Total Sugars 8.3g
Saturated Fat 8.3g 42%	Total Carbs 12.3g 4%	Protein 41.4g

Cauliflower Turkey Casserole

Serves: 4/Prep Time: 35 mins
Ingredients

- 1 tablespoon Italian seasoning
- 2 cups cauliflower rice, uncooked
- 2 cups cooked turkey, diced
- ¼ cup heavy whipping cream
- ½ cup parmesan and garlic cheese

Directions

1. Preheat the oven to 360°F and grease a casserole dish with nonstick cooking spray.
2. Mix together cauliflower rice, Italian seasoning and turkey in a large bowl.
3. Transfer this mixture into the prepared casserole dish.
4. Combine cream, parmesan and garlic cheese in another bowl until mixed.
5. Pour over the cauliflower rice mixture and transfer to the oven.
6. Bake for about 20 minutes and remove from the oven to serve hot.

Nutrition Amount per serving

Calories 184	Cholesterol 66mg 22%	Dietary Fiber 0g 0%
Total Fat 8.3g 11%	Sodium 114mg 5%	Total Sugars 2.3g
Saturated Fat 3.4g 17%	Total Carbs 4.1g 1%	Protein 22.6g

Keto Chicken Parmesan

Serves: 3/Prep Time: 55 mins
Ingredients

- ¾ cup parmesan cheese
- 1 oz. pork rinds
- 1 pound chicken breasts
- Salt, black pepper, oregano and garlic powder
- ½ cup marinara sauce

Directions

1. Preheat the oven to 360°F.
2. Put half of parmesan cheese and the pork rinds in a food processor and process until coarse.
3. Transfer this mixture into a dish and dredge the chicken breasts.
4. Season the chicken breasts with salt, black pepper, oregano and garlic powder.
5. Transfer into the oven and bake for about 25 minutes until golden brown in color.
6. Remove from the oven and pour marinara sauce over each chicken breast.

7. Top with the remaining parmesan cheese and return to the oven.
8. Bake for about 15 more minutes and dish out to serve warm.

Nutrition Amount per serving

Calories 357	Cholesterol 131mg 44%	Dietary Fiber 1.4g 5%
Total Fat 14.3g 18%	Sodium 691mg 30%	Total Sugars 3.9g
Saturated Fat 5.7g 28%	Total Carbs 7.7g 3%	Protein 48.1g

Creamy Garlic Turkey Soup

Serves: 4/Prep Time: 30 mins

Ingredients
- 2 cups turkey, shredded
- 2 tablespoons butter, melted
- 1 cup heavy cream
- Garlic seasoning and salt, to taste
- 14.5 oz chicken broth

Directions
1. Heat butter over medium heat in a saucepan and add shredded turkey.
2. Coat with melted butter and add heavy cream, chicken broth and garlic seasoning.
3. Mix well and bring to a boil.
4. Reduce heat to low and simmer for about 4 minutes.
5. Season with salt and serve hot.

Nutrition Amount per serving

Calories 290	Cholesterol 109mg 36%	Dietary Fiber 0g 0%
Total Fat 21g 27%	Sodium 428mg 19%	Total Sugars 0.3g
Saturated Fat 11.9g 59%	Total Carbs 2.1g 1%	Protein 23.3g

Chicken Asparagus Sheet Pan

Serves: 8/Prep Time: 40 mins

Ingredients
- ½ pound asparagus, trimmed
- 2 pounds chicken breasts, cut in half to make 4 thin pieces
- 4 sundried tomatoes, cut into strips
- 8 provolone cheese slices
- Salt and black pepper, to taste

Directions
1. Preheat the oven to 400°F and grease a large sheet pan.
2. Arrange chicken breasts and asparagus on the sheet pan and top with sundried tomatoes.
3. Season with salt and black pepper and transfer to the oven.
4. Bake for about 25 minutes and remove from the oven.
5. Top with provolone cheese slices and bake for about 3 more minutes.
6. Dish out and serve hot.

Nutrition Amount per serving

Calories 322	Cholesterol 120mg 40%	Dietary Fiber 0.7g 3%
Total Fat 15.9g 20%	Sodium 364mg 16%	Total Sugars 1.1g
Saturated Fat 7.1g 36%	Total Carbs 2.3g 1%	Protein 40.7g

Turkey Breasts Stuffed with Pimiento Cheese

Serves: 4/Prep Time: 40 mins

Ingredients
- 1 tablespoon pimientos, sliced and chopped
- Paprika, salt and black pepper, divided
- ½ cup Gouda cheese, smoked and shredded
- 4 small boneless, skinless turkey breasts, trimmed
- 1 tablespoon extra-virgin olive oil

Directions
1. Preheat the oven to 400°F.
2. Mix together pimientos, Gouda cheese and paprika in a bowl.

3. Cut slits in the turkey breasts horizontally and add the pimientos mixture inside the slits.
4. Season the turkey breasts with paprika, salt and black pepper.
5. Heat oil over medium high heat in a large ovenproof skillet and add turkey.
6. Cook for about 2 minutes on each side until browned and transfer to the oven.
7. Bake for about 15 minutes and remove from the oven to serve hot.

Nutrition Amount per serving

Calories 270	Cholesterol 102mg 34%	Dietary Fiber 0.4g 1%
Total Fat 11.9g 15%	Sodium 288mg 13%	Total Sugars 2.1g
Saturated Fat 5.5g 27%	Total Carbs 2.9g 1%	Protein 35.4g

Beef Recipes

Hamburger Patties

Serves: 6/Prep Time: 30 mins

Ingredients
- 1 egg
- 25 oz. ground beef
- 3 oz. feta cheese, crumbled
- 2 oz. butter, for frying
- Salt and black pepper, to taste

Directions
1. Mix together egg, ground beef, feta cheese, salt and black pepper in a bowl.
2. Combine well and form equal sized patties.
3. Heat butter in a pan and add patties.
4. Cook on medium low heat for about 3 minutes per side.
5. Dish out and serve warm.

Nutrition Amount per serving

Calories 335	Cholesterol 166mg 55%	Dietary Fiber 0g 0%
Total Fat 18.8g 24%	Sodium 301mg 13%	Total Sugars 0.7g
Saturated Fat 10g 50%	Total Carbs 0.7g 0%	Protein 38.8g

Buttery Beef Curry

Serves: 2/Prep Time: 30 mins

Ingredients
- ½ cup butter
- ½ pound grass fed beef
- ½ pound onions
- Salt and red chili powder, to taste
- ½ pound celery, chopped

Directions
1. Put some water in a pressure cooker and add all the ingredients.
2. Lock the lid and cook on High Pressure for about 15 minutes.
3. Naturally release the pressure and dish out the curry to a bowl to serve.

Nutrition Amount per serving

Calories 450	Cholesterol 132mg 44%	Dietary Fiber 3.1g 11%
Total Fat 38.4g 49%	Sodium 340mg 15%	Total Sugars 4.3g
Saturated Fat 22.5g 113%	Total Carbs 9.8g 4%	Protein 17.2g

Cheesy Beef

Serves: 6/Prep Time: 40 mins

Ingredients
- 1 teaspoon garlic salt
- 2 pounds beef
- 1 cup cream cheese
- 1 cup mozzarella cheese, shredded
- 1 cup low carb Don Pablo's sauce

Directions
1. Season the meat with garlic salt and add to the instant pot.

2. Put the remaining ingredients in the pot and set the instant pot on low.
3. Cook for about 2 hours and dish out.

Nutrition Amount per serving

Calories 471	Cholesterol 187mg 62%	Dietary Fiber 0.1g 0%
Total Fat 27.7g 36%	Sodium 375mg 16%	Total Sugars 1.5g
Saturated Fat 14.6g 73%	Total Carbs 2.9g 1%	Protein 50.9g

Beef Quiche

Serves: 3/Prep Time: 30 mins

Ingredients

- ¼ cup grass fed beef, minced
- 2 slices bacon, cooked and crumbled
- ¼ cup goat cheddar cheese, shredded
- ¼ cup coconut milk
- 3 large pastured eggs

Directions

1. Preheat the oven to 365°F and grease 3 quiche molds.
2. Whisk together eggs and coconut milk in a large bowl.
3. Put beef in quiche molds and stir in the egg mixture.
4. Top with the crumbled bacon and cheddar cheese.
5. Transfer quiche molds to the oven and bake for about 20 minutes.
6. Remove from the oven and serve warm.

Nutrition Amount per serving

Calories 293	Cholesterol 232mg 77%	Dietary Fiber 0.4g 2%
Total Fat 21.4g 27%	Sodium 436mg 19%	Total Sugars 1.1g
Saturated Fat 10.4g 52%	Total Carbs 2.7g 1%	Protein 21.8g

Chili Beef

Serves: 8/Prep Time: 50 mins

Ingredients

- 3 celery ribs, finely diced
- 2 pounds grass fed beef, ground
- 2 tablespoons chili powder
- 2 tablespoons avocado oil, divided
- 2 cups grass fed beef broth

Directions

1. Heat avocado oil in a skillet on medium heat and add beef.
2. Sauté for about 3 minutes on each side and stir in broth and chili powder.
3. Cover the lid and cook for about 30 minutes on medium low heat.
4. Add celery and dish out in a bowl to serve.

Nutrition Amount per serving

Calories 223	Cholesterol 75mg 25%	Dietary Fiber 1.2g 4%
Total Fat 11.8g 15%	Sodium 198mg 9%	Total Sugars 0.5g
Saturated Fat 4.7g 23%	Total Carbs 2.4g 1%	Protein 24.8g

Smoked Brisket with Maple Syrup

Serves: 8/Prep Time: 40 mins

Ingredients

- 1 tablespoon sugar free maple syrup
- 3 pounds grass fed beef briskets
- 3 tablespoons almond oil
- 2 cups bone broth
- 4 tablespoons liquid smoke

Directions

1. Heat almond oil in a skillet on medium heat and add beef briskets.
2. Sauté for about 4 minutes per side and stir in the bone broth and liquid smoke.
3. Cover the lid and cook for about 30 minutes on medium low heat.
4. Dish out in a platter and drizzle with sugar free maple syrup to serve.

Nutrition Amount per serving

Calories 422	Cholesterol 117mg 39%	Dietary Fiber 0g 0%
Total Fat 17g 22%	Sodium 130mg 6%	Total Sugars 1.5g
Saturated Fat 4.9g 25%	Total Carbs 1.7g 1%	Protein 61.6g

Keto Beef Sirloin Steak

Serves: 3/Prep Time: 45 mins

Ingredients

- 3 tablespoons butter
- ½ teaspoon garlic powder
- 1 pound beef top sirloin steaks
- Salt and black pepper, to taste
- 1 garlic clove, minced

Directions

1. Heat butter in a large grill pan and add beef top sirloin steaks.
2. Brown the steaks on both sides by cooking for about 3 minutes per side.
3. Season the steaks with garlic powder, salt and black pepper and cook for about 30 minutes, flipping once.
4. Dish out the steaks to a serving platter and serve hot.

Nutrition Amount per serving

Calories 386	Cholesterol 166mg 55%	Dietary Fiber 0.1g 0%
Total Fat 21g 27%	Sodium 182mg 8%	Total Sugars 0.1g
Saturated Fat 10.9g 54%	Total Carbs 0.7g 0%	Protein 46.1g

Bacon Swiss Beef Steaks

Serves: 4/Prep Time: 25 mins

Ingredients

- ½ cup Swiss cheese, shredded
- 4 beef top sirloin steaks
- 6 bacon strips, cut in half
- Salt and black pepper, to taste
- 1 tablespoon butter

Directions

1. Season the beef steaks generously with salt and black pepper.
2. Put butter in the skillet and heat on medium low heat.
3. Add beef top sirloin steaks and cook for about 5 minutes per side.
4. Add bacon strips and cook for about 15 minutes.
5. Top with Swiss cheese and cook for about 5 minutes on low heat.
6. Remove from heat and dish out on a platter to serve.

Nutrition Amount per serving

Calories 385	Cholesterol 96mg 32%	Dietary Fiber 0g 0%
Total Fat 25.4g 33%	Sodium 552mg 24%	Total Sugars 0.2g
Saturated Fat 10.7g 54%	Total Carbs 0.8g 0%	Protein 35.5g

Mexican Taco Casserole

Serves: 3/Prep Time: 35 mins

Ingredients

- ½ cup cheddar cheese, shredded
- ½ cup low carb salsa
- ½ cup cottage cheese
- 1 pound ground beef
- 1 tablespoon taco seasoning

Directions

1. Preheat the oven to 425°F and lightly grease a baking dish.
2. Mix together the taco seasoning and ground beef in a bowl.
3. Stir in the cottage cheese, salsa and cheddar cheese.
4. Transfer the ground beef mixture to the baking dish and top with cheese mixture.
5. Bake for about 25 minutes and remove from the oven to serve warm.

Nutrition Amount per serving

Calories 432	Cholesterol 165mg 55%	Dietary Fiber 0g 0%
Total Fat 20.4g 26%	Sodium 526mg 23%	Total Sugars 1.6g
Saturated Fat 10g 50%	Total Carbs 3.2g 1%	Protein 56.4g

Mustard Beef Steaks

Serves: 4/Prep Time: 40 mins

Ingredients

- 2 tablespoons butter
- 2 tablespoons Dijon mustard
- 4 beef steaks
- Salt and black pepper, to taste
- 1 tablespoon fresh rosemary, coarsely chopped

Directions

1. Marinate the beef steaks with Dijon mustard, fresh rosemary, salt and black pepper for about 2 hours.
2. Put the butter and marinated beef steaks in a nonstick skillet.
3. Cover the lid and cook for about 30 minutes on medium low heat.
4. Dish out when completely cooked and serve hot.

Nutrition Amount per serving

Calories 217	Cholesterol 91mg 30%	Dietary Fiber 0.6g 2%
Total Fat 11.5g 15%	Sodium 186mg 8%	Total Sugars 0.1g
Saturated Fat 5.7g 29%	Total Carbs 1g 0%	Protein 26.3g

Beef Roast

Serves: 6/Prep Time: 55 mins

Ingredients

- 2 pounds beef
- Salt and black pepper, to taste
- 1 cup onion soup
- 2 teaspoons lemon juice
- 1 cups beef broth

Directions

1. Put the beef in a pressure cooker and stir in the beef broth, lemon juice, onion soup, salt and black pepper.
2. Lock the lid and cook at High Pressure for about 40 minutes.
3. Naturally release the pressure and dish out on a platter to serve.

Nutrition Amount per serving

Calories 307	Cholesterol 135mg 45%	Dietary Fiber 0.3g 1%
Total Fat 10.2g 13%	Sodium 580mg 25%	Total Sugars 1.3g
Saturated Fat 3.7g 19%	Total Carbs 2.9g 1%	Protein 47.9g

Keto Minced Meat

Serves: 4/Prep Time: 30 mins

Ingredients

- 1 pound ground lamb meat
- 1 cup onions, chopped
- 2 tablespoons ginger garlic paste
- 3 tablespoons butter
- Salt and cayenne pepper, to taste

Directions

1. Put the butter in a pot and add garlic, ginger and onions.
2. Sauté for about 3 minutes and add ground meat and all the spices.
3. Cover the lid and cook for about 20 minutes on medium high heat.
4. Dish out to a large serving bowl and serve hot.

Nutrition Amount per serving

Calories 459	Cholesterol 133mg 44%	Dietary Fiber 0.6g 2%
Total Fat 35.3g 45%	Sodium 154mg 7%	Total Sugars 1.2g
Saturated Fat 14.7g 73%	Total Carbs 4.8g 2%	Protein 28.9g

Keto Taco Casserole

Serves: 8/Prep Time: 55 mins
Ingredients
- 2 pounds ground beef
- 1 tablespoon extra-virgin olive oil
- Taco seasoning mix, kosher salt and black pepper
- 2 cups Mexican cheese, shredded
- 6 large eggs, lightly beaten

Directions
1. Preheat the oven to 360°F and grease a 2 quart baking dish.
2. Heat oil over medium heat in a large skillet and add ground beef.
3. Season with taco seasoning mix, kosher salt and black pepper.
4. Cook for about 5 minutes on each side and dish out to let cool slightly.
5. Whisk together eggs in the beef mixture and transfer the mixture to the baking dish.
6. Top with Mexican cheese and bake for about 25 minutes until set.
7. Remove from the oven and serve warm.

Nutrition Amount per serving

Calories 382	Cholesterol 266mg 89%	Dietary Fiber 0g 0%
Total Fat 21.6g 28%	Sodium 363mg 16%	Total Sugars 0.4g
Saturated Fat 9.1g 45%	Total Carbs 1.7g 1%	Protein 45.3g

Keto Burger Fat Bombs

Serves: 10/Prep Time: 30 mins
Ingredients
- ½ teaspoon garlic powder
- 1 pound ground beef
- Kosher salt and black pepper, to taste
- ¼ (8 oz.) block cheddar cheese, cut into 20 pieces
- 2 tablespoons cold butter, cut into 20 pieces

Directions
1. Preheat the oven to 375°F and grease mini muffin tins with cooking spray.
2. Season the beef with garlic powder, kosher salt and black pepper in a medium bowl.
3. Press about 1 tablespoon of beef into each muffin tin, covering the bottom completely.
4. Layer with small piece of butter and add 1 more tablespoon of beef.
5. Top with a piece of cheese in each cup and press the remaining beef.
6. Transfer to the oven and bake for about 20 minutes.
7. Allow to slightly cool and dish out to serve hot.

Nutrition Amount per serving

Calories 128	Cholesterol 53mg 18%	Dietary Fiber 0g 0%
Total Fat 7g 9%	Sodium 81mg 4%	Total Sugars 0.1g
Saturated Fat 3.7g 19%	Total Carbs 0.2g 0%	Protein 15.2g

Ice-Burgers

Serves: 4/Prep Time: 30 mins
Ingredients
- 4 slices bacon, cooked and crisped
- 1 large head iceberg lettuce, sliced into 8 rounds
- 1 pound ground beef
- 4 slices cheddar cheese
- Kosher salt and black pepper, to taste

Directions
1. Make 4 large patties out of ground beef and season both sides with salt and black pepper.
2. Grill for about 10 minutes per side and top with cheddar cheese slices.
3. Place one iceberg round on a plate and layer with grilled beef.
4. Place a slice of bacon and close with second iceberg round.
5. Repeat with the remaining ingredients and serve warm.

Nutrition Amount per serving

Calories 452	Cholesterol 152mg 51%	Dietary Fiber 1.2g 4%
Total Fat 24.6g 32%	Sodium 698mg 30%	Total Sugars 2g
Saturated Fat 11.2g 56%	Total Carbs 6.3g 2%	Protein 49.3g

Beef in Cheese Taco Shells

Serves: 4/Prep Time: 30 mins

Ingredients
- 2 cups cheddar cheese, shredded
- 1 tablespoon olive oil
- 1 tablespoon taco seasoning
- Freshly ground black pepper, to taste
- 1 pound ground beef

Directions
1. Preheat the oven to 375°F and grease a baking dish.
2. Arrange cheddar cheese on the baking sheet and season with black pepper.
3. Bake for about 7 minutes until cheese melts and becomes slightly crispy.
4. Form shells with the help of a wooden spoon and allow them to cool.
5. Meanwhile, heat oil in a large skillet over medium heat and add ground beef.
6. Cook for about 10 minutes and season with taco seasoning.
7. Place beef in the shells and serve.

Nutrition Amount per serving

Calories 478	Cholesterol 161mg 54%	Dietary Fiber 0g 0%
Total Fat 29.3g 38%	Sodium 636mg 28%	Total Sugars 0.8g
Saturated Fat 15.1g 75%	Total Carbs 2.7g 1%	Protein 48.5g

Mexican Ground Beef

Serves: 3/Prep Time: 30 mins

Ingredients
- 1 pound ground beef
- ½ cup cheddar cheese, shredded
- ¼ cup water
- Salt and black pepper, to taste
- 2 tablespoons organic Mexican seasoning

Directions
1. Put beef in a nonstick pan and season with salt and black pepper.
2. Cook for about 8 minutes until brown and pour in the water and Mexican seasoning.
3. Cook for about 5 minutes and dish out in a bowl to serve.

Nutrition Amount per serving

Calories 372	Cholesterol 155mg 52%	Dietary Fiber 0g 0%
Total Fat 15.7g 20%	Sodium 527mg 23%	Total Sugars 0.1g
Saturated Fat 7.5g 38%	Total Carbs 3.2g 1%	Protein 51.1g

Cheesesteak Stuffed Peppers

Serves: 4/Prep Time: 55 mins

Ingredients
- 16 oz. cremini mushrooms, sliced
- 4 bell peppers, halved
- Italian seasoning, kosher salt and black pepper
- 16 provolone cheese slices
- 1½ pounds sirloin steak, thinly sliced

Directions
1. Preheat the oven to 325°F and grease a large baking dish.
2. Arrange bell peppers in the baking dish and transfer to the oven.
3. Bake for about 30 minutes until tender and dish out.
4. Grease a nonstick pan and add mushrooms, Italian seasoning, kosher salt and black pepper.
5. Cook for about 6 minutes and add sirloin steak.

6. Cook for about 3 minutes, stirring occasionally and dish out.
7. Put provolone cheese to the bottom of baked bell peppers and top with steak mixture.
8. Top with the rest of provolone cheese and broil for about 3 minutes until golden.
9. Serve and enjoy.

Nutrition Amount per serving

Calories 521	Cholesterol 153mg 51%	Dietary Fiber 1.5g 5%
Total Fat 27.5g 35%	Sodium 736mg 32%	Total Sugars 5.8g
Saturated Fat 15.5g 77%	Total Carbs 10.8g 4%	Protein 56.2g

Beef with Green Olives and Prunes

Serves: 4/Prep Time: 40 mins
Ingredients
- 2 tablespoons salted butter
- 1¼ pounds beef
- 1 cup reduced sodium chicken broth
- ¼ cup prunes, pitted and chopped
- ¼ cup green olives, pitted and chopped

Directions
1. Heat butter in a large nonstick skillet over medium high heat and add beef.
2. Cook for about 2 minutes per side until browned and add broth.
3. Bring to a simmer, stirring occasionally and add olives and prunes.
4. Reduce heat to low and cover with lid.
5. Cook until the beef is tender and no longer pink in the center, 12 to 15 minutes.
6. Transfer beef to a plate and serve hot.

Nutrition Amount per serving

Calories 350	Cholesterol 142mg 47%	Dietary Fiber 0.8g 3%
Total Fat 15g 19%	Sodium 328mg 14%	Total Sugars 4.2g
Saturated Fat 7.1g 35%	Total Carbs 7g 3%	Protein 44.5g

Stir Fried Spicy Beef Steaks

Serves: 7/Prep Time: 30 mins
Ingredients
- Cayenne pepper, paprika, salt and black pepper
- 3 tablespoons olive oil
- 1 scoop Stevia
- 1½ pounds top round steaks
- 1 (16 ounce) package frozen bell pepper and onion mix

Directions
1. Mix together Stevia, cayenne pepper, paprika, salt and black pepper in a bowl.
2. Add top round steaks and toss to coat well.
3. Cover and refrigerate overnight.
4. Heat olive oil in a large nonstick skillet over high heat and add bell pepper and onion mix.
5. Cook for about 7 minutes, stirring occasionally and add the spice rubbed steaks.
6. Cook for about 15 minutes and dish out to serve hot.

Nutrition Amount per serving

Calories 311	Cholesterol 82mg 27%	Dietary Fiber 2.9g 10%
Total Fat 14.8g 19%	Sodium 60mg 3%	Total Sugars 6.2g
Saturated Fat 3.9g 20%	Total Carbs 11.6g 4%	Protein 32.5g

Keto Sausage Balls

Serves: 6/Prep Time: 35 mins
Ingredients
- 1 cup blanched almond flour
- 1 pound bulk Italian sausage
- 1¼ cups sharp cheddar cheese, shredded
- 2 teaspoons baking powder
- 1 large egg

Directions

1. Preheat the oven to 350°F and place a wire rack on the baking sheet.
2. Mix together all the ingredients in a large bowl until well incorporated.
3. Form small meatballs out of the meat mixture and arrange them on the wire rack.
4. Bake for about 20 minutes until golden brown and remove from the oven to serve hot.

Nutrition Amount per serving

Calories 477	Cholesterol 119mg 40%	Dietary Fiber 2g 7%
Total Fat 39g 50%	Sodium 732mg 32%	Total Sugars 0.2g
Saturated Fat 12.8g 64%	Total Carbs 5.1g 2%	Protein 25.6g

Cumin Spiced Beef Wraps

Serves: 6/Prep Time: 25 mins

Ingredients

- 2 pounds ground beef
- Salt and black pepper, to taste
- 3 tablespoons coconut oil
- 2 teaspoons cumin
- 8 large cabbage leaves, boiled for 20 seconds and plunged in cold water

Directions

1. Heat coconut oil in a pan on medium heat and add the ground beef.
2. Sauté for about 5 minutes and add cumin, salt and black pepper.
3. Place the cabbage leaves on a plate and spoon the ground beef mixture on it.
4. Fold into a roll and serve warm.

Nutrition Amount per serving

Calories 353	Cholesterol 135mg 45%	Dietary Fiber 1.2g 4%
Total Fat 16.4g 21%	Sodium 109mg 5%	Total Sugars 1.4g
Saturated Fat 9.5g 47%	Total Carbs 2.9g 1%	Protein 46.6g

Creamy Mexican Beef

Serves: 6/Prep Time: 9 hours 5 mins

Ingredients

- ½ cup beef stock
- 2 tablespoons homemade taco seasoning
- 1 cup sour cream
- 1 (14 oz) can diced tomatoes and green chilies
- 2 pounds boneless beef

Directions

1. Put all the ingredients in a slow cooker and close the lid.
2. Cover and cook on LOW for about 9 hours.
3. Dish out and serve hot.

Nutrition Amount per serving

Calories 521	Cholesterol 98mg 33%	Dietary Fiber 0.6g 2%
Total Fat 47.3g 61%	Sodium 280mg 12%	Total Sugars 1.7g
Saturated Fat 21.8g 109%	Total Carbs 4.7g 2%	Protein 17.6g

Beef with Carrots

Serves: 8/Prep Time: 8 hours 10 mins

Ingredients

- 1 large onion, thinly sliced
- 2 pounds beef, boneless
- 4 medium carrots, peeled and sliced lengthwise
- Salt and black pepper, to taste
- 1 teaspoon dried oregano, crushed

Directions

1. Season the beef with dried oregano, salt and black pepper.
2. Transfer beef to a bowl and set aside for at least 3 hours.
3. Place onion and carrots at the bottom of a slow cooker and top with beef.

4. Cover the lid and cook on LOW for about 8 hours. Dish out and serve hot.

Nutrition Amount per serving

Calories 231	Cholesterol 101mg 34%	Dietary Fiber 1.2g 4%
Total Fat 7.1g 9%	Sodium 96mg 4%	Total Sugars 2.3g
Saturated Fat 2.7g 13%	Total Carbs 4.9g 2%	Protein 34.9g

Creamy Garlic Beef Soup

Serves: 8/Prep Time: 40 mins

Ingredients
- 2 cups beef meat, shredded
- 2 cups chicken broth
- Salt, to taste
- 1 cup cream cheese, cubed
- ¼ cup heavy cream

Directions
1. Put beef along with all other ingredients in a pressure cooker.
2. Cover the lid and cook on High Pressure for about 30 minutes.
3. Naturally release the pressure and dish out to serve hot.

Nutrition Amount per serving

Calories 388	Cholesterol 109mg 36%	Dietary Fiber 0g 0%
Total Fat 35.1g 45%	Sodium 990mg 43%	Total Sugars 1.4g
Saturated Fat 19.1g 95%	Total Carbs 3.1g 1%	Protein 14g

Paprika Mushroom Beef

Serves: 8/Prep Time: 45 mins

Ingredients
- 2 tablespoons butter
- 2 pounds beef
- ¾ cup sour cream
- Paprika, salt and black pepper, to taste
- 1 cup white mushrooms

Directions
1. Season the beef with paprika, salt and black pepper.
2. Put butter in a skillet and add seasoned beef.
3. Sauté for about 4 minutes and add mushrooms and sour cream.
4. Cover the lid and cook for about 30 minutes. Dish out and serve hot.

Nutrition Amount per serving

Calories 284	Cholesterol 118mg 39%	Dietary Fiber 0.1g 0%
Total Fat 14.5g 19%	Sodium 107mg 5%	Total Sugars 0.2g
Saturated Fat 7.3g 37%	Total Carbs 1.2g 0%	Protein 35.4g

Pesto Parmesan Beef Steaks

Serves: 6/Prep Time: 8 hours 10 mins

Ingredients
- 1 cup parmesan cheese, shredded
- 6 beef steaks
- 6 tablespoons pesto sauce
- Salt and black pepper, to taste
- ½ cup parsley, chopped

Directions
1. Season the beef steaks with salt and black pepper.
2. Drizzle with pesto sauce and put in the slow cooker.
3. Cover and cook on Low for about 7 hours. Top with Parmesan cheese and parsley.
4. Cook again on Low for about 1 hour and dish out to serve.

Nutrition Amount per serving

Calories 385	Cholesterol 86mg 29%	Dietary Fiber 0.4g 2%
Total Fat 30.4g 39%	Sodium 327mg 14%	Total Sugars 1g
Saturated Fat 11.4g 57%	Total Carbs 2g 1%	Protein 25.6g

Bacon Garlic Beef Tenderloins

Serves: 6/Prep Time: 40 mins

Ingredients

- 2 pounds beef tenderloins
- 6 garlic cloves, minced
- 1 tablespoon canola oil
- 6 slices bacon, thick cut
- Salt and black pepper, to taste

Directions

1. Rub the beef tenderloins with garlic, salt and black pepper.
2. Wrap the beef tenderloins with the bacon slices.
3. Put the canola oil and wrapped beef in a skillet.
4. Cook on all sides for about 30 minutes on medium low heat.
5. Dish out and serve hot.

Nutrition Amount per serving

Calories 439	Cholesterol 160mg 53%	Dietary Fiber 0.1g 0%
Total Fat 24.1g 31%	Sodium 529mg 23%	Total Sugars 0g
Saturated Fat 8g 40%	Total Carbs 1.3g 0%	Protein 51g

Keto Italian Beef Steaks

Serves: 5/Prep Time: 50 mins

Ingredients

- ¾ cup cream cheese
- 1½ pounds beef steaks
- 1 tablespoon butter
- 1 teaspoon Italian seasoning
- ¾ cup mozzarella cheese, grated

Directions

1. Mix the mozzarella cheese, Italian seasoning and cream cheese in a bowl.
2. Heat butter in a skillet and add beef steaks.
3. Sauté for about 3 minutes on each side and stir in the cheese mixture.
4. Cover and cook for about 30 minutes on medium low heat.
5. Dish out and serve hot.

Nutrition Amount per serving

Calories 409	Cholesterol 169mg 56%	Dietary Fiber 0g 0%
Total Fat 23.9g 31%	Sodium 235mg 10%	Total Sugars 0.2g
Saturated Fat 12.8g 64%	Total Carbs 1.2g 0%	Protein 45.1g

BLT Burgers

Serves: 4/Prep Time: 35 mins

Ingredients

- 1 pound ground beef
- 1 pound bacon slices, halved
- Kosher salt and black pepper, to taste
- 4 butterhead lettuce, for serving
- ½ cup mayonnaise

Directions

1. Preheat a grill pan to medium high heat.
2. Season the ground beef with kosher salt and black pepper.
3. Make large patties out of this mixture and transfer to the grill pan.
4. Grill for about 4 minutes on each side and dish out.
5. Place bacon slices at the bottom of a plate and spread with mayonnaise.
6. Top with beef and lettuce and close with the bacon slices.
7. Serve immediately.

Nutrition Amount per serving

Calories 372	Cholesterol 114mg 38%	Dietary Fiber 1.8g 6%
Total Fat 19.2g 25%	Sodium 401mg 17%	Total Sugars 3.4g
Saturated Fat 4.8g 24%	Total Carbs 10.7g 4%	Protein 38.6g

Pork Recipes

Pork Filled Egg Muffins

Serves: 6/Prep Time: 25 mins

Ingredients

- 4 eggs
- 4 slices pork, precooked
- ½ teaspoon lemon pepper seasoning
- 4 tablespoons goat cheddar cheese, shredded
- 1 green onion, diced

Directions

1. Preheat the oven to 375°F and grease 6 muffin molds lightly.
2. Mix together eggs, onion, pork, lemon pepper seasoning and cheddar cheese in a bowl.
3. Pour the batter into the muffin molds and transfer to the oven.
4. Bake for about 15 minutes and take the muffins from oven to serve.

Nutrition Amount per serving

Calories 136	Cholesterol 161mg 54%	Dietary Fiber 0.1g 0%
Total Fat 9.6g 12%	Sodium 359mg 16%	Total Sugars 0.1g
Saturated Fat 3.4g 17%	Total Carbs 1.7g 1%	Protein 10.1g

Pork Bread

Serves: 6/Prep Time: 35 mins

Ingredients

- ½ cup almond milk
- ½ cup almond oil
- 2 pastured eggs
- ½ pound pork, precooked and shredded
- ¼ teaspoon baking soda

Directions

1. Preheat the oven to 375°F and grease a baking dish with almond oil.
2. Mix eggs, almond milk, baking soda and pork in a bowl.
3. Pour the batter into the baking dish and transfer the oven.
4. Bake for about 20 minutes and remove from the oven.
5. Slice and serve hot.

Nutrition Amount per serving

Calories 284	Cholesterol 99mg 33%	Dietary Fiber 0.4g 2%
Total Fat 25.8g 33%	Sodium 98mg 4%	Total Sugars 0.7g
Saturated Fat 6.7g 33%	Total Carbs 1.5g 1%	Protein 12.4g

Garlic Creamy Pork Chops

Serves: 8/Prep Time: 45 mins

Ingredients

- ½ cup butter
- Salt and black pepper, to taste
- 4 garlic cloves, minced
- 2 pounds pork chops
- 1½ cups heavy cream

Directions

1. Rub the pork chops with garlic, salt and black pepper.
2. Marinate the chops with butter and cream and set aside for 1 hour.
3. Preheat the grill to medium high heat and transfer the steaks to it.
4. Grill for about 15 minutes on each side and transfer to a plate and serve hot.

Nutrition Amount per serving

Calories 545	Cholesterol 159mg 53%	Dietary Fiber 0g 0%
Total Fat 48g 62%	Sodium 170mg 7%	Total Sugars 0.1g
Saturated Fat 23g 115%	Total Carbs 1.2g 0%	Protein 26.2g

Pork Fajitas

Serves: 4/Prep Time: 40 minutes

Ingredients

- 1 tablespoon butter
- 1 bell pepper, sliced
- 1 pound pork tenderloins, sliced
- 1 tablespoon fajita seasoning
- 1 onion, sliced

Directions

1. Put the butter in the bottom of a skillet and add onions.
2. Sauté for about 3 minutes and add bell pepper.
3. Cook for about 2 minutes and stir in pork tenderloins and fajita seasoning.
4. Cover with lid and cook for about 25 minutes on medium low heat.
5. Dish out the delicious pork fajitas and serve hot.

Nutrition Amount per serving

Calories 265	Cholesterol 109mg 36%	Dietary Fiber 1g 4%
Total Fat 10.1g 13%	Sodium 228mg 10%	Total Sugars 2.7g
Saturated Fat 4.5g 22%	Total Carbs 6.4g 2%	Protein 35g

Jamaican Jerk Pork Roast

Serves: 3/Prep Time: 35 mins

Ingredients

- 1 tablespoon butter
- 1/8 cup beef broth
- 1 pound pork shoulder
- 1/8 cup Jamaican jerk spice blend
- Salt, to taste

Directions

1. Season the pork with Jamaican jerk spice blend.
2. Heat the butter in the pot and add seasoned pork.
3. Cook for about 5 minutes and add beef broth.
4. Cover with lid and cook for about 20 minutes on low heat.
5. Dish out on a serving platter and serve hot.

Nutrition Amount per serving

Calories 477	Cholesterol 146mg 49%	Dietary Fiber 0g 0%
Total Fat 36.2g 46%	Sodium 212mg 9%	Total Sugars 0g
Saturated Fat 14.3g 72%	Total Carbs 0g 0%	Protein 35.4g

Pork Carnitas

Serves: 3/Prep Time: 40 mins

Ingredients

- 1 pound pork shoulder, bone-in
- Salt and black pepper, to taste
- 1 tablespoon butter
- 1 orange, juiced
- ½ teaspoon garlic powder

Directions

1. Season the pork with salt and black pepper.
2. Put butter in the pressure cooker and add garlic powder.
3. Sauté for 1 minute and add seasoned pork. Sauté for 3 minutes and pour orange juice.
4. Lock the lid and cook on high pressure for about 20 minutes.
5. Naturally release the pressure and dish out.
6. Shred the pork with a fork and transfer back to the cooker.
7. Sauté for about 3 minutes and serve warm.

Nutrition Amount per serving

Calories 506	Cholesterol 146mg 49%	Dietary Fiber 1.5g 5%
Total Fat 36.3g 46%	Sodium 130mg 6%	Total Sugars 5.8g
Saturated Fat 14.3g 72%	Total Carbs 7.6g 3%	Protein 35.9g

Zesty Pork Chops

Serves: 4/Prep Time: 50 mins

Ingredients

- 4 tablespoons butter
- 3 tablespoons lemon juice
- 4 pork chops, bone-in
- 2 tablespoons low carb flour mix
- 1 cup picante sauce

Directions

1. Coat the pork chops with low carb flour mix.
2. Mix picante sauce and lemon juice in a bowl.
3. Heat oil in a skillet on medium heat and add the chops and picante mixture.
4. Cook covered for about 35 minutes and dish out to serve hot.

Nutrition Amount per serving

Calories 398	Cholesterol 99mg 33%	Dietary Fiber 0.7g 3%
Total Fat 33.4g 43%	Sodium 441mg 19%	Total Sugars 2.1g
Saturated Fat 15g 75%	Total Carbs 4g 1%	Protein 19.7g

Greek Pork Gyros

Serves: 4/Prep Time: 40 mins

Ingredients

- 4 garlic cloves
- 3 teaspoons ground marjoram
- 1 pound pork meat, ground
- Salt and black pepper, to taste
- ½ small onion, chopped

Directions

1. Preheat the oven to 400°F and grease a loaf pan lightly.
2. Put onions, garlic, marjoram, salt and black pepper in a food processor and process until well combined. Add ground pork meat and process again.
3. Press meat mixture into the loaf pan until compact and very tight.
4. Tightly cover with tin foil and poke some holes in the foil.
5. Bake in the oven for about 25 minutes and dish out to serve warm.

Nutrition Amount per serving

Calories 310	Cholesterol 80mg 27%	Dietary Fiber 0.4g 2%
Total Fat 24.2g 31%	Sodium 66mg 3%	Total Sugars 0.4g
Saturated Fat 9g 45%	Total Carbs 2.1g 1%	Protein 19.4g

Garlic Rosemary Pork Chops

Serves: 4/Prep Time: 30 mins

Ingredients

- 1 tablespoon rosemary, freshly minced
- 2 garlic cloves, minced
- 4 pork loin chops
- ½ cup butter, melted
- Salt and black pepper, to taste

Directions

1. Preheat the oven to 375°F and season pork chops with salt and black pepper.
2. Mix together ¼ cup butter, rosemary and garlic in a small bowl.
3. Heat the rest of the butter in an oven safe skillet and add pork chops.
4. Sear for about 4 minutes per side until golden and brush pork chops generously with garlic butter.
5. Place skillet in the oven and bake for about 15 minutes until cooked through.
6. Dish out and serve hot.

Nutrition Amount per serving

Calories 465	Cholesterol 130mg 43%	Dietary Fiber 0.4g 1%
Total Fat 43g 55%	Sodium 220mg 10%	Total Sugars 0g
Saturated Fat 22.1g 110%	Total Carbs 1.1g 0%	Protein 18.4g

Lemony Grilled Pork Chops

Serves: 4/Prep Time: 20 mins

Ingredients

- 2 tablespoons extra-virgin olive oil
- 4 pork chops
- 2 tablespoons butter
- Kosher salt and black pepper, to taste
- 2 lemons, sliced

Directions

1. Preheat the grill to high heat.
2. Brush pork chops with olive oil and season with salt and black pepper.
3. Put the pork chops on grill and top with lemon slices.
4. Grill for about 10 minutes per side until lemons are charred and chops are cooked through. Dish out on a platter and serve hot.

Nutrition Amount per serving

Calories 375	Cholesterol 84mg 28%	Dietary Fiber 0.8g 3%
Total Fat 32.7g 42%	Sodium 97mg 4%	Total Sugars 0.7g
Saturated Fat 12.1g 61%	Total Carbs 2.7g 1%	Protein 18.4g

Cheddar Maple Squash

Serves: 4/Prep Time: 30 mins

Ingredients

- 1½ pounds summer squash, peeled, halved, seeded, and cut into 1½ inch cubes
- 1 cup aged white cheddar cheese, coarsely grated
- 1 tablespoon sugar free maple syrup
- 1 tablespoon fresh sage, chopped and crushed
- 2 slices pork bacon, cooked and chopped

Directions

1. Boil the summer squash for about 15 minutes and mash with a potato masher.
2. Stir in cheddar cheese, sage and maple syrup and top with cooked pork bacon to serve.

Nutrition Amount per serving

Calories 196	Cholesterol 40mg 13%	Dietary Fiber 2.1g 7%
Total Fat 13.7g 18%	Sodium 414mg 18%	Total Sugars 3.1g
Saturated Fat 7.4g 37%	Total Carbs 7.1g 3%	Protein 12.7g

Spinach Pork Roll Ups

Serves: 8/Prep Time: 15 mins

Ingredients

- 2 teaspoons honey mustard
- 8 thin slices bacon, smoked
- 1 cup Monterey Jack cheese, cut lengthwise into quarters
- 1 cup fresh baby spinach leaves
- ½ medium red bell pepper, seeded and cut into thin strips

Directions

1. Spread the honey mustard over bacon slices.
2. Divide spinach leaves among 8 plates and place bacon slices on it.
3. Top with red bell pepper and cheese to serve.

Nutrition Amount per serving

Calories 161	Cholesterol 33mg 11%	Dietary Fiber 0.2g 1%
Total Fat 12.3g 16%	Sodium 524mg 23%	Total Sugars 0.7g
Saturated Fat 5.3g 27%	Total Carbs 1.6g 1%	Protein 10.7g

Stuffed Pork Chops

Serves: 6/Prep Time: 40 mins
Ingredients
- 4 garlic cloves, minced
- 2 pounds cut boneless pork chops
- 1½ teaspoons salt
- 8 oz. provolone cheese
- 2 cups baby spinach

Directions
1. Preheat the oven to 350°F and grease a baking sheet.
2. Mix garlic with salt and rub on one side of the pork chops.
3. Place half of the pork chops garlic side down on a baking sheet and top with spinach and provolone cheese. Top with rest of the pork chops garlic side up and place in the oven.
4. Bake for about 30 minutes and dish out to serve hot.

Nutrition Amount per serving

Calories 430	Cholesterol 165mg 55%	Dietary Fiber 0.3g 1%
Total Fat 20.2g 26%	Sodium 1005mg 44%	Total Sugars 0.3g
Saturated Fat 9.8g 49%	Total Carbs 1.8g 1%	Protein 57.2g

Pork with Butternut Squash Stew

Serves: 4/Prep Time: 40 mins
Ingredients
- ½ pound butternut squash, peeled and cubed
- 1 pound lean pork
- 2 tablespoons butter
- Salt and black pepper, to taste
- 1 cup beef stock

Directions
1. Put the butter and lean pork in a skillet and cook for about 5 minutes.
2. Add butternut squash, beef stock and season with salt and black pepper.
3. Cover with lid and cook for about 25 minutes on medium low heat.
4. Dish out to a bowl and serve hot.

Nutrition Amount per serving

Calories 319	Cholesterol 105mg 35%	Dietary Fiber 1.1g 4%
Total Fat 17.1g 22%	Sodium 311mg 14%	Total Sugars 1.3g
Saturated Fat 7.9g 39%	Total Carbs 6.7g 2%	Protein 33.7g

Keto Sweet Mustard Pork

Serves: 4/Prep Time: 40 mins
Ingredients
- ¼ cup Dijon mustard
- 4 pork chops
- 1 tablespoon granular Erythritol
- 2 tablespoons olive oil
- ½ cup sour cream

Directions
1. Preheat the oven to 350°F.
2. Mix together Dijon mustard, Erythritol and sour cream in a bowl.
3. Combine the pork chops and half of the mustard dressing in a bowl.
4. Marinate the pork chops overnight in the refrigerator.
5. Heat olive oil over medium high heat in a large oven proof skillet and add pork.
6. Cook for about 4 minutes on both sides until brown and pour in the remaining mustard dressing. Place the skillet into the oven and bake for about 20 minutes.
7. Dish out and serve hot.

Nutrition Amount per serving

Calories 388	Cholesterol 81mg 27%	Dietary Fiber 0.5g 2%
Total Fat 33.5g 43%	Sodium 249mg 11%	Total Sugars 3.9g
Saturated Fat 12.2g 61%	Total Carbs 5.8g 2%	Protein 19.6g

Barbecue Dry Rub Ribs

Serves: 8/Prep Time: 2 hours 50 mins

Ingredients

- 2 tablespoons olive oil
- 2 pounds pork baby back ribs
- 1½ tablespoons smoked paprika
- 1 tablespoon Erythritol
- Garlic powder, onion powder, chili powder and sea salt

Directions

1. Preheat the oven to 300°F and line a baking sheet with aluminum foil.
2. Mix together garlic powder, onion powder, chili powder, sea salt, Erythritol and smoked paprika in a bowl. Place the pork baby back ribs on the baking sheet and brush with olive oil.
3. Sprinkle the dry rub over both sides of the ribs and place in the oven.
4. Bake for about 2 hours until the ribs are juicy and tender.
5. Dish out onto a platter and serve hot.

Nutrition Amount per serving

Calories 451	Cholesterol 96mg 32%	Dietary Fiber 0.6g 2%
Total Fat 37.5g 48%	Sodium 77mg 3%	Total Sugars 2.2g
Saturated Fat 14.2g 71%	Total Carbs 3.3g 1%	Protein 26g

Pork Enchilada Casserole

Serves: 5/Prep Time: 1 hour

Ingredients

- 1 pound boneless pork
- 1½ cups enchilada sauce
- 3 cups cheddar cheese, shredded
- Salt and black pepper, to taste
- ½ cup fresh cilantro, minced

Directions

1. Preheat the oven to 450°F and grease a casserole dish with olive oil.
2. Season pork with salt and black pepper. Put the pork and 1 cup enchilada sauce in a saucepan and cook on medium low heat for about 30 minutes. Dish out the pork and shred with a fork. Combine shredded pork, ½ cup enchilada sauce and cilantro in the casserole dish and top with cheddar cheese.
3. Transfer to the oven and bake for about 15 minutes. Dish out and serve hot.

Nutrition Amount per serving

Calories 433	Cholesterol 137mg 46%	Dietary Fiber 3.1g 11%
Total Fat 26g 33%	Sodium 479mg 21%	Total Sugars 0.4g
Saturated Fat 15.5g 78%	Total Carbs 8.4g 3%	Protein 41.9g

Cheesy Bacon Pork Chops

Serves: 6/Prep Time: 50 mins

Ingredients

- ½ pound bacon, cut strips in half
- 6 pork chops
- 1 cup cheddar cheese, shredded
- Salt and black pepper, to taste
- 2 tablespoons paprika, smoked

Directions

1. Preheat the oven to 360°F and grease a baking dish. Season the pork chops with paprika, salt and black pepper. Put the pork chops in the baking dish and top with bacon.
2. Sprinkle the cheese over the pork chops and bacon and transfer to the oven.
3. Bake for about 35 minutes and dish out to serve hot.

Nutrition Amount per serving

Calories 543	Cholesterol 130mg 43%	Dietary Fiber 0.9g 3%
Total Fat 42.2g 54%	Sodium 1047mg 46%	Total Sugars 0.3g
Saturated Fat 16.7g 83%	Total Carbs 2.1g 1%	Protein 37g

Ketogenic Easy Pork Briskets

Serves: 6/Prep Time: 7 hours 10 mins

Ingredients
- 1 tablespoon butter
- 2 pounds pork briskets
- 2 garlic cloves, minced
- Salt and black pepper, to taste
- 1 small onion, sliced

Directions
1. Put all the ingredients in a large slow cooker and cover the lid.
2. Cook on low for about 7 hours and dish out the pork briskets onto a cutting board.
3. Slice with a knife into desired slices to serve.

Nutrition Amount per serving

Calories 304
Total Fat 11.4g 15%
Saturated Fat 4.8g 24%

Cholesterol 140mg 47%
Sodium 114mg 5%
Total Carbs 1.4g 1%

Dietary Fiber 0.3g 1%
Total Sugars 0.5g
Protein 46.1g

Ground Pork with Zucchini

Serves: 6/Prep Time: 35 mins

Ingredients
- 2 large zucchinis, chopped
- 2 pounds lean ground pork
- 3 tablespoons butter
- Salt and black pepper, to taste
- ½ cup homemade bone broth

Directions
1. Put the butter and pork in a skillet and cook for about 5 minutes.
2. Add the bone broth, zucchini, salt and black pepper.
3. Cook for about 20 minutes and dish out to serve hot.

Nutrition Amount per serving

Calories 164
Total Fat 12g 15%
Saturated Fat 5.5g 28%

Cholesterol 50mg 17%
Sodium 90mg 4%
Total Carbs 3.6g 1%

Dietary Fiber 1.2g 4%
Total Sugars 1.9g
Protein 10.9g

Creamy BBQ Pork

Serves: 6/Prep Time: 55 mins

Ingredients
- ½ cup BBQ sauce
- 2 pounds pork, boneless
- 4 tablespoons butter
- Salt, to taste
- 1 cup cream

Directions
1. Heat butter in a skillet and add pork and salt.
2. Cook for about 5 minutes and stir in the BBQ sauce and cream.
3. Cover and cook for about 35 minutes.
4. Dish out in a bowl and serve hot.

Nutrition Amount per serving

Calories 406
Total Fat 19.4g 25%
Saturated Fat 9.8g 49%

Cholesterol 163mg 54%
Sodium 427mg 19%
Total Carbs 8.8g 3%

Dietary Fiber 0.1g 0%
Total Sugars 6.2g
Protein 46.3g

Ketogenic Lime Chili Pork Briskets

Serves: 4/Prep Time: 8 hours 10 mins

Ingredients

- 4 green chilies, chopped
- Salt, to taste
- 1 pound pork briskets
- 1 tablespoon lime juice
- 1 cup bone broth

Directions

1. Season the pork briskets with salt and lime juice.
2. Add the seasoned beef, green chilies and broth to the slow cooker.
3. Set the slow cooker on low and cook for about 8 hours.
4. Dish out onto a platter and serve hot.

Nutrition Amount per serving

Calories 124	Cholesterol 30mg 10%	Dietary Fiber 0.2g 1%
Total Fat 1.9g 2%	Sodium 666mg 29%	Total Sugars 1.5g
Saturated Fat 0.1g 1%	Total Carbs 3g 1%	Protein 25.6g

Keto Broccoli Pork

Serves: 4/Prep Time: 45 mins

Ingredients

- 3 cups broccoli florets
- 1 pound pork, thinly sliced and chopped into 2 inch pieces
- 2 tablespoons butter
- 2 tablespoons cornstarch + 4 tablespoons cold water
- 1 cup bone broth

Directions

1. Heat butter on medium heat in a skillet and add pork.
2. Sauté for about 3 minutes on each side and add broccoli and bone broth.
3. Cook for about 30 minutes and stir in the cornstarch with water.
4. Cover the skillet and cook for about 4 minutes.
5. Dish out and serve hot.

Nutrition Amount per serving

Calories 261	Cholesterol 98mg 33%	Dietary Fiber 1.8g 6%
Total Fat 10.3g 13%	Sodium 319mg 14%	Total Sugars 1.3g
Saturated Fat 5.1g 26%	Total Carbs 8.4g 3%	Protein 32.9g

Home Style Pork Meatloaf

Serves: 4/Prep Time: 30 mins

Ingredients

- 1 large onion, sliced
- 1 cup tomato sauce
- 1 pound ground pork
- 1 egg
- Salt and black pepper, to taste

Directions

1. Put the ground pork, salt, black pepper, egg and onion in a grinder and grind well.
2. Mold the ground mixture into loaves.
3. Put the tomato sauce and loaves in the pressure cooker.
4. Cook on High Pressure for about 20 minutes and dish out to serve.

Nutrition Amount per serving

Calories 208	Cholesterol 124mg 41%	Dietary Fiber 1.7g 6%
Total Fat 5.2g 7%	Sodium 403mg 18%	Total Sugars 4.3g
Saturated Fat 1.7g 9%	Total Carbs 6.9g 3%	Protein 32.3g

Italian Pork with Veggies

Serves: 5/Prep Time: 40 mins

Ingredients

- 2 bell peppers, sliced
- 1½ pounds pork, sliced
- 2 tablespoons butter
- 1 onion, sliced
- 2 tablespoons Italian seasoning

Directions

1. Heat butter on medium heat in a skillet and add pork.
2. Sauté for about 3 minutes and add bell pepper, onion, and Italian seasoning.
3. Cover with lid and cook for about 25 minutes.
4. Dish out and serve hot.

Nutrition Amount per serving

Calories 330	Cholesterol 134mg 45%	Dietary Fiber 1.1g 4%
Total Fat 13.2g 17%	Sodium 334mg 15%	Total Sugars 3.3g
Saturated Fat 6.1g 31%	Total Carbs 8.2g 3%	Protein 42.1g

Pork Taco Casserole

Serves: 6/Prep Time: 40 mins

Ingredients

- 1 cup cottage cheese
- 2 pounds ground pork
- 2 tablespoons taco seasoning
- 1 cup salsa
- ½ cup cheddar cheese, shredded

Directions

1. Preheat the oven to 375°F and grease a casserole dish.
2. Mix the ground pork and taco seasoning in a bowl.
3. Mix together the cottage cheese, cheddar cheese and salsa.
4. Put the ground pork mixture in the casserole dish and top with the cheese mixture.
5. Transfer to the oven and bake for about 30 minutes.
6. Remove from the oven and serve hot.

Nutrition Amount per serving

Calories 310	Cholesterol 123mg 41%	Dietary Fiber 0.7g 2%
Total Fat 9.2g 12%	Sodium 768mg 33%	Total Sugars 2g
Saturated Fat 4.3g 21%	Total Carbs 6.2g 2%	Protein 47.8g

Slow Cooker Pork Stew

Serves: 6/Prep Time: 7 hours 10 mins

Ingredients

- 2 medium onions, chopped
- 2 pounds salmon fillet, cubed
- 2 tablespoons butter
- 2 cups homemade fish broth
- Salt and black pepper, to taste

Directions

1. Put all the ingredients in the slow cooker and mix well.
2. Cover the lid and cook on low for about 7 hours.
3. Dish out to a bowl and serve hot.

Nutrition Amount per serving

Calories 272	Cholesterol 82mg 27%	Dietary Fiber 1.1g 4%
Total Fat 14.2g 18%	Sodium 275mg 12%	Total Sugars 1.9g
Saturated Fat 4.1g 20%	Total Carbs 4.4g 2%	Protein 32.1g

Buttered Chili Pork Chops

Serves: 6/Prep Time: 40 mins

Ingredients

- 6 green chilies, chopped
- 2 pounds pork chops
- 1½ cups butter
- Salt and black pepper, to taste
- 1 teaspoon paprika

Directions

1. Season the pork chops evenly with paprika, salt and black pepper.
2. Put 3 tablespoons of butter in a skillet and add pork chops.
3. Cook for about 4 minutes on each side and top with butter and chilies.
4. Cover the skillet and cook on medium low heat for about 25 minutes.
5. Dish out and serve hot.

Nutrition Amount per serving

Calories 670	Cholesterol 189mg 63%	Dietary Fiber 0.2g 1%
Total Fat 62.8g 80%	Sodium 325mg 14%	Total Sugars 0.2g
Saturated Fat 32.4g 162%	Total Carbs 0.5g 0%	Protein 25.9g

Ketogenic Pork in Gravy

Serves: 6/Prep Time: 45 mins

Ingredients

- 4 tablespoons butter
- Salt and black pepper, to taste
- 2 pounds pork, cubed
- 1 large onion, sliced
- 1 cup homemade tomato puree

Directions

1. Heat butter on medium heat in a skillet and add onions.
2. Sauté for about 3 minutes and add pork, tomato puree, salt and black pepper.
3. Cover the skillet and cook for about 30 minutes on medium low heat.
4. Dish out and serve hot.

Nutrition Amount per serving

Calories 304	Cholesterol 131mg 44%	Dietary Fiber 1.2g 4%
Total Fat 13g 17%	Sodium 148mg 6%	Total Sugars 2.4g
Saturated Fat 6.7g 33%	Total Carbs 4.4g 2%	Protein 40.3g

Pork Asparagus Roll Ups

Serves: 1/Prep Time: 20 mins

Ingredients

- 1 tablespoon mozzarella cheese
- 2 teaspoons cream cheese
- 2 thin slices pork meat, smoked
- 2 asparagus spears, boiled
- Ground black pepper, to taste

Directions

1. Mix together cream cheese and mozzarella cheese in a bowl.
2. Put the cheese mixture between pork slices and season lightly with black pepper.
3. Place an asparagus spear on each pork slice and roll up to serve.

Nutrition Amount per serving

Calories 453	Cholesterol 172mg 57%	Dietary Fiber 1g 4%
Total Fat 23.4g 30%	Sodium 361mg 16%	Total Sugars 0.9g
Saturated Fat 10.5g 52%	Total Carbs 3.1g 1%	Protein 53.6g

Fish and Seafood Recipes

Garlic Butter Salmon

Serves: 8/Prep Time: 40 mins

Ingredients

- Kosher salt and black pepper, to taste
- 1 pound (3 pounds) salmon fillet, skin removed
- 4 tablespoons butter, melted
- 2 garlic cloves, minced
- ¼ cup parmesan cheese, freshly grated

Directions

1. Preheat the oven to 350°F and lightly grease a large baking sheet.
2. Season the salmon with salt and black pepper and transfer to the baking sheet.
3. Mix together butter, garlic and parmesan cheese in a small bowl.
4. Marinate salmon in this mixture for about 1 hour.
5. Transfer to the oven and bake for about 25 minutes.
6. Additionally, broil for about 2 minutes until top becomes lightly golden.
7. Dish out onto a platter and serve hot.

Nutrition Amount per serving

Calories 172	Cholesterol 50mg 17%	Dietary Fiber 0g 0%
Total Fat 12.3g 16%	Sodium 196mg 9%	Total Sugars 0g
Saturated Fat 6.2g 31%	Total Carbs 0.8g 0%	Protein 15.6g

Tuscan Butter Salmon

Serves: 4/Prep Time: 35 mins

Ingredients

- 4 (6 oz) salmon fillets, patted dry with paper towels
- 3 tablespoons butter
- ¾ cup heavy cream
- Kosher salt and black pepper
- 2 cups baby spinach

Directions

1. Season the salmon with salt and black pepper.
2. Heat 1½ tablespoons butter over medium high heat in a large skillet and add salmon skin side up.
3. Cook for about 10 minutes on both sides until deeply golden and dish out onto a plate.
4. Heat the rest of the butter in the skillet and add spinach.
5. Cook for about 5 minutes and stir in the heavy cream.
6. Reduce heat to low and simmer for about 3 minutes.
7. Return the salmon to the skillet and mix well with the sauce.
8. Allow to simmer for about 3 minutes until salmon is cooked through.
9. Dish out and serve hot.

Nutrition Amount per serving

Calories 382	Cholesterol 129mg 43%	Dietary Fiber 0.3g 1%
Total Fat 27.5g 35%	Sodium 157mg 7%	Total Sugars 0.1g
Saturated Fat 12.2g 61%	Total Carbs 1.2g 0%	Protein 34g

Mahi Mahi Stew

Serves: 3/Prep Time: 45 mins

Ingredients

- 2 tablespoons butter
- 2 pounds Mahi Mahi fillets, cubed
- 1 onion, chopped
- Salt and black pepper, to taste
- 2 cups homemade fish broth

Directions

1. Season the Mahi Mahi fillets with salt and black pepper.
2. Heat butter in a pressure cooker and add onion.

3. Sauté for about 3 minutes and stir in the seasoned Mahi Mahi fillets and fish broth.
4. Lock the lid and cook on High Pressure for about 30 minutes.
5. Naturally release the pressure and dish out to serve hot.

Nutrition Amount per serving

Calories 398	Cholesterol 290mg 97%	Dietary Fiber 1.5g 5%
Total Fat 12.5g 16%	Sodium 803mg 35%	Total Sugars 2.2g
Saturated Fat 6.4g 32%	Total Carbs 5.5g 2%	Protein 62.3g

Sour Cream Tilapia

Serves: 3/Prep Time: 3 hours 10 mins
Ingredients
- ¾ cup homemade chicken broth
- 1 pound tilapia fillets
- 1 cup sour cream
- Salt and black pepper, to taste
- 1 teaspoon cayenne pepper

Directions
1. Put tilapia fillets in the slow cooker along with rest of the ingredients.
2. Cover the lid and cook on low for about 3 hours. Dish out and serve hot.

Nutrition Amount per serving

Calories 300	Cholesterol 107mg 36%	Dietary Fiber 0.2g 1%
Total Fat 17.9g 23%	Sodium 285mg 12%	Total Sugars 0.4g
Saturated Fat 10.7g 54%	Total Carbs 3.9g 1%	Protein 31.8g

Tilapia with Herbed Butter

Serves: 6/Prep Time: 35 mins
Ingredients
- 2 pounds tilapia fillets
- 12 garlic cloves, chopped finely
- 6 green broccoli, chopped
- 2 cups herbed butter
- Salt and black pepper, to taste

Directions
1. Season the tilapia fillets with salt and black pepper.
2. Put the seasoned tilapia along with all other ingredients in an Instant Pot and mix well.
3. Cover the lid and cook on High Pressure for about 25 minutes.
4. Dish out in a platter and serve hot.

Nutrition Amount per serving

Calories 281	Cholesterol 109mg 36%	Dietary Fiber 2.5g 9%
Total Fat 10.4g 13%	Sodium 178mg 8%	Total Sugars 1.9g
Saturated Fat 4.3g 21%	Total Carbs 9g 3%	Protein 38.7g

Roasted Trout

Serves: 4/Prep Time: 45 mins
Ingredients
- ½ cup fresh lemon juice
- 1 pound trout fish fillets
- 4 tablespoons butter
- Salt and black pepper, to taste
- 1 teaspoon dried rosemary, crushed

Directions
1. Put ½ pound trout fillets in a dish and sprinkle with lemon juice and dried rosemary.
2. Season with salt and black pepper and transfer into a skillet.
3. Add butter and cook, covered on medium low heat for about 35 minutes.
4. Dish out the fillets in a platter and serve with a sauce.

Nutrition Amount per serving

Calories 349	Cholesterol 31mg 10%	Dietary Fiber 0.3g 1%
Total Fat 28.2g 36%	Sodium 88mg 4%	Total Sugars 0.9g
Saturated Fat 11.7g 58%	Total Carbs 1.1g 0%	Protein 23.3g

Sour Fish with Herbed Butter

Serves: 3/Prep Time: 45 mins

Ingredients

- 2 tablespoons herbed butter
- 3 cod fillets
- 1 tablespoon vinegar
- Salt and black pepper, to taste
- ½ tablespoon lemon pepper seasoning

Directions

1. Preheat the oven to 375°F and grease a baking tray.
2. Mix together cod fillets, vinegar, lemon pepper seasoning, salt and black pepper in a bowl.
3. Marinate for about 3 hours and then arrange on the baking tray.
4. Transfer into the oven and bake for about 30 minutes.
5. Remove from the oven and serve with herbed butter.

Nutrition Amount per serving

Calories 234	Cholesterol 77mg 26%	Dietary Fiber 0g 0%
Total Fat 11.8g 15%	Sodium 119mg 5%	Total Sugars 0.1g
Saturated Fat 2.4g 12%	Total Carbs 0.4g 0%	Protein 31.5g

Cod Coconut Curry

Serves: 6/Prep Time: 35 mins

Ingredients

- 1 onion, chopped
- 2 pounds cod
- 1 cup dry coconut, chopped
- Salt and black pepper, to taste
- 1 cup fresh lemon juice

Directions

1. Put the cod along with all other ingredients in a pressure cooker.
2. Add 2 cups of water and cover the lid.
3. Cook on High Pressure for about 25 minutes and naturally release the pressure.
4. Open the lid and dish out the curry to serve hot.

Nutrition Amount per serving

Calories 223	Cholesterol 83mg 28%	Dietary Fiber 1.8g 6%
Total Fat 6.1g 8%	Sodium 129mg 6%	Total Sugars 2.5g
Saturated Fat 4.5g 23%	Total Carbs 4.6g 2%	Protein 35.5g

Garlic Shrimp with Goat Cheese

Serves: 4/Prep Time: 30 mins

Ingredients

- 4 tablespoons herbed butter
- Salt and black pepper, to taste
- 1 pound large raw shrimp
- 4 ounces goat cheese
- 4 garlic cloves, chopped

Directions

1. Preheat the oven to 375°F and grease a baking dish.
2. Mix together herbed butter, garlic, raw shrimp, salt and black pepper in a bowl.
3. Put the marinated shrimp on the baking dish and top with the shredded cheese.
4. Place in the oven and bake for about 25 minutes.
5. Take the shrimp out and serve hot.

Nutrition Amount per serving

Calories 294	Cholesterol 266mg 89%	Dietary Fiber 0.1g 0%
Total Fat 15g 19%	Sodium 392mg 17%	Total Sugars 0.8g
Saturated Fat 8.9g 44%	Total Carbs 2.1g 1%	Protein 35.8g

Grain Free Salmon Bread

Serves: 6/Prep Time: 35 mins

Ingredients
- ½ cup olive oil
- ¼ teaspoon baking soda
- ½ cup coconut milk
- 2 pounds salmon, steamed and shredded
- 2 pastured eggs

Directions
1. Preheat the oven to 375°F and grease a baking dish with olive oil.
2. Mix together coconut milk, eggs, baking soda and salmon in a bowl.
3. Pour the batter of salmon bread in the baking dish and transfer into the oven.
4. Bake for about 20 minutes and remove from the oven to serve hot.

Nutrition Amount per serving

Calories 413	Cholesterol 138mg 46%	Dietary Fiber 0.4g 2%
Total Fat 32.4g 42%	Sodium 143mg 6%	Total Sugars 0.7g
Saturated Fat 8.5g 42%	Total Carbs 1.5g 1%	Protein 31.8g

Buttered Mahi Mahi Slices

Serves: 3/Prep Time: 30 mins

Ingredients
- ½ cup butter
- 1 pound Mahi Mahi, steamed and shredded
- ½ onion, chopped
- Salt and black pepper, to taste
- 1 mushroom, chopped

Directions
1. Preheat the oven to 375°F and grease a baking dish.
2. Mix together butter, onion, mushrooms, salt and black pepper in a bowl.
3. Make slices from the batter and place them on the baking dish.
4. Transfer to the oven and bake for about 20 minutes.
5. Remove from the oven and serve with a sauce.

Nutrition Amount per serving

Calories 445	Cholesterol 224mg 75%	Dietary Fiber 0.5g 2%
Total Fat 32.1g 41%	Sodium 390mg 17%	Total Sugars 0.9g
Saturated Fat 19.8g 99%	Total Carbs 2g 1%	Protein 36.6g

Salmon Stew

Serves: 3/Prep Time: 20 mins

Ingredients
- 1 cup homemade fish broth
- 1 medium onion, chopped
- 1 pound salmon fillets, cubed
- Salt and black pepper, to taste
- 1 tablespoon butter

Directions
1. Season the salmon with salt and black pepper.
2. Heat butter in a skillet on medium heat and add onions.
3. Sauté for about 3 minutes and add seasoned salmon.
4. Cook about 2 minutes on each side and stir in the fish broth.
5. Cover with lid and cook for about 7 minutes.
6. Dish out and serve hot.

Nutrition Amount per serving

Calories 272	Cholesterol 82mg 27%	Dietary Fiber 1.1g 4%
Total Fat 14.2g 18%	Sodium 275mg 12%	Total Sugars 1.9g
Saturated Fat 4.1g 20%	Total Carbs 4.4g 2%	Protein 32.1g

Paprika Shrimp

Serves: 6/Prep Time: 25 mins

Ingredients

- 1 teaspoon smoked paprika
- 6 tablespoons butter
- 2 pounds tiger shrimp
- Salt, to taste
- 2 tablespoons sour cream

Directions

1. Preheat the oven to 400°F and grease a baking dish with butter.
2. Mix together all the ingredients with tiger shrimp in a large bowl and marinate well.
3. Place the seasoned shrimp on the baking dish and transfer to the oven.
4. Bake for about 15 minutes and dish out on a platter to serve hot.

Nutrition Amount per serving

Calories 261	Cholesterol 327mg 109%	Dietary Fiber 0.1g 0%
Total Fat 14g 18%	Sodium 450mg 20%	Total Sugars 0.1g
Saturated Fat 8.3g 41%	Total Carbs 0.4g 0%	Protein 31.9g

Ketogenic Butter Fish

Serves: 3/Prep Time: 40 mins

Ingredients

- 2 tablespoons ginger garlic paste
- 3 green chilies, chopped
- 1 pound salmon fillets
- Salt and black pepper, to taste
- ¾ cup butter

Directions

1. Season the salmon fillets with ginger garlic paste, salt and black pepper.
2. Place the salmon fillets in the pot and top with green chilies and butter.
3. Cover the lid and cook on medium low heat for about 30 minutes.
4. Dish out in a platter to serve hot.

Nutrition Amount per serving

Calories 676	Cholesterol 189mg 63%	Dietary Fiber 0.2g 1%
Total Fat 61.2g 78%	Sodium 394mg 17%	Total Sugars 0.2g
Saturated Fat 30.5g 152%	Total Carbs 3.2g 1%	Protein 30.4g

Shrimp Magic

Serves: 3/Prep Time: 25 mins

Ingredients

- 2 tablespoons butter
- ½ teaspoon smoked paprika
- 1 pound shrimp, peeled and deveined
- Lemongrass stalks
- 1 red chili pepper, seeded and chopped

Directions

1. Preheat the oven to 390°F and grease a baking dish.
2. Mix together all the ingredients in a bowl except lemongrass and marinate for about 3 hours.
3. Thread the shrimp onto lemongrass stalks and place in the baking dish.
4. Bake for about 15 minutes and dish out to serve immediately.

Nutrition Amount per serving

Calories 251	Cholesterol 339mg 113%	Dietary Fiber 0.2g 1%
Total Fat 10.3g 13%	Sodium 424mg 18%	Total Sugars 0.1g
Saturated Fat 5.7g 28%	Total Carbs 3g 1%	Protein 34.6g

Sweet and Sour Cod

Serves: 3/Prep Time: 35 mins

Ingredients

- ¼ cup butter
- 2 drops liquid Stevia
- 1 pound cod, chunked
- Salt and black pepper, to taste
- 1 tablespoon vinegar

Directions

1. Heat butter in a large skillet and add cod chunks.
2. Sauté for about 3 minutes and stir in liquid Stevia, vinegar, salt and black pepper.
3. Cook for about 20 minutes at medium low heat, stirring continuously.
4. Dish out to a serving bowl and serve hot.

Nutrition Amount per serving

Calories 296	Cholesterol 124mg 41%	Dietary Fiber 0g 0%
Total Fat 16.7g 21%	Sodium 227mg 10%	Total Sugars 0g
Saturated Fat 10g 50%	Total Carbs 0.1g 0%	Protein 34.7g

Buttered Scallops

Serves: 6/Prep Time: 15 mins

Ingredients

- 4 tablespoons fresh rosemary, chopped
- 4 garlic cloves, minced
- 2 pounds sea scallops
- Salt and black pepper, to taste
- ½ cup butter

Directions

1. Season the sea scallops with salt and black pepper.
2. Put butter, rosemary and garlic on medium high heat in a skillet.
3. Sauté for about 2 minutes and stir in the seasoned sea scallops.
4. Cook for about 3 minutes per side and dish out to serve hot.

Nutrition Amount per serving

Calories 279	Cholesterol 91mg 30%	Dietary Fiber 1g 4%
Total Fat 16.8g 22%	Sodium 354mg 15%	Total Sugars 0g
Saturated Fat 10g 50%	Total Carbs 5.7g 2%	Protein 25.8g

Buffalo Fish

Serves: 3/Prep Time: 20 mins

Ingredients

- 3 tablespoons butter
- 1/3 cup Franks Red Hot sauce
- 3 fish fillets
- Salt and black pepper, to taste
- 1 teaspoon garlic powder

Directions

1. Heat butter in a large skillet and add fish fillets.
2. Cook for about 2 minutes on each side and add salt, black pepper and garlic powder.
3. Cook for about 1 minute and add Franks Red Hot sauce.
4. Cover with lid and cook for about 6 minutes on low heat.
5. Dish out on a serving platter and serve hot.

Nutrition Amount per serving

Calories 342	Cholesterol 109mg 36%	Dietary Fiber 0.1g 0%
Total Fat 22.5g 29%	Sodium 254mg 11%	Total Sugars 0.2g
Saturated Fat 8.9g 44%	Total Carbs 0.9g 0%	Protein 34.8g

Garlicky Lemon Scallops

Serves: 6/Prep Time: 30 mins
Ingredients
- 2 pounds scallops
- 3 garlic cloves, minced
- 5 tablespoons butter, divided
- Red pepper flakes, kosher salt and black pepper
- 1 lemon, zest and juice

Directions
1. Heat 2 tablespoons butter over medium heat in a large skillet and add scallops, kosher salt and black pepper.
2. Cook for about 5 minutes per side until golden and transfer to a plate.
3. Heat remaining butter in a skillet and add garlic and red pepper flakes.
4. Cook for about 1 minute and stir in lemon juice and zest.
5. Return the scallops to the skillet and stir well. Dish out on a platter and serve hot.

Nutrition Amount per serving

Calories 224	Cholesterol 75mg 25%	Dietary Fiber 0.4g 1%
Total Fat 10.8g 14%	Sodium 312mg 14%	Total Sugars 0.3g
Saturated Fat 6.2g 31%	Total Carbs 5.2g 2%	Protein 25.7g

Garlic Parmesan Cod

Serves: 6/Prep Time: 35 mins
Ingredients
- 1 tablespoon extra-virgin olive oil
- 1 (2½) pound cod fillet
- ¼ cup parmesan cheese, finely grated
- Salt and black pepper, to taste
- 5 garlic cloves, minced

Directions
1. Preheat the oven to 400°F and grease a baking dish with cooking spray.
2. Mix together olive oil, garlic, parmesan cheese, salt and black pepper in a bowl.
3. Marinate the cod fillets in this mixture for about 1 hour.
4. Transfer to the baking dish and cover with foil.
5. Place in the oven and bake for about 20 minutes.
6. Remove from the oven and serve warm.

Nutrition Amount per serving

Calories 139	Cholesterol 37mg 12%	Dietary Fiber 0.1g 0%
Total Fat 8g 10%	Sodium 77mg 3%	Total Sugars 0g
Saturated Fat 1.7g 8%	Total Carbs 1g 0%	Protein 16.3g

Energetic Cod Platter

Serves: 6/Prep Time: 40 mins
Ingredients
- 1 pound cherry tomatoes, halved
- 6 (4 ounce) cod fillets
- 3 garlic cloves, minced
- Salt and black pepper, to taste
- 2 tablespoons olive oil

Directions
1. Preheat the oven to 375°F and grease a baking dish.
2. Put half the cherry tomatoes in the baking dish and layer with cod fillets.
3. Season with garlic, salt and black pepper and drizzle with olive oil.
4. Arrange remaining tomatoes on the cod fillets and transfer to the oven.
5. Bake for about 30 minutes and dish out to serve hot.

Nutrition Amount per serving

Calories 147	Cholesterol 56mg 19%	Dietary Fiber 1g 3%
Total Fat 5.8g 7%	Sodium 75mg 3%	Total Sugars 2g
Saturated Fat 0.7g 3%	Total Carbs 3.5g 1%	Protein 21g

Keto Dinner Mussels

Serves: 6/Prep Time: 20 mins

Ingredients

- 4 tablespoons olive oil
- 2 pounds mussels, cleaned and debearded
- 2 garlic cloves, minced
- Salt and black pepper, to taste
- 1 cup homemade chicken broth

Directions

1. Heat olive oil in a skillet over medium heat and add garlic.
2. Sauté for about 1 minute and add mussels.
3. Cook for about 5 minutes and stir in the broth, salt and black pepper.
4. Cover with lid and cook for about 5 minutes on low heat.
5. Dish out to a bowl and serve hot.

Nutrition Amount per serving

Calories 218	Cholesterol 42mg 14%	Dietary Fiber 0g 0%
Total Fat 13g 17%	Sodium 560mg 24%	Total Sugars 0.1g
Saturated Fat 2g 10%	Total Carbs 6.1g 2%	Protein 18.9g

3 Cheese Mussels

Serves: 6/Prep Time: 15 mins

Ingredients

- 1 tablespoon salted butter
- 2 pounds mussels, cleaned and debearded
- ¼ cup mozzarella cheese
- ¼ cup parmesan cheese
- ¼ cup cheddar cheese

Directions

1. Heat butter in a skillet on medium heat and add mussels.
2. Cover with lid and cook for about 5 minutes.
3. Stir in all the cheeses and cook for about 3 minutes.
4. Dish out to a bowl to serve hot.

Nutrition Amount per serving

Calories 184	Cholesterol 56mg 19%	Dietary Fiber 0g 0%
Total Fat 8.1g 10%	Sodium 526mg 23%	Total Sugars 0g
Saturated Fat 3.7g 18%	Total Carbs 5.9g 2%	Protein 21g

Buttered Lobster

Serves: 6/Prep Time: 20 mins

Ingredients

- 2 pounds lobster tails, cut in half
- ½ cup unsalted butter, melted
- 1 garlic clove, minced
- Salt, to taste
- ¼ cup parsley

Directions

1. Preheat the oven to 375°F and lightly grease a baking tray.
2. Place the lobster tails, shell side on the baking tray and season with salt.
3. Top with garlic, butter and parsley and transfer to the oven.
4. Bake for about 15 minutes and dish out to serve hot.

Nutrition Amount per serving

Calories 272	Cholesterol 261mg 87%	Dietary Fiber 0.1g 0%
Total Fat 16.6g 21%	Sodium 845mg 37%	Total Sugars 0g
Saturated Fat 10g 50%	Total Carbs 0.2g 0%	Protein 29g

Creamed Crab Legs

Serves: 4/Prep Time: 25 mins

Ingredients

- 2 tablespoons butter, melted
- 2 pounds crab legs, frozen
- 1 medium onion, thinly sliced
- Salt, to taste
- 1 cup sour cream

Directions

1. Heat butter in a skillet over medium heat and add onion.
2. Sauté for about 3 minutes and add crab legs and salt.
3. Cook for about 3 minutes per side and stir in the sour cream.
4. Cook for about 2 minutes and dish out to serve hot.

Nutrition Amount per serving

Calories 414	Cholesterol 167mg 56%	Dietary Fiber 0.6g 2%
Total Fat 21.3g 27%	Sodium 2540mg 110%	Total Sugars 1.3g
Saturated Fat 11.2g 56%	Total Carbs 5g 2%	Protein 45.7g

Prosciutto Wrapped Salmon Skewers

Serves: 4/Prep Time: 20 mins

Ingredients

- 1 pound salmon, frozen in pieces
- ¼ cup fresh basil, finely chopped
- Black pepper, to taste
- 1 tablespoon olive oil
- 3 oz. prosciutto, in slices

Directions

1. Soak 4 skewers in water and season the salmon fillets with black pepper.
2. Mount the salmon fillets lengthwise on the skewers.
3. Roll the skewers in the chopped basil and wrap with prosciutto slices.
4. Drizzle with olive oil and fry in a nonstick pan for about 5-10 minutes on all sides.
5. Dish out and immediately serve.

Nutrition Amount per serving

Calories 211	Cholesterol 61mg 20%	Dietary Fiber 0g 0%
Total Fat 11.7g 15%	Sodium 306mg 13%	Total Sugars 0g
Saturated Fat 1.9g 9%	Total Carbs 0.4g 0%	Protein 26.5g

Garlic Butter Broiled Lobster Tails

Serves: 4/Prep Time: 25 mins

Ingredients

- 10 tablespoons butter
- 2 lemons, juiced
- 4 lobster tails, top removed and deveined
- ½ cup garlic, minced
- Sea salt, smoked paprika and white pepper

Directions

1. Preheat the broiler to high and grease a baking sheet.
2. Heat 4 tablespoons butter in a medium skillet and add garlic.
3. Sauté for about 2 minutes and set aside.
4. Mix together sea salt, smoked paprika and white pepper in a bowl.
5. Arrange the lobster tails on the baking sheet and sprinkle with the spice mixture.
6. Drizzle with half the garlic butter and transfer to the oven. Bake for about 10 minutes, drizzling rest of the garlic butter in between. Remove from the oven and serve warm.

Nutrition Amount per serving

Calories 367	Cholesterol 200mg 67%	Dietary Fiber 1.6g 6%
Total Fat 29.8g 38%	Sodium 621mg 27%	Total Sugars 1g
Saturated Fat 18.5g 92%	Total Carbs 8.9g 3%	Protein 18g

5 Ingredient Clam Chowder

Serves: 6/Prep Time: 30 mins

Ingredients

- 1 pound cauliflower florets, cut into small pieces
- 2 (6.5 oz) cans clams, finely chopped and liquid retained
- 2½ cups almond milk, unsweetened
- Sea salt and black pepper, to taste
- 1½ cups chicken broth

Directions

1. Put cauliflower florets, clams, almond milk, chicken broth, sea salt and black pepper in a skillet and mix well. Bring to a boil and lower the heat.
2. Allow to simmer for about 20 minutes and dish out in a bowl to serve hot.

Nutrition Amount per serving

Calories 311	Cholesterol 17mg 6%	Dietary Fiber 4.1g 15%
Total Fat 25.6g 33%	Sodium 404mg 18%	Total Sugars 5.3g
Saturated Fat 21.5g 108%	Total Carbs 12.1g 4%	Protein 12.3g

Ginger Butter Prawns

Serves: 1/Prep Time: 20 mins

Ingredients

- ¼ pound prawns
- 2 tablespoons butter
- ½ lemon, juiced
- Salt, black pepper, cayenne pepper
- 2 tablespoons ginger

Directions

1. Marinate the prawns with salt, black pepper, and cayenne pepper and mix well.
2. Heat butter in a pan on medium low heat and add ginger and lemon juice.
3. Cook for about 8 minutes and dish out to a bowl and serve hot.

Nutrition Amount per serving

Calories 384	Cholesterol 300mg 100%	Dietary Fiber 2.2g 8%
Total Fat 25.7g 33%	Sodium 599mg 26%	Total Sugars 1.1g
Saturated Fat 15.4g 77%	Total Carbs 12.1g 4%	Protein 27.4g

Keto Grilled Shrimp with Creole Butter

Serves: 4/Prep Time: 20 mins

Ingredients

- ½ cup salted butter, softened
- 1 pound shrimp, threaded onto skewers
- 2 teaspoons fresh garlic, minced
- 2 tablespoons fresh parsley, chopped
- 1 tablespoon Creole seasoning

Directions

1. Preheat the grill to about 400°F.
2. Mix together butter, parsley, Creole seasoning and garlic in a bowl until well combined.
3. Place the skewers shrimp side down over the grill and grill for about 3 minutes.
4. Flip over the shrimp and baste generously with the Creole butter.
5. Cook for 4 more minutes and dish out to serve.

Nutrition Amount per serving

Calories 341	Cholesterol 300mg 100%	Dietary Fiber 0.1g 0%
Total Fat 25g 32%	Sodium 1251mg 54%	Total Sugars 0.1g
Saturated Fat 15.2g 76%	Total Carbs 2.3g 1%	Protein 26.2g

Vegetable Recipes

Browned Butter Cauliflower Mash

Serves: 4/Prep Time: 35 mins
Ingredients

- 1 yellow onion, finely chopped
- ¾ cup heavy whipping cream
- 1½ pounds cauliflower, shredded
- Sea salt and black pepper, to taste
- 3½ oz. butter

Directions

1. Heat 2 tablespoons butter in a skillet on medium heat and add onions.
2. Sauté for about 3 minutes and dish out to a bowl.
3. Mix together cauliflower, heavy whipping cream, sea salt and black pepper in the same skillet. Cover with lid and cook on medium low heat for about 15 minutes.
4. Season with salt and black pepper and stir in sautéed onions.
5. Dish out to a bowl and heat the rest of the butter in the skillet.
6. Cook until the butter is brown and nutty and serve with cauliflower mash.

Nutrition Amount per serving

Calories 309	Cholesterol 84mg 28%	Dietary Fiber 4.8g 17%
Total Fat 28.7g 37%	Sodium 204mg 9%	Total Sugars 5.3g
Saturated Fat 18g 90%	Total Carbs 12.2g 4%	Protein 4.3g

Cauliflower Gratin

Serves: 6/Prep Time: 35 mins
Ingredients

- 20 oz. cauliflower, chopped
- 2 oz. salted butter, for frying
- 5 oz. cheddar cheese, shredded
- 15 oz. sausages in links, precooked and chopped into 1 inch pieces
- 1 cup crème fraiche

Directions

1. Preheat the oven to 375°F and grease a baking dish lightly.
2. Heat 1 oz. butter in a pan on medium low heat and add chopped cauliflower.
3. Sauté for about 4 minutes and transfer to the baking dish.
4. Heat the rest of the butter in a pan on medium low heat and add sausage links.
5. Sauté for about 3 minutes and transfer to the baking dish on top of cauliflower.
6. Pour the crème fraiche in the baking dish and top with cheddar cheese.
7. Transfer into the oven and bake for about 15 minutes. Dish out to a bowl and serve hot.

Nutrition Amount per serving

Calories 509	Cholesterol 122mg 41%	Dietary Fiber 2.4g 8%
Total Fat 43.7g 56%	Sodium 781mg 34%	Total Sugars 2.5g
Saturated Fat 21.3g 107%	Total Carbs 7g 3%	Protein 22.8g

Beefless Ground Tofu

Serves: 2/Prep Time: 20 mins
Ingredients

- 2 tablespoons tamari
- 1 (16 ounce) package extra firm tofu, drained, crumbled and patted dry
- ½ teaspoon garlic powder
- 1 tablespoon extra-virgin olive oil
- ½ teaspoon paprika

Directions

1. Mix together tofu, garlic powder, tamari and paprika in a bowl.
2. Heat olive oil over medium high heat in a nonstick skillet and add the tofu mixture.
3. Cook for about 10 minutes until nicely browned, stirring occasionally.
4. Dish out to a bowl and serve hot.

Nutrition Amount per serving

Calories 281	Cholesterol 0mg 0%	Dietary Fiber 1.3g 5%
Total Fat 20.3g 26%	Sodium 1024mg 45%	Total Sugars 1.7g
Saturated Fat 2.2g 11%	Total Carbs 6.4g 2%	Protein 24.5g

Browned Butter Asparagus

Serves: 4/Prep Time: 25 mins

Ingredients

- ½ cup sour cream
- 25 oz. green asparagus
- 3 oz. parmesan cheese, grated
- Salt and cayenne pepper, to taste
- 3 oz. butter

Directions

1. Season the asparagus with salt and cayenne pepper.
2. Heat 1 oz. butter in a skillet over medium heat and add seasoned asparagus.
3. Sauté for about 5 minutes and dish out to a bowl.
4. Heat the rest of the butter in a skillet and cook until it is light brown and has a nutty smell. Add asparagus to the butter along with sour cream and parmesan cheese.
5. Dish out to a bowl and serve hot.

Nutrition Amount per serving

Calories 319	Cholesterol 74mg 25%	Dietary Fiber 3.8g 14%
Total Fat 28.1g 36%	Sodium 339mg 15%	Total Sugars 3.4g
Saturated Fat 17.8g 89%	Total Carbs 9.1g 3%	Protein 11.9g

Baked Mini Bell Peppers

Serves: 4/Prep Time: 30 mins

Ingredients

- 1 oz. chorizo, air dried and thinly sliced
- 8 oz. mini bell peppers, sliced lengthwise
- 8 oz. cream cheese
- 1 cup cheddar cheese, shredded
- 1 tablespoon mild chipotle paste

Directions

1. Preheat the oven to 400°F and grease a large baking dish.
2. Mix together cream cheese, chipotle paste, bell peppers and chorizo in a small bowl.
3. Stir the mixture until smooth and transfer to the baking dish.
4. Top with cheddar cheese and place in the oven.
5. Bake for about 20 minutes until the cheese is golden brown and dish onto a platter.

Nutrition Amount per serving

Calories 364	Cholesterol 98mg 33%	Dietary Fiber 0.7g 2%
Total Fat 31.9g 41%	Sodium 491mg 21%	Total Sugars 2.9g
Saturated Fat 19.4g 97%	Total Carbs 6g 2%	Protein 13.8g

Lemon Cream Bok Choy

Serves: 4/Prep Time: 45 mins

Ingredients

- 28 oz. bok choy
- 1 large lemon, juice and zest
- ¾ cup heavy whipping cream
- 1 cup parmesan cheese, freshly grated
- 1 teaspoon black pepper

Directions

1. Preheat the oven to 350°F and lightly grease a baking dish.
2. Pour the cream over the bok choy evenly and drizzle with the lemon juice.
3. Mix well and transfer to the baking dish.
4. Top with parmesan cheese, lemon zest and black pepper and place in the oven.
5. Bake for about 30 minutes until lightly browned and remove from the oven to serve hot.

Nutrition Amount per serving

Calories 199	Cholesterol 51mg 17%	Dietary Fiber 2.5g 9%
Total Fat 14.8g 19%	Sodium 398mg 17%	Total Sugars 2.7g
Saturated Fat 9.3g 46%	Total Carbs 7.7g 3%	Protein 12.7g

Butter Fried Green Cabbage

Serves: 4/Prep Time: 30 mins

Ingredients

- 3 oz. butter
- Salt and black pepper, to taste
- 25 oz. green cabbage, shredded
- 1 tablespoon basil
- ¼ teaspoon red chili flakes

Directions

1. Heat butter in a large skillet over medium heat and add cabbage.
2. Sauté for about 15 minutes, stirring occasionally, until the cabbage is golden brown.
3. Stir in basil, red chili flakes, salt and black pepper and cook for about 3 minutes.
4. Dish out to a bowl and serve hot.

Nutrition Amount per serving

Calories 197	Cholesterol 46mg 15%	Dietary Fiber 4.5g 16%
Total Fat 17.4g 22%	Sodium 301mg 13%	Total Sugars 5.7g
Saturated Fat 11g 55%	Total Carbs 10.3g 4%	Protein 2.5g

Broccoli and Cheese

Serves: 4/Prep Time: 20 mins

Ingredients

- 5½ oz. cheddar cheese, shredded
- 23 oz. broccoli, chopped
- 2 oz. butter
- Salt and black pepper, to taste
- 4 tablespoons sour cream

Directions

1. Heat butter in a large skillet over medium high heat and add broccoli, salt and black pepper.
2. Cook for about 5 minutes and stir in the sour cream and cheddar cheese.
3. Cover with lid and cook for about 8 minutes on medium low heat.
4. Dish out to a bowl and serve hot.

Nutrition Amount per serving

Calories 340	Cholesterol 77mg 26%	Dietary Fiber 4.3g 15%
Total Fat 27.5g 35%	Sodium 384mg 17%	Total Sugars 3g
Saturated Fat 17.1g 85%	Total Carbs 11.9g 4%	Protein 14.8g

Broccoli Gratin

Serves: 4/Prep Time: 35 mins

Ingredients

- 2 oz. salted butter, for frying
- 5 oz. parmesan cheese, shredded
- 20 oz. broccoli, in florets
- 2 tablespoons Dijon mustard
- ¾ cup crème fraiche

Directions

1. Preheat the oven to 400°F and grease a baking dish lightly.
2. Heat half the butter in a pan on medium low heat and add chopped broccoli.
3. Sauté for about 5 minutes and transfer to the baking dish.
4. Mix the rest of the butter with Dijon mustard and crème fraiche.
5. Pour this mixture in the baking dish and top with parmesan cheese.
6. Transfer to the oven and bake for about 18 minutes.
7. Dish out to a bowl and serve hot.

Nutrition Amount per serving

Calories 338
Total Fat 27.4g 35%
Saturated Fat 12.4g 62%

Cholesterol 56mg 19%
Sodium 546mg 24%
Total Carbs 11.1g 4%

Dietary Fiber 4g 14%
Total Sugars 2.5g
Protein 16.2g

Fried Mac and Cheese

Serves: 4/Prep Time: 25 mins
Ingredients
- 1½ cups cheddar cheese, shredded
- 1 medium cauliflower, riced
- 3 large eggs
- 1 tablespoon olive oil
- 2 teaspoons paprika

Directions
1. Microwave cauliflower rice for about 5 minutes and dry completely on a kitchen towel.
2. Mix cheddar cheese, eggs, turmeric and paprika with the cauliflower rice.
3. Make small patties out of the cauliflower mixture.
4. Heat olive oil in a pan on medium heat and add patties.
5. Fry on each side for about 3 minutes until crisp and dish onto a platter to serve.

Nutrition Amount per serving

Calories 293
Total Fat 21.6g 28%
Saturated Fat 10.6g 53%

Cholesterol 184mg 61%
Sodium 359mg 16%
Total Carbs 9g 3%

Dietary Fiber 4g 14%
Total Sugars 4.1g
Protein 18.3g

Low Carb Cauliflower Rice

Serves: 4/Prep Time: 20 mins
Ingredients
- 25 oz. cauliflower, riced in a processor
- ½ teaspoon turmeric powder
- 3 oz. coconut oil
- ½ teaspoon salt
- ¼ teaspoon paprika

Directions
1. Heat coconut oil on medium heat in a skillet and add cauliflower rice.
2. Cook for about 10 minutes and season with salt, paprika and turmeric powder.
3. Dish out to a bowl and serve warm.

Nutrition Amount per serving

Calories 229
Total Fat 21.5g 28%
Saturated Fat 18.4g 92%

Cholesterol 0mg 0%
Sodium 344mg 15%
Total Carbs 9.6g 4%

Dietary Fiber 4.5g 16%
Total Sugars 4.3g
Protein 3.6g

Creamed Green Cabbage

Serves: 4/Prep Time: 20 mins
Ingredients
- 25 oz. green cabbage, shredded
- 2 oz. butter
- 1¼ cups heavy whipping cream
- ½ cup fresh parsley, finely chopped
- Salt and black pepper, to taste

Directions
1. Heat butter over medium high heat in a pan and add the cabbage.
2. Sauté for about 6 minutes until soft and golden brown and stir in the cream.
3. Reduce the heat and season with salt and black pepper.
4. Cook for about 3 minutes and add parsley. Dish out to a bowl and serve warm.

Nutrition Amount per serving

Calories 278
Total Fat 25.6g 33%
Saturated Fat 16g 80%

Cholesterol 82mg 27%
Sodium 132mg 6%
Total Carbs 11.8g 4%

Dietary Fiber 4.7g 17%
Total Sugars 5.8g
Protein 3.4g

Roasted Brussels Sprouts

Serves: 5/Prep Time: 30 mins

Ingredients

- 4 tablespoons olive oil
- 23 oz. Brussels sprouts
- 1 teaspoon dried rosemary
- 4 oz. parmesan cheese, shaved
- Salt and black pepper, to taste

Directions

1. Preheat the oven to 450°F and grease a baking dish with 2 tablespoons of olive oil.
2. Season the Brussels sprouts with dried rosemary, salt and black pepper.
3. Arrange the seasoned Brussels sprouts in a baking dish and sprinkle with olive oil and parmesan cheese.
4. Roast in the oven for about 20 minutes and remove from the oven to serve.

Nutrition Amount per serving

Calories 226	Cholesterol 16mg 5%	Dietary Fiber 5g 18%
Total Fat 16.5g 21%	Sodium 243mg 11%	Total Sugars 2.8g
Saturated Fat 5g 25%	Total Carbs 12.8g 5%	Protein 11.8g

Baked Rutabaga Wedges

Serves: 4/Prep Time: 35 mins

Ingredients

- 4 tablespoons olive oil
- 15 oz. rutabaga, peeled and cut into wedges
- 1 teaspoon chili powder
- ½ cup sour cream
- Salt and black pepper, to taste

Directions

1. Preheat the oven to 400°F and grease a baking sheet.
2. Arrange the wedges on a baking sheet and season with chili powder, salt and black pepper.
3. Drizzle with olive oil and transfer to the oven.
4. Bake for about 20 minutes and remove from the oven to serve with sour cream.

Nutrition Amount per serving

Calories 222	Cholesterol 13mg 4%	Dietary Fiber 2.9g 10%
Total Fat 20.4g 26%	Sodium 43mg 2%	Total Sugars 6.1g
Saturated Fat 5.8g 29%	Total Carbs 10.3g 4%	Protein 2.3g

Zucchini Fettuccine

Serves: 1/Prep Time: 15 mins

Ingredients

- 1 oz. olive oil
- 1 zucchini, spiralized into noodles
- ¼ cup parmesan cheese
- Salt and black pepper, to taste
- ¼ teaspoon red chili flakes

Directions

1. Boil the zucchini noodles and dish out in a microwave safe serving bowl.
2. Season with red chili flakes, salt and black pepper and drizzle with olive oil.
3. Top with parmesan cheese and microwave for about 5 minutes.
4. Remove from the oven and serve hot.

Nutrition Amount per serving

Calories 348	Cholesterol 20mg 7%	Dietary Fiber 2.2g 8%
Total Fat 32.8g 42%	Sodium 860mg 37%	Total Sugars 3.4g
Saturated Fat 7.9g 39%	Total Carbs 7.6g 3%	Protein 11.4g

Low Carb Cauliflower Mash

Serves: 4/Prep Time: 12 mins

Ingredients
- 3 oz. parmesan cheese, grated
- 1 pound cauliflower, cut into florets
- 4 oz. salted butter
- ½ lemon, juice and zest
- 2 tablespoons olive oil

Directions
1. Boil the cauliflower in salted water until tender and drain well.
2. Put the cauliflower in a food processor along with rest of the ingredients.
3. Pulse until smooth and dish out in a bowl to serve.

Nutrition Amount per serving

Calories 362	Cholesterol 76mg 25%	Dietary Fiber 3g 11%
Total Fat 34.7g 44%	Sodium 395mg 17%	Total Sugars 2.9g
Saturated Fat 18.6g 93%	Total Carbs 7.5g 3%	Protein 9.4g

Whipped Lemon Butter Artichokes

Serves: 5/Prep Time: 45 mins

Ingredients
- 1½ lemons, juice and zest
- ½ teaspoon red chili flakes
- 7 oz. butter
- Salt and black pepper, to taste
- 2 fresh artichokes

Directions
1. Boil the artichokes in salted water for about 35 minutes with ½ a lemon.
2. Melt the butter in a microwave oven and beat until fluffy.
3. Season with red chili flakes, salt and black pepper and squeeze in juice from 1 lemon.
4. Mix in lemon zest and whip well.
5. Dip the artichokes in this lemon butter and serve warm.

Nutrition Amount per serving

Calories 320	Cholesterol 85mg 28%	Dietary Fiber 4g 14%
Total Fat 32.3g 41%	Sodium 522mg 23%	Total Sugars 1.1g
Saturated Fat 20.4g 102%	Total Carbs 8.5g 3%	Protein 2.7g

Low Carb Cauliflower Cheese

Serves: 8/Prep Time: 1 hour 10 mins

Ingredients
- 8 oz. cream cheese
- 1 cup heavy whipping cream
- Garlic powder, salt and black pepper, to taste
- 2¾ pounds cauliflower, cut into small florets
- 2 cups cheddar cheese, shredded

Directions
1. Preheat the oven to 350°F and grease a baking dish.
2. Boil the cauliflower in water for about 20 minutes until tender and drain well.
3. Add the heavy whipping cream, cream cheese, garlic powder, salt and black pepper to an immersion blender.
4. Blend until smooth and transfer into a baking dish.
5. Top with cheddar cheese and place in the oven.
6. Bake for about 40 minutes until the cauliflower is golden brown and dish out to serve hot.

Nutrition Amount per serving

Calories 304	Cholesterol 81mg 27%	Dietary Fiber 3.9g 14%
Total Fat 25g 32%	Sodium 312mg 14%	Total Sugars 4g
Saturated Fat 15.7g 78%	Total Carbs 9.8g 4%	Protein 12.6g

Brussels Sprouts with Caramelized Red Onions

Serves: 4/Prep Time: 30 mins

Ingredients

- 4 oz. butter
- 1 red onion, cut into wedges
- 1 tablespoon red wine vinegar
- 15 oz. Brussels sprouts
- Salt and black pepper, to taste

Directions

1. Heat butter in a medium skillet on low heat and add onions.
2. Sauté for about 10 minutes until the onions are caramelized.
3. Stir in the Brussels sprouts, vinegar, salt and black pepper and cover the skillet.
4. Cook on medium low heat for about 15 minutes and dish out to a bowl to serve hot.

Nutrition Amount per serving

Calories 261	Cholesterol 61mg 20%	Dietary Fiber 4.6g 16%
Total Fat 23.4g 30%	Sodium 191mg 8%	Total Sugars 3.5g
Saturated Fat 14.7g 73%	Total Carbs 12.3g 4%	Protein 4.2g

Keto Stuffed Mushrooms

Serves: 3/Prep Time: 35 mins

Ingredients

- 4 oz. bacon, cooked and crisped
- 1 tablespoon butter
- Salt and black pepper, to taste
- 6 mushrooms, chopped
- 3.5 oz. cream cheese

Directions

1. Preheat the oven to 400°F and grease a baking dish lightly.
2. Mix bacon with butter, cream cheese, salt and black pepper in a bowl.
3. Stuff this mixture inside the mushrooms and arrange on a baking dish.
4. Transfer to the oven and bake for about 20 minutes.
5. Remove from the oven and serve warm.

Nutrition Amount per serving

Calories 362	Cholesterol 88mg 29%	Dietary Fiber 0.4g 1%
Total Fat 31.3g 40%	Sodium 1000mg 43%	Total Sugars 0.7g
Saturated Fat 14.9g 74%	Total Carbs 2.6g 1%	Protein 17.7g

Thai Curry Cabbage

Serves: 5/Prep Time: 20 mins

Ingredients

- 1 tablespoon Thai red curry paste
- 3 tablespoons coconut oil
- 30 oz. green cabbage, shredded
- 1 tablespoon sesame oil
- 1 teaspoon salt

Directions

1. Heat coconut oil in a wok over high heat and add Thai curry paste.
2. Cook for about 1 minute and add green cabbage.
3. Sauté for about 5 minutes until golden brown and lower the heat.
4. Season with salt and drizzle with sesame oil.
5. Sauté for 2 more minutes and dish out to serve hot.

Nutrition Amount per serving

Calories 149	Cholesterol 0mg 0%	Dietary Fiber 4.3g 15%
Total Fat 12g 15%	Sodium 652mg 28%	Total Sugars 5.4g
Saturated Fat 7.8g 39%	Total Carbs 10.5g 4%	Protein 2.2g

Low Carb Broccoli Mash

Serves: 4/Prep Time: 15 mins

Ingredients

- 4 tablespoons fresh parsley, finely chopped
- 25 oz. broccoli florets, boiled and drained
- 3 oz. butter
- Salt and black pepper, to taste
- 1 garlic clove

Directions

1. Blend broccoli with other ingredients in an immersion blender.
2. Blend until smooth and serve.

Nutrition Amount per serving

Calories 215	Cholesterol 46mg 15%	Dietary Fiber 4.8g 17%
Total Fat 17.9g 23%	Sodium 183mg 8%	Total Sugars 3.1g
Saturated Fat 10.9g 55%	Total Carbs 12.3g 4%	Protein 5.3g

Creamy Lemon Green Beans

Serves: 4/Prep Time: 25 mins

Ingredients

- 3 oz. butter
- 1 cup heavy whipping cream
- 10 oz. fresh green beans
- Sea salt and black pepper, to taste
- ½ lemon zest

Directions

1. Heat butter on medium heat in a frying pan and add green beans.
2. Sauté for about 4 minutes over medium high heat and lower the heat.
3. Season with sea salt and black pepper and cook for about 1 minute.
4. Stir in the heavy cream and lemon zest and cook for about 3 minutes.
5. Dish out to a bowl and serve hot.

Nutrition Amount per serving

Calories 284	Cholesterol 87mg 29%	Dietary Fiber 2.4g 9%
Total Fat 28.4g 36%	Sodium 138mg 6%	Total Sugars 2.5g
Saturated Fat 17.9g 89%	Total Carbs 7.5g 3%	Protein 2.1g

Oven Baked Tofu

Serves: 2/Prep Time: 50 mins

Ingredients

- 1 tablespoon soy sauce
- 15 ounces extra firm tofu, pressed and dried
- 1 tablespoon sesame oil
- 2 tablespoons rice wine vinegar
- 2 teaspoons garlic, minced

Directions

1. Preheat the oven to 350°F and line a baking sheet with parchment paper
2. Mix together soy sauce, sesame oil, garlic and rice wine vinegar in a bowl.
3. Marinate tofu in this mixture for about 2 hours and arrange on the baking sheet.
4. Transfer into the oven and bake for about 35 minutes.
5. Remove from the oven and serve hot.

Nutrition Amount per serving

Calories 227	Cholesterol 0mg 0%	Dietary Fiber 2g 7%
Total Fat 15.7g 20%	Sodium 477mg 21%	Total Sugars 1.5g
Saturated Fat 2.8g 14%	Total Carbs 5.1g 2%	Protein 18.1g

Cauliflower Mac and Cheese

Serves: 7/Prep Time: 30 mins

Ingredients

- 6 ounces cream cheese, cubed
- Salt and black pepper, to taste
- 2 pounds cauliflower florets, boiled
- 8 ounces cheddar cheese, shredded
- 1 teaspoon Dijon mustard

Directions

1. Put the cream cheese in a bowl and bring to a simmer.
2. Stir in Dijon mustard, 6 ounces of the cheddar cheese, salt and black pepper and mix until the cheese is melted.
3. Add cauliflower to the cheese sauce and coat well.
4. Top with the remaining 2 ounces of cheddar cheese and stir well until the cheese is melted. Dish out to a bowl and serve hot.

Nutrition Amount per serving

Calories 248	Cholesterol 61mg 20%	Dietary Fiber 3.3g 12%
Total Fat 19.4g 25%	Sodium 320mg 14%	Total Sugars 3.3g
Saturated Fat 12.2g 61%	Total Carbs 8g 3%	Protein 12.5g

Avocado Walnut Pesto

Serves: 4/Prep Time: 10 mins

Ingredients

- 2 cups fresh basil leaves
- 1 large avocado
- ½ cup walnuts
- ½ cup parmesan cheese, grated
- 4 garlic cloves, peeled

Directions

1. Put avocado with all other ingredients into the food processor and process until smooth.
2. Dish out to a bowl and serve.

Nutrition Amount per serving

Calories 296	Cholesterol 20mg 7%	Dietary Fiber 4.7g 17%
Total Fat 25.1g 32%	Sodium 264mg 11%	Total Sugars 0.5g
Saturated Fat 6.6g 33%	Total Carbs 8.2g 3%	Protein 14.3g

Cheesy Hearts of Palm Dip

Serves: 4/Prep Time: 35 mins

Ingredients

- 3 stalks green onions, chopped
- 1 (14 ounce) can hearts of palm, drained
- ¼ cup mayonnaise
- ½ cup parmesan cheese, shredded
- 2 tablespoons Italian seasoning

Directions

1. Preheat the oven to 350°F and grease a small baking dish.
2. Mix together green onions, hearts of palm, mayonnaise, Italian seasoning and parmesan cheese in the food processor.
3. Pulse until well chopped and transfer into prepared baking dish.
4. Bake for about 20 minutes and remove from the oven to serve.

Nutrition Amount per serving

Calories 153	Cholesterol 19mg 6%	Dietary Fiber 2.5g 9%
Total Fat 10.6g 14%	Sodium 660mg 29%	Total Sugars 1.6g
Saturated Fat 3.2g 16%	Total Carbs 9.6g 4%	Protein 7.2g

Zucchini Parmesan Chips

Serves: 4/Prep Time: 30 mins

Ingredients

- ¾ cup parmesan cheese
- 4 small zucchinis, sliced into small rounds
- ¾ cup cheddar cheese
- Salt and black pepper, to taste
- ¼ teaspoon turmeric powder

Directions

1. Preheat the oven to 425°F and grease a small baking sheet.
2. Season the zucchini with turmeric powder, salt and black pepper.
3. Arrange the sliced zucchini rounds on the baking sheet and sprinkle evenly with parmesan cheese and cheddar cheese.
4. Transfer to the oven and bake for about 20 minutes until the cheese turns golden brown.
5. Remove from the oven and serve warm.

Nutrition Amount per serving

Calories 172	Cholesterol 37mg 12%	Dietary Fiber 1.3g 5%
Total Fat 11.7g 15%	Sodium 338mg 15%	Total Sugars 2.2g
Saturated Fat 7.5g 38%	Total Carbs 5.1g 2%	Protein 13.5g

Buttery Bacon and Cabbage Stir Fry

Serves: 4/Prep Time: 15 mins

Ingredients

- ¼ cup butter
- 2½ cups Chinese cabbage, shredded
- 2 rashers bacon
- 1 pinch salt
- 1 pinch cayenne pepper

Directions

1. Heat half the butter in a pan and add bacon.
2. Cook until the bacon becomes crispy and add cabbage.
3. Cook for about 3 minutes and add the rest of the butter, salt and cayenne pepper.
4. Dish out to a bowl and serve hot.

Nutrition Amount per serving

Calories 159	Cholesterol 41mg 14%	Dietary Fiber 0.5g 2%
Total Fat 15.6g 20%	Sodium 368mg 16%	Total Sugars 0.5g
Saturated Fat 8.6g 43%	Total Carbs 1.1g 0%	Protein 4.3g

Baked Artichokes

Serves: 9/Prep Time: 25 mins

Ingredients

- 4 tablespoons olive oil
- 3 pounds bok choy, boiled
- Salt and black pepper, to taste
- 2 tablespoons thyme
- ½ cup sour cream

Directions

1. Preheat the oven to 350°F and grease a baking dish lightly with olive oil.
2. Place the bok choy on the baking sheet and season with thyme, salt and black pepper.
3. Drizzle with olive oil and place in the oven.
4. Bake for about 15 minutes and remove from the oven to serve with sour cream.

Nutrition Amount per serving

Calories 102	Cholesterol 6mg 2%	Dietary Fiber 1.7g 6%
Total Fat 9.3g 12%	Sodium 105mg 5%	Total Sugars 1.8g
Saturated Fat 2.6g 13%	Total Carbs 4.2g 2%	Protein 2.7g

Vegan Recipes

Vegan Tofu Scramble

Serves: 2/Prep Time: 20 mins

Ingredients

- 1½ tablespoons olive oil
- 1 block firm tofu, drained, pressed and chopped
- Black salt and black pepper, to taste
- ¼ cup dairy free milk, unsweetened
- 2 teaspoons ground turmeric

Directions

1. Heat olive oil in a skillet over medium heat and add tofu, turmeric, black salt and black pepper.
2. Cook for about 7 minutes and stir in the dairy free milk.
3. Cover the skillet and cook for about 5 more minutes.
4. Dish out to a bowl and serve hot.

Nutrition Amount per serving

Calories 135	Cholesterol 0mg 0%	Dietary Fiber 1g 4%
Total Fat 13.2g 17%	Sodium 6mg 0%	Total Sugars 0.3g
Saturated Fat 2.5g 12%	Total Carbs 2.5g 1%	Protein 3.9g

Vegan Keto Porridge

Serves: 4/Prep Time: 10 mins

Ingredients

- 3 tablespoons golden flaxseed meal
- 2 tablespoons coconut flour
- 2 tablespoons vegan vanilla protein powder
- 1 scoop Stevia
- 1½ cups almond milk, unsweetened

Directions

1. Mix together the golden flaxseed meal, coconut flour and vanilla protein powder in a bowl.
2. Put this mixture in the saucepan along with almond milk and cook for about 10 minutes over medium heat. Stir in the Stevia and dish out to a bowl and serve hot.

Nutrition Amount per serving

Calories 274	Cholesterol 0mg 0%	Dietary Fiber 5g 18%
Total Fat 23.7g 30%	Sodium 61mg 3%	Total Sugars 3g
Saturated Fat 19.5g 97%	Total Carbs 10.2g 4%	Protein 8.9g

Vegan Sesame Tofu and Eggplant

Serves: 4/Prep Time: 25 mins

Ingredients

- 4 tablespoons toasted sesame oil
- 1 pound block firm tofu
- 1 whole eggplant, peeled and julienned
- ¼ cup sesame seeds
- Salt and black pepper, to taste

Directions

1. Put the sesame seeds on a plate and coat both sides of tofu with them.
2. Heat sesame oil in a skillet and add eggplant.
3. Cook for about 5 minutes and season the coated tofu with salt and black pepper.
4. Cover with lid and cook for about 10 minutes on medium low heat.
5. Dish out to a bowl and serve hot.

Nutrition Amount per serving

Calories 264	Cholesterol 0mg 0%	Dietary Fiber 3g 11%
Total Fat 22.9g 29%	Sodium 103mg 4%	Total Sugars 1.9g
Saturated Fat 3.6g 18%	Total Carbs 7.1g 3%	Protein 11.2g

Mint Chocolate Coffee Creamer

Serves: 24/Prep Time: 5 mins

Ingredients
- 1 cup full fat coconut milk
- ½ cup unsweetened vanilla almond milk
- ¼ teaspoon peppermint extract
- 2 tablespoons cacao powder
- 5 drops Stevia

Directions
1. Put all the ingredients in a highspeed blender and blend until smooth.
2. Dish out to a jar and pour in your coffee.

Nutrition Amount per serving

Calories 22
Total Fat 2.1g 3%
Saturated Fat 1.9g 9%
Cholesterol 0mg 0%
Sodium 6mg 0%
Total Carbs 0.6g 0%
Dietary Fiber 0.2g 1%
Total Sugars 0.2g
Protein 0.3g

Coconut Bacon

Serves: 4/Prep Time: 5 mins

Ingredients
- 2 tablespoons liquid smoke
- 3½ cups flaked coconut, unsweetened
- 1 tablespoon Braggs liquid aminos
- 3 tablespoons heavy whipping cream
- 1 tablespoon water

Directions
1. Preheat the oven to 325°F and grease a baking sheet lightly.
2. Mix together coconut flakes, liquid smoke, liquid aminos, water and cream in a bowl.
3. Pour this mixture onto a baking sheet and place in the oven.
4. Bake for about 25 minutes, flipping every 5 minutes.
5. Dish out to a plate and serve.

Nutrition Amount per serving

Calories 372
Total Fat 37.5g 48%
Saturated Fat 29.3g 146%
Cholesterol 15mg 5%
Sodium 253mg 11%
Total Carbs 3.6g 1%
Dietary Fiber 8.3g 30%
Total Sugars 3.3g
Protein 3.9g

Dark Saltwater Truffles

Serves: 2/Prep Time: 30 mins

Ingredients
- 1 scoop Stevia
- 150g dark chocolate, broken into small pieces
- 55ml water
- Cocoa powder, for dusting
- Pinch of salt

Directions
1. Heat water and salt in a pot and bring to a boil.
2. Remove from heat and add chocolate pieces and Stevia.
3. Stir well until the chocolate is dissolved and ladle into a bowl.
4. Refrigerate for about 4 hours.
5. Put cocoa powder in a bowl and dust it on your hands.
6. Make small balls out of the chocolate mixture and roll into cocoa powder.
7. Put these truffles in the fridge for 1 more hour then serve and enjoy.

Nutrition Amount per serving

Calories 118
Total Fat 10g 13%
Saturated Fat 6.3g 31%
Cholesterol 0mg 0%
Sodium 79mg 3%
Total Carbs 4.6g 2%
Dietary Fiber 3.4g 12%
Total Sugars 2g
Protein 2.3g

Zucchini Noodles with Avocado Sauce

Serves: 2/Prep Time: 20 mins

Ingredients

- 1¼ cups basil
- 1 zucchini, spiralized with noodles
- 4 tablespoons pine nuts
- 1 avocado
- 2 tablespoons lemon juice

Directions

1. Put basil, pine nuts, avocado and lemon juice in a blender along with 1/3 cup water.
2. Blend until smooth and dish into a bowl. Add zucchini noodles to the avocado sauce.

Nutrition Amount per serving

Calories 166	Cholesterol 0mg 0%	Dietary Fiber 3.5g 13%
Total Fat 14.7g 19%	Sodium 14mg 1%	Total Sugars 2.7g
Saturated Fat 1.5g 8%	Total Carbs 7.8g 3%	Protein 4.6g

Mushroom Brussels Sprouts

Serves: 6/Prep Time: 30 mins

Ingredients

- 3 tablespoons olive oil
- 2 cups brown mushrooms, thinly sliced
- 2 tablespoons sour cream
- 1½ pounds Brussels sprouts, trimmed and outer leaves removed
- Salt and smoked paprika, to taste

Directions

1. Mix together mushrooms, sour cream, salt and smoked paprika in a bowl.
2. Heat 1 tablespoon of olive oil in a skillet on medium high heat and add mushrooms mixture. Cook for about 10 minutes and dish out.
3. Heat the rest of the oil in a saucepan and add the Brussels sprouts.
4. Coat well and add ¼ cup hot water.
5. Cover with a lid and cook on medium heat for about 8 minutes.
6. Stir in the mushrooms mixture and cook for about 2 minutes.
7. Dish out and serve hot.

Nutrition Amount per serving

Calories 125	Cholesterol 2mg 1%	Dietary Fiber 4.5g 16%
Total Fat 8.3g 11%	Sodium 32mg 1%	Total Sugars 2.9g
Saturated Fat 1.7g 8%	Total Carbs 11.7g 4%	Protein 4.7g

Vegan Almond and Cinnamon Cookies

Serves: 5/Prep Time: 30 mins

Ingredients

- ⅔ cup coconut sugar
- 2 cups ground almonds
- 2 tablespoons chia seeds
- 3 tablespoons orange juice
- 2 tablespoons cinnamon

Directions

1. Preheat the oven to 360°F and grease a baking sheet.
2. Put chia seeds and coconut sugar in a food processor and process until smooth.
3. Dish into a bowl and add almonds and cinnamon.
4. Stir in orange juice and mix well to form a dough.
5. Form small balls out of this mixture and transfer to a baking sheet.
6. Press with a fork and place in the oven.
7. Bake for about 15 minutes until golden brown and remove from baking sheet to serve.

Nutrition Amount per serving

Calories 150	Cholesterol 0mg 0%	Dietary Fiber 6.8g 24%
Total Fat 9.5g 12%	Sodium 6mg 0%	Total Sugars 1.2g
Saturated Fat 0.9g 4%	Total Carbs 12.3g 4%	Protein 5.2g

Vegan Mashed Cauliflower

Serves: 4/Prep Time: 15 mins

Ingredients
- 1 cup vegetable broth
- 1 large head cauliflower, cored and roughly chopped
- ¼ cup vegan parmesan
- Sea salt and black pepper, to taste
- 2 tablespoons non-dairy butter

Directions
1. Put cauliflower and vegetable broth in the pressure cooker and close the lid.
2. Cook on High Pressure for about 5 minutes. Quickly release the pressure and drain well.
3. Transfer to a food processor and add parmesan, butter, salt and black pepper.
4. Process until smooth and dish into a bowl and serve immediately.

Nutrition Amount per serving

Calories 145	Cholesterol 5mg 2%	Dietary Fiber 5.3g 19%
Total Fat 8.9g 11%	Sodium 319mg 14%	Total Sugars 5.2g
Saturated Fat 2.4g 12%	Total Carbs 11.6g 4%	Protein 7.6g

Crispy Tofu and Cauliflower Stir Fry

Serves: 4/Prep Time: 15 mins

Ingredients
- 3 tablespoons toasted sesame oil
- 12 ounces extra firm tofu, pressed
- 1 small head cauliflower, riced
- ¼ cup low sodium soy sauce
- 2 garlic cloves, minced

Directions
1. Preheat the oven to 400°F and grease a baking sheet.
2. Put the tofu on the baking sheet and place in the oven.
3. Bake for about 25 minutes and dish into a bowl.
4. Heat sesame oil in a large skillet over medium high heat and add garlic.
5. Sauté for about 1 minute and add tofu and soy sauce.
6. Sauté for about 5 minutes and stir in cauliflower rice.
7. Cover the skillet and cook on medium low heat for about 6 minutes.
8. Dish out to a bowl and serve warm.

Nutrition Amount per serving

Calories 195	Cholesterol 0mg 0%	Dietary Fiber 2.2g 8%
Total Fat 15.3g 20%	Sodium 558mg 24%	Total Sugars 2.3g
Saturated Fat 1.9g 10%	Total Carbs 7.1g 3%	Protein 10.6g

Tofu in Purgatory

Serves: 2/Prep Time: 30 mins

Ingredients
- 1 can diced tomatoes
- 2 teaspoons dried herbs
- 2 tablespoons olive oil
- Garlic powder, salt and black pepper, to taste
- 1 block unpressed medium tofu, cut into rounds

Directions
1. Heat olive oil in a skillet on medium heat and add tofu.
2. Sauté for about 3 minutes and add tomatoes.
3. Sauté for about 2 minutes and sprinkle with dried herbs, garlic powder, salt and black pepper. Lower the heat and let it simmer for about 15 minutes. Dish into a bowl and serve hot.

Nutrition Amount per serving

Calories 165	Cholesterol 0mg 0%	Dietary Fiber 1.7g 6%
Total Fat 15.7g 20%	Sodium 130mg 6%	Total Sugars 2.4g
Saturated Fat 2.4g 12%	Total Carbs 4.6g 2%	Protein 4.1g

Low Carb Maple Oatmeal

Serves: 4/Prep Time: 40 mins

Ingredients

- ¼ cup sunflower seeds
- 1 cup nuts (walnuts and pecans)
- ¼ cup coconut flakes
- 2 scoops Stevia
- 4 cups unsweetened almond milk

Directions

1. Put nuts and sunflower seeds in a food processor and pulse until crumbled.
2. Transfer this mixture into a large pot along with rest of the ingredients.
3. Allow to simmer for about 30 minutes, stirring occasionally.
4. Dish into a bowl and allow it to cool down before serving.

Nutrition Amount per serving

Calories 268	Cholesterol 0mg 0%	Dietary Fiber 3.8g 14%
Total Fat 25.1g 32%	Sodium 182mg 8%	Total Sugars 0.7g
Saturated Fat 3g 15%	Total Carbs 6.4g 2%	Protein 9.3g

Keto Crackers

Serves: 8/Prep Time: 3 hours 25 mins

Ingredients

- 3 tablespoons chia seeds
- 1 cup whole flaxseeds
- 3 tablespoons hemp hearts
- ½ teaspoon sea salt
- 3 tablespoons dried rosemary

Directions

1. Preheat the oven to 200°F and line a baking tray with parchment paper.
2. Combine the chia seeds and flaxseeds with water in a bowl.
3. Mix well and allow it to sit for about 20 minutes.
4. Stir in the rest of the ingredients and spread in a thin layer on the baking tray.
5. Bake for about 1½ hours and then flip over the cracker mixture.
6. Bake for another 1½ hours and turn off the oven.
7. Allow to stay in the warmed oven for about 20 minutes.
8. Remove from oven and allow the crackers to cool and serve.

Nutrition Amount per serving

Calories 149	Cholesterol 0mg 0%	Dietary Fiber 7.5g 27%
Total Fat 9.6g 12%	Sodium 118mg 5%	Total Sugars 1.3g
Saturated Fat 1.1g 5%	Total Carbs 9.3g 3%	Protein 5.9g

Mushroom Spaghetti Squash

Serves: 6/Prep Time: 20 mins

Ingredients

- 8 ounces mushrooms, sliced
- 6 cups spaghetti squash, cooked and shredded
- ¼ cup pine nuts, toasted
- Kosher salt and black pepper, to taste
- 3 tablespoons olive oil

Directions

1. Heat olive oil over medium heat in a large pan and add mushrooms.
2. Sauté for about 4 minutes and add cooked spaghetti squash.
3. Cook for about 2 minutes and stir in pine nuts, salt and black pepper.
4. Mix well and dish into a bowl to serve.

Nutrition Amount per serving

Calories 138	Cholesterol 0mg 0%	Dietary Fiber 0.6g 2%
Total Fat 11.6g 15%	Sodium 19mg 1%	Total Sugars 0.9g
Saturated Fat 1.4g 7%	Total Carbs 9g 3%	Protein 2.6g

Garlic Roasted Radishes

Serves: 3/Prep Time: 30 mins
Ingredients
- ½ cup low sodium vegetable broth
- 3 garlic cloves, minced
- 3 radish bunches, chopped
- ½ teaspoon dried rosemary
- Himalayan pink sea salt and black pepper, to taste

Directions
1. Preheat the oven to 400°F and grease a medium sized casserole dish.
2. Put vegetable broth, garlic cloves, dried rosemary, pink sea salt and black pepper in a bowl.
3. Put the radishes in the casserole and top with the broth mixture.
4. Transfer to the oven and bake for about 20 minutes.
5. Dish into a platter and serve hot.

Nutrition Amount per serving

Calories 26	Cholesterol 0mg 0%	Dietary Fiber 2g 7%
Total Fat 0.2g 0%	Sodium 58mg 3%	Total Sugars 2.2g
Saturated Fat 0.1g 0%	Total Carbs 5.2g 2%	Protein 1.3g

Mashed Cauliflower with Garlic and Herbs

Serves: 3/Prep Time: 20 mins
Ingredients
- 1 tablespoon olive oil
- 1 head cauliflower, boiled
- 2 garlic cloves, minced
- Salt and black pepper, to taste
- 2 teaspoons fresh herbs, chopped

Directions
1. Heat olive oil on medium heat in a small pan and add garlic.
2. Sauté for about 1 minute and add boiled cauliflower and fresh herbs.
3. Season with salt and black pepper and cook for about 3 minutes.
4. Mash the cauliflower with a potato masher and dish into a bowl to serve.

Nutrition Amount per serving

Calories 66	Cholesterol 0mg 0%	Dietary Fiber 2.5g 9%
Total Fat 4.8g 6%	Sodium 27mg 1%	Total Sugars 2.2g
Saturated Fat 0.7g 3%	Total Carbs 5.7g 2%	Protein 2g

Roasted Cabbage with Lemon

Serves: 4/Prep Time: 40 mins
Ingredients
- 2 tablespoons olive oil
- 1 large head green cabbage, cut into 8 wedges
- 3 tablespoons lemon juice, freshly squeezed
- 6 lemon slices, for serving
- Sea salt and black pepper, to taste

Directions
1. Preheat the oven to 450°F and grease a roasting pan with olive oil.
2. Whisk together lemon juice and olive oil in a bowl and brush onto the cabbage wedges.
3. Season generously with salt and black pepper and arrange the cabbage wedges on a roasting pan.
4. Roast for about 30 minutes, flipping once after 15 minutes.
5. Dish onto a platter and top with lemon slices to serve.

Nutrition Amount per serving

Calories 96	Cholesterol 0mg 0%	Dietary Fiber 1.1g 4%
Total Fat 9.5g 12%	Sodium 10mg 0%	Total Sugars 1.7g
Saturated Fat 1.5g 7%	Total Carbs 3.3g 1%	Protein 0.6g

Balsamic Glazed Mushrooms

Serves: 6/Prep Time: 3 hours 15 minutes
Ingredients

- ¼ cup extra-virgin olive oil
- 2 pounds portobello mushrooms
- 2 tablespoons balsamic vinegar
- 2 tablespoons tamari
- Sea salt and black pepper, to taste

Directions

1. Put the portobello mushrooms along with rest of the ingredients in a slow cooker.
2. Mix well and cover with lid.
3. Cook on low for about 3 hours and dish out to serve hot.

Nutrition Amount per serving

Calories 113	Cholesterol 0mg 0%	Dietary Fiber 1.9g 7%
Total Fat 8.4g 11%	Sodium 335mg 15%	Total Sugars 0.1g
Saturated Fat 1.2g 6%	Total Carbs 5.8g 2%	Protein 6g

Vegan Garlic Aioli

Serves: 4/Prep Time: 10 mins
Ingredients

- 3 fresh garlic cloves, minced
- ¾ cup vegenaise
- 2½ tablespoons fresh lemon juice
- ¼ teaspoon black pepper
- ¼ teaspoon pink sea salt

Directions

1. Put all the ingredients in a bowl and mix well until combined.
2. Cover and refrigerate for about 1 hour before serving.

Nutrition Amount per serving

Calories 276	Cholesterol 0mg 0%	Dietary Fiber 0.1g 0%
Total Fat 27.1g 35%	Sodium 384mg 17%	Total Sugars 0.2g
Saturated Fat 1.6g 8%	Total Carbs 1g 0%	Protein 0.2g

Basil Pesto

Serves: 6/Prep Time: 5 mins
Ingredients

- 2 cups fresh organic basil leaves
- 1 large garlic clove, peeled
- 1/3 cup extra virgin olive oil
- Sea salt and black pepper, to taste
- 1/3 cup pine nuts, toasted

Directions

1. Place garlic in a food processor and pulse until chopped.
2. Add basil leaves, olive oil, pine nuts, salt and black pepper and process until smooth.
3. Dish into a bowl and serve with your favorite dish.

Nutrition Amount per serving

Calories 151	Cholesterol 0mg 0%	Dietary Fiber 0.5g 2%
Total Fat 16.4g 21%	Sodium 1mg 0%	Total Sugars 0.3g
Saturated Fat 2g 10%	Total Carbs 1.7g 1%	Protein 1.4g

Mexican Spiced Keto Chocolate

Serves: 4/Prep Time: 20 mins

Ingredients
- ¼ teaspoon chili powder
- 25 drops liquid Stevia
- ½ cup cocoa powder
- 1 pinch fine sea salt, black pepper and cinnamon
- ¼ cup cacao butter, melted

Directions
1. Whisk together cocoa powder and salt in a small bowl.
2. Microwave cacao butter for about 30 seconds on high until melted.
3. Mix chili powder and liquid Stevia with cacao butter.
4. Stir in the cocoa powder mixture and mix well.
5. Pour the mixture into greased mini loaf pans and allow to set until firm.

Nutrition Amount per serving

Calories 54	Cholesterol 0mg 0%	Dietary Fiber 3.3g 12%
Total Fat 4.9g 6%	Sodium 62mg 3%	Total Sugars 0.2g
Saturated Fat 2.8g 14%	Total Carbs 6g 2%	Protein 2g

BLT Sushi

Serves: 5/Prep Time: 35 mins

Ingredients
- 1 cup tomatoes, chopped
- 10 bacon slices
- ½ avocado, diced
- Kosher salt and black pepper, to taste
- 1 cup romaine lettuce, shredded

Directions
1. Preheat the oven to 400°F and put a wire rack over a baking sheet.
2. Make a weave with the bacon slices and place on the baking sheet.
3. Bake for about 20 minutes until bacon is cooked.
4. Put tomatoes, avocado and romaine lettuce on the bacon weave and season with salt and black pepper.
5. Roll up tightly and slice crosswise into "sushi rolls".

Nutrition Amount per serving

Calories 255	Cholesterol 42mg 14%	Dietary Fiber 1.9g 7%
Total Fat 19.9g 26%	Sodium 881mg 38%	Total Sugars 1.2g
Saturated Fat 6.1g 30%	Total Carbs 4g 1%	Protein 14.8g

Roasted Mushrooms

Serves: 4/Prep Time: 30 mins

Ingredients
- ½ cup tomato puree
- 18 ounces whole mushrooms, quartered
- 4 tablespoons olive oil
- Salt and black pepper, to taste
- 2 teaspoons ginger garlic paste

Directions
1. Heat olive oil over medium high heat in a nonstick frying pan and add whole mushrooms and ginger garlic paste.
2. Sauté for about 5 minutes and add tomato puree, salt and black pepper.
3. Sauté for about 3 minutes until crisp and tender then dish into a bowl and serve hot.

Nutrition Amount per serving

Calories 176	Cholesterol 0mg 0%	Dietary Fiber 1.9g 7%
Total Fat 15.9g 20%	Sodium 16mg 1%	Total Sugars 3.7g
Saturated Fat 2g 10%	Total Carbs 7.7g 3%	Protein 4.7g

Vegan Cauliflower Pizza Crust

Serves: 5/Prep Time: 1 hour
Ingredients
- 1½ pounds frozen cauliflower rice, thawed
- ½ cup almond flour
- ½ teaspoon dried oregano
- 3 tablespoons flax seeds
- Salt and garlic powder, to taste

Directions
1. Preheat the oven to 390°F and line a baking sheet with parchment paper.
2. Mix together cauliflower rice with rest of the ingredients and add a little water to make a dough.
3. Press this dough on the baking sheet to form a thin crust and transfer into the oven.
4. Bake for about 45 minutes and dish out.
5. Top with your favorite toppings and bake again.

Nutrition Amount per serving

Calories 129	Cholesterol 0mg 0%	Dietary Fiber 6g 21%
Total Fat 6.8g 9%	Sodium 46mg 2%	Total Sugars 3.3g
Saturated Fat 0.6g 3%	Total Carbs 12.1g 4%	Protein 6.1g

Curried Spinach Stuffed Portobello Mushrooms

Serves: 6/Prep Time: 25 mins
Ingredients
- 1 cup coconut cream
- 1 cup spinach
- 4 cups Portobello mushroom caps, stems removed
- Salt and red pepper, to taste
- ¼ cup oil and vinegar salad dressing

Directions
1. Preheat the grill to medium high heat.
2. Rub salad dressing on the Portobello mushrooms and arrange in a pan.
3. Season with salt and black pepper and cover with a plastic wrap.
4. Marinate for at least an hour and then place on the grill, stem side down.
5. Grill for about 10 minutes on both sides and dish out.
6. Mix spinach with coconut cream and fill in the grilled portobellos.
7. Broil for about 5 minutes in the oven and dish out to serve.

Nutrition Amount per serving

Calories 161	Cholesterol 0mg 0%	Dietary Fiber 2.1g 8%
Total Fat 14.9g 19%	Sodium 14mg 1%	Total Sugars 3.7g
Saturated Fat 9.4g 47%	Total Carbs 7.1g 3%	

Keto Tabbouleh

Serves: 4/Prep Time: 15 mins
Ingredients
- ¼ cup lemon juice
- ½ cup extra-virgin olive oil
- ½ teaspoon gray sea salt
- 1⅓ cups Manitoba Harvest Hemp Hearts
- 1 cup fresh parsley, chopped

Directions
1. Whisk together lemon juice, olive oil and sea salt in a large bowl until combined.
2. Stir in Hemp Hearts and fresh parsley to serve.

Nutrition Amount per serving

Calories 404	Cholesterol 0mg 0%	Dietary Fiber 3.1g 11%
Total Fat 39.3g 50%	Sodium 16mg 1%	Total Sugars 2g
Saturated Fat 5.1g 25%	Total Carbs 5.6g 2%	Protein 10.6g

Green Coffee Shake

Serves: 4/Prep Time: 10 mins
Ingredients
- 1½ cups chilled brewed coffee
- 8 ice cubes, for serving
- 1¾ cups full fat coconut milk
- 2 tablespoons almond butter, unsweetened
- 1 tablespoon vegan greens

Directions
1. Put all the ingredients in a blender and blend until smooth.
2. Pour into 4 glasses and serve immediately.

Nutrition Amount per serving

Calories 115	Cholesterol 0mg 0%	Dietary Fiber 1.4g 5%
Total Fat 9.9g 13%	Sodium 9mg 0%	Total Sugars 1.8g
Saturated Fat 5.4g 27%	Total Carbs 4.3g 2%	Protein 3.2g

Vanilla Keto Overnight Oats

Serves: 2/Prep Time: 5 mins
Ingredients
- ½ cup Manitoba Harvest Hemp Hearts
- ⅔ cup full fat coconut milk
- 1 tablespoon chia seed
- ½ teaspoon vanilla extract
- 4 drops liquid Stevia

Directions
1. Put all the ingredients in a large container and stir well.
2. Cover and refrigerate for at least 6 hours.
3. Dish into a bowl and serve.

Nutrition Amount per serving

Calories 231	Cholesterol 0mg 0%	Dietary Fiber 2.7g 10%
Total Fat 19.9g 25%	Sodium 17mg 1%	Total Sugars 3.6g
Saturated Fat 10.8g 54%	Total Carbs 8.6g 3%	

Harissa Portobello Mushrooms Tacos

Serves: 6/Prep Time: 30 mins
Ingredients
- ¼ cup spicy harissa
- 1 pound portobello mushrooms, sliced
- 3 tablespoons olive oil, divided
- 6 collard green leaves, rinsed and chopped
- 1 teaspoon ground cumin

Directions
1. Mix together harissa, 1½ tablespoons olive oil and cumin in a bowl.
2. Rub each portobello mushroom with the harissa mixture and allow the mushrooms to marinade for 15 minutes.
3. Heat remaining olive oil in a pan and add portobello mushrooms.
4. Cook for about 6 minutes on both sides and lower the heat.
5. Allow the mushrooms to rest for about 3 minutes.
6. Fill the portobello mushrooms slices in a collard green leaf and serve.

Nutrition Amount per serving

Calories 87	Cholesterol 1mg 0%	Dietary Fiber 1.3g 4%
Total Fat 7.4g 10%	Sodium 17mg 1%	Total Sugars 0.1g
Saturated Fat 1.1g 5%	Total Carbs 3.6g 1%	Protein 3.3g

Side Dishes Recipes

Brie with Apple

Serves: 3/Prep Time: 10 mins
Ingredients
- 1 tablespoon unsalted butter
- 2 oz. pecans, chopped
- ¼ teaspoon cinnamon
- 4 oz. brie cheese, thinly sliced
- 1 small gala apple, thinly sliced

Directions
1. Mix together apple and brie in a bowl and top with butter, pecans and cinnamon.
2. Serve over low carb crepes.

Nutrition Amount per serving

Calories 310
Total Fat 27.9g 36%
Saturated Fat 10.4g 52%

Cholesterol 48mg 16%
Sodium 265mg 12%
Total Carbs 7.1g 3%

Dietary Fiber 2.6g 9%
Total Sugars 4.4g
Protein 10g

Oven Baked Brie Cheese

Serves: 4/Prep Time: 15 mins
Ingredients
- 2 oz. pecans, chopped
- 9 oz. Brie cheese
- 1 tablespoon fresh rosemary
- Salt and black pepper, to taste
- 1 tablespoon olive oil

Directions
1. Preheat the oven to 400ºF and grease a small baking dish.
2. Mix together pecans with olive oil, fresh rosemary, salt and black pepper.
3. Place Brie cheese on the baking dish and top with pecans mixture.
4. Transfer to the oven and bake for about 10 minutes.
5. Remove from the oven and serve warm.

Nutrition Amount per serving

Calories 345
Total Fat 31.4g 40%
Saturated Fat 12.7g 63%

Cholesterol 64mg 21%
Sodium 402mg 17%
Total Carbs 2.9g 1%

Dietary Fiber 1.9g 7%
Total Sugars 0.8g
Protein 14.8g

Pan Fried Radishes with Bacon

Serves: 8/Prep Time: 30 mins
Ingredients
- 3 pounds radishes, quartered
- 20 oz. bacon, chopped
- 2 garlic cloves, pressed
- 2 tablespoons olive oil
- Salt and black pepper, to taste

Directions
1. Heat olive oil in a large nonstick skillet and add bacon.
2. Fry until crispy and add garlic and radishes.
3. Fry for about 12 minutes, stirring occasionally and season with salt and black pepper to serve.

Nutrition Amount per serving

Calories 442
Total Fat 33.3g 43%
Saturated Fat 10.3g 51%

Cholesterol 78mg 26%
Sodium 1704mg 74%
Total Carbs 7.1g 3%

Dietary Fiber 2.7g 10%
Total Sugars 3.2g
Protein 27.5g

Lemon and Dill Butter

Serves: 6/Prep Time: 10 mins

Ingredients
- 5½ oz. butter
- 2 tablespoons cream cheese
- 3 tablespoons fresh dill, finely chopped
- Salt and black pepper, to taste
- 1 tablespoon lemon juice

Directions
1. Put all the ingredients in a blender and blend until smooth and fluffy.
2. Dish into a bowl to serve with snacks.

Nutrition Amount per serving

Calories 203	Cholesterol 60mg 20%	Dietary Fiber 0.2g 1%
Total Fat 22.3g 29%	Sodium 163mg 7%	Total Sugars 0.1g
Saturated Fat 14.1g 71%	Total Carbs 1g 0%	Protein

Herb Butter

Serves: 6/Prep Time: 10 mins

Ingredients
- 2 garlic cloves, pressed
- 5 oz. butter
- 4 tablespoons fresh parsley, finely chopped
- ½ teaspoon salt
- 1 teaspoon lemon juice

Directions
1. Mix together butter with all other ingredients in a small bowl until well combined.
2. Set aside for about 15 minutes and allow the flavors to infuse well to serve.

Nutrition Amount per serving

Calories 172	Cholesterol 51mg 17%	Dietary Fiber 0.1g 0%
Total Fat 19.2g 25%	Sodium 332mg 14%	Total Sugars 0.1g
Saturated Fat 12.1g 61%	Total Carbs 0.5g 0%	Protein 0.4g

Low Carb Salsa Dressing

Serves: 4/Prep Time: 5 mins

Ingredients
- 4 tablespoons olive oil
- ½ cup low carb salsa
- 4 tablespoons sour cream
- 1 teaspoon chili powder
- 3 tablespoons cider vinegar

Directions
1. Mix together salsa with the rest of the ingredients in a bowl until well combined and smooth. Serve over your favorite salad.

Nutrition Amount per serving

Calories 159	Cholesterol 5mg 2%	Dietary Fiber 0.7g 3%
Total Fat 16.7g 21%	Sodium 208mg 9%	Total Sugars 1.1g
Saturated Fat 3.6g 18%	Total Carbs 3g 1%	Protein 1g

Ginger Asian Slaw

Serves: 8/Prep Time: 15 mins

Ingredients
- 2 cups carrots, shredded
- 6 cups red cabbage, thinly sliced
- 1 cup cilantro, roughly chopped
- 4 tablespoons almond butter
- ¾ cup green onions, sliced

Directions
1. Mix together carrots, cabbage, cilantro and green onions in a large mixing bowl.
2. Top with almond butter and toss to coat well and serve.

Nutrition Amount per serving

Calories 79	Cholesterol 0mg 0%	Dietary Fiber 2.6g 9%
Total Fat 4.8g 6%	Sodium 67mg 3%	Total Sugars 3.7g
Saturated Fat 0.5g 2%	Total Carbs 8.2g 3%	Protein 2.3g

Spiralized Zucchini Asian Salad

Serves: 10/Prep Time: 15 mins

Ingredients

- 1 pound cabbage, shredded
- 1 medium zucchini, thinly spiralized
- 2 cups sunflower seeds, shelled
- 1/3 cup rice vinegar
- ¾ cup avocado oil

Directions

1. Combine sunflower seeds, zucchini and cabbage in a bowl.
2. Mix together avocado oil and rice vinegar in another bowl to make a dressing.
3. Pour the dressing over the salad and mix well.
4. Refrigerate for at least 2 hours and serve.

Nutrition Amount per serving

Calories 96	Cholesterol 0mg 0%	Dietary Fiber 2.9g 10%
Total Fat 7g 9%	Sodium 12mg 1%	Total Sugars 2.1g
Saturated Fat 0.9g 4%	Total Carbs 6.1g 2%	Protein 2.9g

Strawberry Matcha Chia Pudding

Serves: 4/Prep Time: 15 mins

Ingredients

- 1½ cups coconut milk
- 1 teaspoon matcha powder
- 3 tablespoons chia seeds
- 4 scoops Stevia
- 4 strawberries, diced small

Directions

1. Whisk together coconut milk with chia seeds, matcha powder and Stevia.
2. Pour mixture into 4 glasses and refrigerate for about 4 hours.
3. Stir the strawberries into the pudding and serve chilled.

Nutrition Amount per serving

Calories 248	Cholesterol 0mg 0%	Dietary Fiber 5.4g 19%
Total Fat 23.7g 30%	Sodium 15mg 1%	Total Sugars 3.6g
Saturated Fat 19.3g 96%	Total Carbs 8.9g 3%	Protein 4.1g

Eggplant Hole in the Head

Serves: 6/Prep Time: 30 mins

Ingredients

- 2 tablespoons extra-virgin olive oil
- 2 eggplants, sliced half lengthwise
- 2 teaspoons salted butter
- Salt and black pepper, to taste
- 8 eggs, whole

Directions

1. Preheat the grill to high heat.
2. Drizzle eggplant slices with olive oil and season with salt and black pepper.
3. Transfer to the grill and grill for about 4 minutes on each side.
4. Cut a hole in the center of each slice of eggplant and place in the frying pan.
5. Sauté for about 4 minutes with butter over medium heat.
6. Crack egg in the eggplant hole and cook for about 3 minutes.
7. Flip carefully and cook for 3 more minutes.
8. Season with salt and black pepper and serve immediately.

Nutrition Amount per serving

Calories 156	Cholesterol 290mg 97%	Dietary Fiber 0.8g 3%
Total Fat 12g 15%	Sodium 175mg 8%	Total Sugars 1.1g
Saturated Fat 3.5g 17%	Total Carbs 4.1g 1%	Protein 8.3g

Keto Bagels

Serves: 6/Prep Time: 55 mins
Ingredients
- ½ cup tahini
- ¾ cup ground flax seed
- 1/8 cup psyllium husks
- 1 teaspoon baking powder
- 1 cup water

Directions
1. Preheat the oven to 375°F and grease a baking tray.
2. Mix together ground flax seed, psyllium husks and baking powder in a bowl until combined.
3. Whisk together tahini with water and pour into the flax seed mixture.
4. Knead well to make the dough and form patties out of this mixture.
5. Arrange the patties on the baking tray and place in the oven.
6. Bake for about 40 minutes until golden brown and remove from the oven to serve.

Nutrition Amount per serving

Calories 202	Cholesterol 0mg 0%	Dietary Fiber 8.9g 32%
Total Fat 15.3g 20%	Sodium 32mg 1%	Total Sugars 0.3g
Saturated Fat 2.1g 11%	Total Carbs 8.6g 3%	Protein 6.1g

Hemp Heart Porridge

Serves: 4/Prep Time: 5 mins
Ingredients
- 1 cup nondairy milk
- 3 tablespoons flax seed, freshly ground
- ½ cup Manitoba Harvest Hemp Hearts
- ¼ cup almonds, crushed
- 5 drops Stevia

Directions
1. Put the milk, flax seed, Hemp Hearts and Stevia in a saucepan and mix well.
2. Heat over medium heat until boiling and allow to simmer for about 2 minutes.
3. Dish into a bowl and top with almonds to serve.

Nutrition Amount per serving

Calories 157	Cholesterol 0mg 0%	Dietary Fiber 3.4g 12%
Total Fat 11g 14%	Sodium 34mg 1%	Total Sugars 2.8g
Saturated Fat 1.1g 5%	Total Carbs 6.8g 2%	Protein 8g

Kelp Noodles with Avocado Pesto

Serves: 4/Prep Time: 20 mins
Ingredients
- ½ cup extra-virgin olive oil
- 1 Hass avocado
- 1¼ cups fresh baby spinach leaves
- 1 package kelp noodles, soaked in water for at least 30 minutes
- 1 teaspoon salt

Directions
1. Put avocado, olive oil, baby spinach leaves and salt in a blender.
2. Blend until smooth and dish out in a bowl.
3. Stir in the kelp noodles and mix well to serve.

Nutrition Amount per serving

Calories 317	Cholesterol 0mg 0%	Dietary Fiber 4.7g 17%
Total Fat 34g 44%	Sodium 611mg 27%	Total Sugars 0.3g
Saturated Fat 4.9g 24%	Total Carbs 5.8g 2%	Protein 1.5g

Parmesan Zucchini Pasta

Serves: 6/Prep Time: 20 mins

Ingredients

- 1 pint cherry tomatoes, halved
- 2 pounds zucchini, spiralized
- ¼ cup extra virgin olive oil
- ½ cup parmesan cheese, shredded
- Salt and black pepper, to taste

Directions

1. Heat olive oil over medium low heat in a large pot and add cherry tomatoes.
2. Cook for about 3 minutes and stir in the zucchini noodles.
3. Season with salt and black pepper and cover the lid.
4. Cook for about 4 minutes on low heat and stir in the parmesan cheese.
5. Cook for about 2 minutes and dish out to serve hot.

Nutrition Amount per serving

Calories 137	Cholesterol 7mg 2%	Dietary Fiber 2.4g 9%
Total Fat 10.8g 14%	Sodium 105mg 5%	Total Sugars 4.2g
Saturated Fat 2.6g 13%	Total Carbs 7.7g 3%	Protein 5.4g

Keto Crack Slaw

Serves: 4/Prep Time: 20 mins

Ingredients

- ½ cup macadamia nuts, chopped
- 3 tablespoons liquid aminos
- 4 cups green cabbage, shredded
- 1 teaspoon Sriracha paste
- 1 tablespoon sesame oil

Directions

1. Mix together cabbage with sesame oil, Sriracha paste and liquid aminos in a bowl.
2. Top with macadamia nuts and serve immediately.

Nutrition Amount per serving

Calories 168	Cholesterol 0mg 0%	Dietary Fiber 3.2g 11%
Total Fat 16.2g 21%	Sodium 737mg 32%	Total Sugars 3g
Saturated Fat 2.5g 13%	Total Carbs 6.8g 2%	Protein 3.6g

Keto Kale Pate and Spread

Serves: 10/Prep Time: 20 mins

Ingredients

- ½ cup raw organic sesame seeds
- ½ cup extra-virgin olive oil
- 6 cups kale, chopped
- 8 green onions, green part only
- 1¼ teaspoons grey sea salt

Directions

1. Heat 1 tablespoon olive oil in a skillet and add kale.
2. Cook for about 7 minutes until crispy and transfer to a food processor.
3. Process until smooth and add green onions, sesame seeds and grey sea salt.
4. Blend until smooth and dish out in a bowl to serve.

Nutrition Amount per serving

Calories 149	Cholesterol 0mg 0%	Dietary Fiber 1.6g 6%
Total Fat 13.7g 18%	Sodium 79mg 3%	Total Sugars 0.2g
Saturated Fat 1.9g 10%	Total Carbs 6.3g 2%	Protein 2.6g

Crumbly Almond Feta

Serves: 3/Prep Time: 40 mins
Ingredients
- 3 tablespoons lemon juice
- 1 cup almonds, soaked for at least 8 hours and skins removed
- 3 tablespoons olive oil
- ½ teaspoon salt
- 1 garlic clove

Directions
1. Preheat the oven to 400°F and grease a baking sheet.
2. Put almonds, lemon juice, olive oil, salt and garlic in a high powered blender and blend until smooth. Place a colander over a bowl and cover with a few layers of cheesecloth. Pour the pureed nut cheese into the colander and fold the cloth around the cheese to squeeze. Allow to sit for about 24 hours at room temperature and place the cheese on the baking sheet.
3. Transfer to the oven and bake for about 30 minutes until firm and golden brown.
4. Allow it to cool and refrigerate for about 2 hours to serve.

Nutrition Amount per serving

Calories 308
Total Fat 30g   38%
Saturated Fat 3.3g   17%

Cholesterol 0mg   0%
Sodium 391mg   17%
Total Carbs 7.4g   3%

Dietary Fiber 4g   14%
Total Sugars 1.7g
Protein 6.9g

Creamy Spinach with Dill

Serves: 4/Prep Time: 25 mins
Ingredients
- 1 pound spinach, large stems removed, coarsely chopped
- 1 tablespoon unsalted butter
- 1/3 cup heavy cream
- 1/3 cup fresh dill, coarsely chopped
- Salt, black pepper and nutmeg, to taste

Directions
1. Heat butter over medium heat in a large pot and add the spinach.
2. Cover and cook for about 3 minutes, stirring occasionally.
3. Dish into a bowl and drain the spinach.
4. Return to the pot over medium heat and stir in the cream and nutmeg.
5. Cook on low heat for about 4 minutes and season with salt and black pepper.
6. Sprinkle with fresh dill and cook for about 3 minutes. Dish out and serve hot.

Nutrition Amount per serving

Calories 129
Total Fat 9.7g   12%
Saturated Fat 5.7g   28%

Cholesterol 28mg   9%
Sodium 163mg   7%
Total Carbs 8.9g   3%

Dietary Fiber 4.1g   15%
Total Sugars 0.7g
Protein 5.7g

Keto Cheese Bread

Serves: 2/Prep Time: 15 mins
Ingredients
- 2 large eggs
- 2 tablespoons olive oil
- 4 tablespoons coconut flour
- ½ teaspoon baking powder
- ½ cup cheddar cheese, grated

Directions
1. Whisk together eggs, coconut flour, 1 tablespoon olive oil, cheddar cheese and baking powder in a small bowl. Stir well and pour into a microwave safe mug.
2. Microwave for about 1 minute 30 seconds and invert the mug onto a cutting board.
3. Cut the bread crosswise into ½ inch thick slices.
4. Heat the rest of the oil over medium heat in a small skillet and add slices.
5. Toast for about 30 seconds on each side until golden brown and serve.

Nutrition Amount per serving

Calories 367
Total Fat 29.8g 38%
Saturated Fat 10.5g 53%
Cholesterol 216mg 72%
Sodium 247mg 11%
Total Carbs 11.3g 4%
Dietary Fiber 6g 22%
Total Sugars 0.5g
Protein 15.3g

Saucy Chili Garlic Cucumber Noodles

Serves: 3/Prep Time: 15 mins
Ingredients

- 1 tablespoon sesame oil, toasted
- 3 tablespoons rice vinegar
- 2 teaspoons Asian chili garlic sauce
- 2 teaspoons sesame seeds, toasted
- 1½ pounds English cucumbers, spiralizes into noodles

Directions

1. Whisk together sesame oil, rice vinegar and chili garlic sauce in a large bowl.
2. Put the cucumber noodles in a bowl and drizzle with the dressing.
3. Top with the sesame seeds and immediately serve.

Nutrition Amount per serving

Calories 96
Total Fat 5.8g 7%
Saturated Fat 0.9g 4%
Cholesterol 0mg 0%
Sodium 51mg 2%
Total Carbs 8.7g 3%
Dietary Fiber 1.4g 5%
Total Sugars 3.8g
Protein 1.8g

Garlic Butter Mushrooms

Serves: 6/Prep Time: 25 mins
Ingredients

- 2 pounds white button mushrooms, stems trimmed but not removed
- 6 tablespoons unsalted butter
- Salt and black pepper, to taste
- 4 teaspoons fresh thyme leaves
- 4 garlic cloves, minced

Directions

1. Heat butter over medium heat in a large skillet and add button mushrooms.
2. Season with salt and black pepper and cook for about 10 minutes until browned on both sides. Stir in the thyme and garlic and sauté for about 1 minute.
3. Dish into a bowl and serve immediately.

Nutrition Amount per serving

Calories 139
Total Fat 12g 15%
Saturated Fat 7.3g 37%
Cholesterol 31mg 10%
Sodium 91mg 4%
Total Carbs 6.1g 2%
Dietary Fiber 1.8g 6%
Total Sugars 2.6g
Protein 5.1g

Kale with Lemon and Garlic

Serves: 6/Prep Time: 20 mins
Ingredients

- 3 tablespoons olive oil
- 6 cups kale, coarsely chopped
- 4 cloves garlic, thinly sliced
- 2 teaspoons lemon juice
- Red pepper flakes, salt and black pepper, to taste

Directions

1. Heat olive oil over medium heat in a large pan and add garlic and red pepper flakes.
2. Sauté for about 1 minute and add kale and season with salt and black pepper.
3. Cover with lid and cook for about 5 minutes, stirring occasionally.
4. Stir in the lemon juice and dish out to serve warm.

Nutrition Amount per serving

Calories 92
Total Fat 7.4g 10%
Saturated Fat 1.1g 5%
Cholesterol 0mg 0%
Sodium 48mg 2%
Total Carbs 6.3g 2%
Dietary Fiber 1.2g 4%
Total Sugars 0.1g
Protein 2g

Oven Roasted Frozen Broccoli

Serves: 4/Prep Time: 25 mins

Ingredients

- 2 tablespoons olive oil
- ¼ cup parmesan cheese, grated
- 1 (16 ounce) bag frozen broccoli florets
- Salt and black pepper, to taste
- 1 medium lemon, halved

Directions

1. Preheat the oven to 450°F and grease a baking sheet lightly.
2. Mix together broccoli, olive oil, salt and black pepper in a bowl until well coated.
3. Arrange the broccoli on the baking sheet and transfer to the oven.
4. Bake for about 15 minutes and top with lemon halves and Parmesan cheese.
5. Place in the oven and bake for about 3 minutes until melted.
6. Remove from the oven and serve hot.

Nutrition Amount per serving

Calories 118	Cholesterol 5mg 2%	Dietary Fiber 0.4g 1%
Total Fat 8.9g 11%	Sodium 96mg 4%	Total Sugars 0.3g
Saturated Fat 2.1g 10%	Total Carbs 7.3g 3%	Protein 5.8g

Creamiest Garlic Mashed Cauliflower

Serves: 9/Prep Time: 30 mins

Ingredients

- 3 tablespoons unsalted butter
- 3 pounds cauliflower, finely chopped
- 2 tablespoons garlic, minced
- 1 teaspoon kosher salt
- 2 cups water

Directions

1. Heat butter over medium high heat in a skillet and add garlic.
2. Sauté for about 1 minute and add cauliflower.
3. Sauté for about 5 minutes, stirring occasionally and add salt and water.
4. Cover with lid and cook for about 10 minutes on low heat until boiled.
5. Drain the cauliflower and reserve ¼ cup of the cooking liquid.
6. Mash the cauliflower in an immersion blender and blend until smooth.
7. Dish into a bowl and serve hot.

Nutrition Amount per serving

Calories 75	Cholesterol 10mg 3%	Dietary Fiber 3.8g 14%
Total Fat 4g 5%	Sodium 333mg 14%	Total Sugars 3.7g
Saturated Fat 2.5g 12%	Total Carbs 8.6g 3%	Protein 3.2g

Roasted Cabbage with Bacon

Serves: 6/Prep Time: 40 mins

Ingredients

- 4 tablespoons olive oil
- 1 head green cabbage, outer leaves removed and quartered into wedges
- Kosher salt and black pepper, to taste
- 3 tablespoons sesame seeds
- 8 ounces thick cut bacon slices

Directions

1. Preheat the oven to 450°F and grease a large roasting pan.
2. Arrange on the baking sheet and drizzle with olive oil.
3. Season with salt and black pepper and top with bacon slices.
4. Place in the oven and roast for about 30 minutes. Remove from the oven and serve hot.

Nutrition Amount per serving

Calories 346	Cholesterol 32mg 11%	Dietary Fiber 3.5g 13%
Total Fat 30.6g 39%	Sodium 694mg 30%	Total Sugars 3.8g
Saturated Fat 9g 45%	Total Carbs 8g 3%	Protein 12.8g

Keto BLT Dip

Serves: 8/Prep Time: 250 mins

Ingredients
- ¼ cup mayonnaise, salted
- 12 oz. cream cheese
- 1/3 cup cheddar cheese, shredded and divided
- 2/3 cup tomatoes, chopped
- 2 cups lettuce, chopped

Directions
1. Mix together mayonnaise and cream cheese in a bowl until combined.
2. Add half of the cheddar cheese and top with tomatoes, lettuce and rest of the cheddar cheese. Dish out to a serving bowl and serve.

Nutrition Amount per serving

Calories 201	Cholesterol 54mg 18%	Dietary Fiber 0.3g 1%
Total Fat 18.9g 24%	Sodium 209mg 9%	Total Sugars 1.1g
Saturated Fat 10.7g 53%	Total Carbs 3.9g 1%	Protein 4.6g

Crispy Baked Garlic Parmesan Wings

Serves: 8/Prep Time: 1 hour 20 mins

Ingredients
- ½ cup butter, melted
- 2 pounds chicken wings
- ½ cup parmesan cheese, grated
- Sea salt, black pepper, garlic powder and onion powder
- 1 garlic clove, minced

Directions
1. Preheat the oven to 250°F and grease a baking sheet lightly.
2. Season the chicken wings with salt and arrange on the baking sheet.
3. Bake for about 20 minutes and increase the temperature to 425°F.
4. Transfer the baking sheet to the middle upper rack.
5. Bake for 45 more minutes until crispy and remove from the oven.
6. Mix together butter, garlic, black pepper, parmesan cheese, garlic powder and onion powder in a bowl.
7. Stir until well combined and serve with the wings.

Nutrition Amount per serving

Calories 342	Cholesterol 136mg 45%	Dietary Fiber 0.1g 0%
Total Fat 21.4g 27%	Sodium 245mg 11%	Total Sugars 0.2g
Saturated Fat 10.6g 53%	Total Carbs 0.9g 0%	

Cheesy Zucchini

Serves: 3/Prep Time: 20 mins

Ingredients
- 1 zucchini, spiralized into noodles
- ½ cup water
- 1 tablespoon salted butter
- 2 tablespoons coconut milk
- 1 cup cheddar cheese, shredded

Directions
1. Put zucchini noodles and water in a saucepan and bring to a boil.
2. Reduce heat to low and add butter, coconut milk and cheddar cheese to the pan.
3. Stir well and dish into a bowl to serve.

Nutrition Amount per serving

Calories 219	Cholesterol 50mg 17%	Dietary Fiber 0.9g 3%
Total Fat 18.8g 24%	Sodium 269mg 12%	Total Sugars 1.7g
Saturated Fat 12.5g 63%	Total Carbs 3.2g 1%	Protein 10.4g

Bacon Wrapped Maple Parmesan Asparagus Bundles

Serves: 8/Prep Time: 55 mins

Ingredients

- ½ cup salted butter
- ½ cup sugar free maple syrup
- 2 pounds fresh asparagus, washed, ends chopped off
- ¼ cup parmesan cheese, grated
- 8 slices thick   cut bacon

Directions

1. Preheat the oven to 425ºF and grease a casserole dish lightly.
2. Heat butter over medium low heat in a small pot and add maple syrup.
3. Bring to a boil and remove from heat.
4. Wrap bacon slices around the asparagus stalks and secure with a toothpick.
5. Place these in the casserole dish and top with butter maple sauce and parmesan cheese.
6. Transfer in the oven and bake for about 40 minutes.
7. Turn on the oven broiler and broil for about 2 minutes.
8. Remove from the oven and serve hot.

Nutrition Amount per serving

Calories 247	Cholesterol 54mg 18%	Dietary Fiber 2.4g 9%
Total Fat 20.3g 26%	Sodium 563mg 24%	Total Sugars 2.1g
Saturated Fat 10.5g 52%	Total Carbs 7.1g 3%	Protein 10.8g

Garlic Broccoli

Serves: 6/Prep Time: 15 mins

Ingredients

- ¼ cup olive oil
- 1½ pounds broccoli florets, steamed and drained
- 1/8 cup fresh lemon juice
- 1 teaspoon salt
- 1 teaspoon garlic powder

Directions

1. Mix together lemon juice, olive oil, salt and garlic powder in a small blender and blend until creamy. Drizzle the broccoli with the lemon garlic dressing and serve.

Nutrition Amount per serving

Calories 113	Cholesterol 0mg 0%	Dietary Fiber 3g 11%
Total Fat 8.8g 11%	Sodium 426mg 19%	Total Sugars 2.2g
Saturated Fat 1.2g 6%	Total Carbs 8g 3%	Protein 3.3g

Snacks Recipes

Caprese Snack

Serves: 4/Prep Time: 5 mins

Ingredients

- 8 oz. mozzarella, mini cheese balls
- 8 oz. cherry tomatoes
- 2 tablespoons green pesto
- Salt and black pepper, to taste
- 1 tablespoon garlic powder

Directions

1. Slice the mozzarella balls and tomatoes in half.
2. Stir in the green pesto and season with garlic powder, salt and pepper to serve.

Nutrition Amount per serving

Calories 407	Cholesterol 30mg 10%	Dietary Fiber 0.9g 3%
Total Fat 34.5g 44%	Sodium 343mg 15%	Total Sugars 2g
Saturated Fat 7.4g 37%	Total Carbs 6.3g 2%	Protein 19.4g

Almond Flour Crackers

Serves: 6/Prep Time: 25 mins

Ingredients

- 2 tablespoons sunflower seeds
- 1 cup almond flour
- ¾ teaspoon sea salt
- 1 tablespoon whole psyllium husks
- 1 tablespoon coconut oil

Directions

1. Preheat the oven to 350°F and grease a baking sheet lightly.
2. Mix together sunflower seeds, almond flour, sea salt, coconut oil, psyllium husks and 2 tablespoons of water in a bowl. Transfer into a blender and blend until smooth.
3. Form a dough out of this mixture and roll it on the parchment paper until 1/16 inch thick.
4. Slice into 1 inch squares and season with some sea salt.
5. Arrange the squares on the baking sheet and transfer to the oven.
6. Bake for about 15 minutes until edges are crisp and brown.
7. Allow to cool and separate into squares to serve.

Nutrition Amount per serving

Calories 141	Cholesterol 0mg 0%	Dietary Fiber 3.1g 11%
Total Fat 11.6g 15%	Sodium 241mg 10%	Total Sugars 0g
Saturated Fat 2.7g 13%	Total Carbs 5.2g 2%	Protein 4.2g

Crispy Baked Zucchini Fries

Serves: 4/Prep Time: 30 mins

Ingredients

- ¾ cup parmesan cheese, grated
- 2 medium zucchinis, chopped into small sticks
- 1 large egg
- ¼ teaspoon black pepper
- ¼ teaspoon garlic powder

Directions

1. Preheat the oven to 425°F and grease a baking sheet lightly.
2. Whisk egg in one bowl and mix together parmesan cheese, black pepper and garlic powder in another bowl.
3. Dip each zucchini stick in the egg and then dredge in the dry mixture.
4. Transfer to the baking sheet and place in the oven.
5. Bake for about 20 minutes until golden and broil for 3 minutes to serve.

Nutrition Amount per serving

Calories 102	Cholesterol 62mg 21%	Dietary Fiber 1.1g 4%
Total Fat 5.9g 8%	Sodium 222mg 10%	Total Sugars 1.8g
Saturated Fat 3.4g 17%	Total Carbs 4.3g 2%	Protein 9.6g

Low Carb Onion Rings

Serves: 6/Prep Time: 30 mins

Ingredients

- 2 medium white onions, sliced into ½ inch thick rings
- ½ cup coconut flour
- 4 large eggs
- 4 oz pork rinds
- 1 cup parmesan cheese, grated

Directions

1. Preheat an Air fryer to 390°F and grease a fryer basket.
2. Put coconut flour in one bowl, eggs in the second bowl and pork rinds and parmesan cheese in the third bowl. Coat the onion rings through the three bowls one by one and repeat.
3. Place the coated onion rings in the fryer basket and cook for about 15 minutes.
4. Dish out to a platter and serve with your favorite low carb sauce.

Nutrition Amount per serving

Calories 270	Cholesterol 164mg 55%	Dietary Fiber 4.8g 17%
Total Fat 15.1g 19%	Sodium 586mg 25%	Total Sugars 1.8g
Saturated Fat 7.1g 35%	Total Carbs 11g 4%	Protein 24.1g

Broccoli Fritters with Cheddar Cheese

Serves: 4/Prep Time: 20 mins

Ingredients

- 1 cup cheddar cheese, shredded
- 8 ounces broccoli, chopped, steamed and drained
- 2 large eggs, beaten
- 1 tablespoon avocado oil
- 2 tablespoons oat fiber

Directions

1. Mix together broccoli with cheddar cheese, eggs and oat fiber in a bowl.
2. Heat avocado oil over medium heat in a nonstick pan and add the broccoli mixture in small chunks.
3. Cook for about 5 minutes on both sides until browned and dish onto a platter to serve.

Nutrition Amount per serving

Calories 178	Cholesterol 123mg 41%	Dietary Fiber 2g 7%
Total Fat 12.6g 16%	Sodium 236mg 10%	Total Sugars 1.4g
Saturated Fat 6.8g 34%	Total Carbs 5.3g 2%	Protein 12.1g

Cheesy Low Carb Creamed Spinach

Serves: 8/Prep Time: 25 mins

Ingredients

- 2 (10 oz) packages frozen chopped spinach, thawed
- 3 tablespoons butter
- 6 ounces cream cheese
- Onion powder, salt and black pepper
- ½ cup parmesan cheese, grated

Directions

1. Mix together 2 tablespoons of butter with cream cheese, parmesan cheese, salt and black pepper in a bowl.
2. Heat the rest of the butter on medium heat in a small pan and add onion powder.
3. Sauté for about 1 minute and add spinach.
4. Cover and cook on low heat for about 5 minutes.
5. Stir in the cheese mixture and cook for about 3 minutes. Dish into a bowl and serve hot.

Nutrition Amount per serving

Calories 141	Cholesterol 37mg 12%	Dietary Fiber 1.6g 6%
Total Fat 12.8g 16%	Sodium 182mg 8%	Total Sugars 0.5g
Saturated Fat 8g 40%	Total Carbs 3.5g 1%	Protein 4.8g

Jicama Fries

Serves: 2/Prep Time: 20 mins

Ingredients

- 2 tablespoons avocado oil
- 1 Jicama, cut into fries
- 1 tablespoon garlic powder
- ½ cup parmesan cheese, grated
- Salt and black pepper, to taste

Directions

1. Preheat the Air fryer to 400°F and grease the fryer basket. Boil jicama fries for about 10 minutes and drain well. Mix jicama fries with garlic powder, salt and black pepper in a bowl.
2. Place in the fryer basket and cook for about 10 minutes.Dish onto a platter and serve .

Nutrition Amount per serving

Calories 145	Cholesterol 20mg 7%	Dietary Fiber 4g 14%
Total Fat 7.8g 10%	Sodium 262mg 11%	Total Sugars 2.6g
Saturated Fat 4.4g 22%	Total Carbs 10.4g 4%	Protein 10.4g

Spicy Tuna Rolls

Serves: 2/Prep Time: 15 mins
Ingredients
- 1 pouch StarKist Selects E.V.O.O. Wild Caught Yellowfin Tuna
- 1 medium cucumber, thinly sliced lengthwise
- 1 teaspoon hot sauce
- 2 slices avocado, diced
- Cayenne, salt and black pepper

Directions
1. Mix together tuna with hot sauce, cayenne, salt and black pepper in a bowl until combined.
2. Put the tuna mixture on the cucumber slices and top with avocado.
3. Roll up the cucumber and secure with 2 toothpicks to serve.

Nutrition Amount per serving

Calories 139	Cholesterol 22mg 7%	Dietary Fiber 2.9g 10%
Total Fat 6.5g 8%	Sodium 86mg 4%	Total Sugars 2.8g
Saturated Fat 1.2g 6%	Total Carbs 8.4g 3%	

Cheesy Radish

Serves: 5/Prep Time: 1 hour
Ingredients
- 16 oz. Monterey jack cheese, shredded
- 2 cups radish
- ½ cup heavy cream
- 1 teaspoon lemon juice
- Salt and white pepper, to taste

Directions
1. Preheat the oven to 300°F and lightly grease a baking sheet.
2. Heat heavy cream in a small saucepan and season with salt and white pepper.
3. Stir in Monterey jack cheese and lemon juice.
4. Place the radish on the baking sheet and top with the cheese mixture.
5. Bake for about 45 minutes and remove from the oven to serve hot.

Nutrition Amount per serving

Calories 387	Cholesterol 97mg 32%	Dietary Fiber 0.7g 3%
Total Fat 32g 41%	Sodium 509mg 22%	Total Sugars 1.3g
Saturated Fat 20.1g 100%	Total Carbs 2.6g 1%	Protein 22.8g

Parmesan Garlic Oven Roasted Mushrooms

Serves: 6/Prep Time: 30 mins
Ingredients
- 3 tablespoons butter
- 12 oz. baby Bella mushrooms
- ¼ cup pork rinds, finely ground
- Pink Himalayan salt and black pepper, to taste
- ¼ cup parmesan cheese, grated

Directions
1. Preheat the oven to 400°F and lightly grease a baking sheet.
2. Heat butter in a large skillet over medium high heat and add mushrooms.
3. Sauté for about 3 minutes and dish out.
4. Mix together pork rinds, parmesan cheese, salt and black pepper in a bowl.
5. Put the mushrooms in this mixture and mix to coat well.
6. Place on the baking sheet and transfer to the oven.
7. Bake for about 15 minutes and dish out to immediately serve.

Nutrition Amount per serving

Calories 94	Cholesterol 22mg 7%	Dietary Fiber 0.9g 3%
Total Fat 7.7g 10%	Sodium 228mg 10%	Total Sugars 1g
Saturated Fat 4.7g 23%	Total Carbs 3g 1%	Protein 4.5g

Garlicky Green Beans Stir Fry

Serves: 4/Prep Time: 25 mins

Ingredients

- 2 tablespoons peanut oil
- 1 pound fresh green beans
- 2 tablespoons garlic, chopped
- Salt and red chili pepper, to taste
- ½ yellow onion, slivered

Directions

1. Heat peanut oil in a wok over high heat and add garlic and onions.
2. Sauté for about 4 minutes add beans, salt and red chili pepper.
3. Sauté for about 3 minutes and add a little water.
4. Cover with lid and cook on low heat for about 5 minutes.
5. Dish out into a bowl and serve hot.

Nutrition Amount per serving

Calories 107	Cholesterol 0mg 0%	Dietary Fiber 4.3g 15%
Total Fat 6.9g 9%	Sodium 8mg 0%	Total Sugars 2.3g
Saturated Fat 1.2g 6%	Total Carbs 10.9g 4%	Protein 2.5g

Collard Greens with Burst Cherry Tomatoes

Serves: 4/Prep Time: 25 mins

Ingredients

- 1 pound collard greens
- 3 strips bacon, cooked and crisped
- ¼ cup cherry tomatoes
- Salt and black pepper, to taste
- 2 tablespoons chicken broth

Directions

1. Put the collard greens, cherry tomatoes and chicken broth in a pot and stir gently.
2. Cook for about 8 minutes and season with salt and black pepper.
3. Cook for about 2 minutes and stir in the bacon.
4. Cook for about 3 minutes and dish out into a bowl to serve hot.

Nutrition Amount per serving

Calories 110	Cholesterol 0mg 0%	Dietary Fiber 3.9g 14%
Total Fat 7.6g 10%	Sodium 268mg 12%	Total Sugars 0.3g
Saturated Fat 2.3g 11%	Total Carbs 6.7g 2%	Protein 5.7g

Basil Parmesan Tomatoes

Serves: 6/Prep Time: 30 mins

Ingredients

- ½ teaspoon dried oregano
- 4 Roma tomatoes
- Spices: onion powder, garlic powder, sea salt and black pepper
- ½ cup parmesan cheese, shredded
- 12 small fresh basil leaves

Directions

1. Preheat the oven to 425°F and grease a baking sheet lightly.
2. Mix together dried oregano, onion powder, garlic powder, sea salt and black pepper in a small bowl.
3. Arrange the tomato slices on a baking sheet and sprinkle with the seasoning blend.
4. Top with parmesan cheese and basil leaves and transfer to the oven.
5. Bake for about 20 minutes and remove from the oven to serve.

Nutrition Amount per serving

Calories 49	Cholesterol 7mg 2%	Dietary Fiber 1.2g 4%
Total Fat 2.2g 3%	Sodium 91mg 4%	Total Sugars 2.4g
Saturated Fat 1.4g 7%	Total Carbs 4.3g 2%	Protein 3.9g

Roasted Spicy Garlic Eggplant Slices

Serves: 4/Prep Time: 35 mins

Ingredients

- 2 tablespoons olive oil
- 1 eggplant, sliced into rounds
- 1 teaspoon garlic powder
- Salt and red pepper
- ½ teaspoon Italian seasoning

Directions

1. Preheat the oven to 400°F and line a baking sheet with parchment paper.
2. Arrange the eggplant slices on a baking sheet and drizzle with olive oil.
3. Season with Italian seasoning, garlic powder, salt and red pepper.
4. Transfer to the oven and bake for about 25 minutes.
5. Remove from the oven and serve hot.

Nutrition Amount per serving

Calories 123	Cholesterol 0mg 0%	Dietary Fiber 5.6g 20%
Total Fat 9.7g 12%	Sodium 3mg 0%	Total Sugars 4.9g
Saturated Fat 1.4g 7%	Total Carbs 10g 4%	Protein 1.7g

Pepper Jack Brussels Sprouts

Serves: 9/Prep Time: 20 mins

Ingredients

- 2 pounds Brussels sprouts, halved and boiled
- 2 tablespoons garlic, minced
- 3 cups pepper jack cheese, shredded
- 2 tablespoons coconut oil
- 1 cup sour cream

Directions

1. Heat oil in a skillet on medium heat and add garlic.
2. Sauté for about 1 minute and stir in the sour cream and pepper jack cheese.
3. Cook for about 5 minutes on medium low heat and add Brussels sprouts.
4. Stir to coat well and cover with the lid.
5. Cook for about 5 minutes and dish out into a bowl to serve.

Nutrition Amount per serving

Calories 274	Cholesterol 51mg 17%	Dietary Fiber 3.8g 14%
Total Fat 20.7g 27%	Sodium 266mg 12%	Total Sugars 2.2g
Saturated Fat 14.1g 70%	Total Carbs 10.9g 4%	Protein 13.7g

Egg Fast Fettuccini Alfredo

Serves: 2/Prep Time: 20 mins

Ingredients

- 1 oz. cream cheese
- 2 eggs
- Garlic powder, salt and black pepper
- 1 tablespoon butter
- 2 oz. Mascarpone cheese

Directions

1. Preheat the oven to 325°F and grease a baking pan lightly.
2. Put the cream cheese, eggs, garlic powder, salt and black pepper in a blender.
3. Pour this mixture into the baking pan and transfer to the oven.
4. Bake for about 8 minutes and remove from the oven.
5. Allow to slightly cool and roll up the baked sheet.
6. Mix together butter and Mascarpone cheese in a small bowl.
7. Microwave for about 1 minute on high and whisk well until smooth.
8. Put the baked sheet in the butter cheese mixture and immediately serve.

Nutrition Amount per serving   Calories 217 Total Fat 18.8g 24% Saturated Fat 10.5g 52% Cholesterol 209mg 70% Sodium 169mg 7% Total Carbs 2.6g 1% Dietary Fiber 0.1g 1% Total Sugars 0.8g Protein 10.1g

Braided Garlic Breadsticks

Serves: 4/Prep Time: 35 mins
Ingredients
- 1 egg
- 2 garlic cloves, crushed
- 10 oz. mozzarella cheese, shredded
- 1 cup ground flax seed
- 2 tablespoons salted butter, melted

Directions
1. Preheat the oven to 400°F and lightly grease a cookie sheet. Mix together garlic and butter in a bowl and set aside. Melt the cheese in microwave and stir in flax seed and egg.
2. Mix well and press into a rectangle and cut lengthwise into small strips.
3. Braid the dough with 3 strips and brush with half of the garlic butter.
4. Transfer onto the cookie sheet and bake for about 15 minutes.
5. Remove from the oven and brush with the rest of the garlic butter.
6. Bake for another 10 minutes and dish out to serve warm.

Nutrition Amount per serving

Calories 417	Cholesterol 94mg 31%	Dietary Fiber 7.6g 27%
Total Fat 28.2g 36%	Sodium 490mg 21%	Total Sugars 0.5g
Saturated Fat 12.7g 63%	Total Carbs 11.1g 4%	Protein 26.7g

Stir Fried Bok Choy

Serves: 4/Prep Time: 15 mins
Ingredients
- 1 tablespoon oyster sauce
- 2 teaspoons soy sauce
- 1 tablespoon butter
- 2 heads bok choy, ends trimmed and cut crosswise into strips
- 2 tablespoons sesame oil

Directions
1. Mix together soy sauce, oyster sauce, sesame oil and 2 tablespoons water in a bowl and set aside. Heat butter in a wok on medium heat and add bok choy.
2. Sauté for about 3 minutes and stir in the soy sauce mixture.
3. Stir fry for about 2 more minutes and dish out onto a platter to serve.

Nutrition Amount per serving

Calories 142	Cholesterol 8mg 3%	Dietary Fiber 4.2g 15%
Total Fat 10.5g 13%	Sodium 470mg 20%	Total Sugars 5g
Saturated Fat 2.9g 15%	Total Carbs 9.5g 3%	Protein 6.5g

Black and White Keto Fat Bombs

Serves: 8/Prep Time: 45 mins
Ingredients
- 1 cup extra-virgin coconut oil
- 2 cups almonds, slivered
- 2 scoops Stevia
- 2 tablespoons unsweetened cocoa powder
- 2 teaspoons sugar free vanilla extract

Directions
1. Put mini liners in 8 cup mini muffin tin.
2. Put the coconut oil, almonds, Stevia and vanilla extract in a food processor and process until coarsely smooth. Dish out half of this mixture into a bowl and add cocoa powder.
3. Put almond mixture in half of the muffin tin and top with the cocoa mixture.
4. Transfer the muffin tray in the freezer and freeze for about 30 minutes before serving.

Nutrition Amount per serving

Calories 394	Cholesterol 0mg 0%	Dietary Fiber 3.4g 12%
Total Fat 40.1g 51%	Sodium 1mg 0%	Total Sugars 1.2g
Saturated Fat 28g 140%	Total Carbs 6g 2%	Protein 5.3g

Keto Cheddar Taco Crisps

Serves: 5/Prep Time: 15 mins

Ingredients

- ¼ cup parmesan cheese, shredded
- ¾ cup full fat sharp cheddar cheese, finely shredded
- ¼ teaspoon chili powder
- 1 pinch cayenne pepper
- ¼ teaspoon ground cumin

Directions

1. Preheat the oven to 400°F and grease a baking sheet lightly.
2. Mix together parmesan cheese, cheddar cheese, chili powder, cayenne pepper and cumin in a bowl.
3. Spoon the cheese mixture 1 inch apart on the baking sheet and transfer to the oven.
4. Bake for about 5 minutes until the cheese is golden brown and remove from the oven to serve.

Nutrition Amount per serving

Calories 99	Cholesterol 18mg 6%	Dietary Fiber 0.4g 2%
Total Fat 8.2g 10%	Sodium 337mg 15%	Total Sugars 0.2g
Saturated Fat 3.5g 18%	Total Carbs 1.5g 1%	Protein 5.1g

Cheesy Cauliflower Breadsticks

Serves: 6/Prep Time: 30 mins

Ingredients

- ½ teaspoon dried Italian seasoning
- 4 cups cauliflower, riced
- 2 large eggs, beaten
- Kosher salt and black pepper, to taste
- 3 cups cheddar cheese, shredded

Directions

1. Preheat the oven to 475°F and grease a baking sheet lightly.
2. Mix together cauliflower, Italian seasoning, eggs, cheddar cheese, salt and black pepper in a bowl.
3. Spread this mixture on the prepared baking sheet and transfer to the oven.
4. Bake for about 20 minutes and remove from the oven to serve.

Nutrition Amount per serving

Calories 269	Cholesterol 122mg 41%	Dietary Fiber 1.7g 6%
Total Fat 20.6g 26%	Sodium 394mg 17%	Total Sugars 2.1g
Saturated Fat 12.5g 62%	Total Carbs 4.4g 2%	Protein 17.5g

Citrus Marinated Olives

Serves: 4/Prep Time: 20 mins

Ingredients

- ¼ lemon, zest and juice
- ¼ cup extra virgin olive oil
- ¼ orange, zest and juice
- 1 cup Castelvetrano olives
- Kosher salt, black pepper and red chili pepper, to taste

Directions

1. Heat olive oil over medium heat in a small saucepan and add olives.
2. Sauté for about 3 minutes and stir in the lemon zest, orange zest, salt, black pepper and red chili pepper.
3. Sauté for about 2 minutes and stir in the lemon juice and orange juice.
4. Dish into a bowl and serve warm.

Nutrition Amount per serving

Calories 120	Cholesterol 0mg 0%	Dietary Fiber 0.4g 2%
Total Fat 13.1g 17%	Sodium 60mg 3%	Total Sugars 1.3g
Saturated Fat 1.8g 9%	Total Carbs 1.8g 1%	Protein 0.2g

Spicy Edamame Dip

Serves: 5/Prep Time: 30 mins
Ingredients
- 1 cup edamame beans, shelled
- 2 tablespoons olive oil
- Salt and cayenne pepper, to taste
- ¼ cup fresh lime juice
- ¼ cup fresh cilantro, finely chopped

Directions
1. Boil edamame beans in water and reserve ¾ cup of the cooking water.
2. Put the boiled beans, reserved cooking water, olive oil, lime juice, cilantro, salt and cayenne pepper in the food processor.
3. Process until smooth and serve with your favorite snacks.

Nutrition Amount per serving

Calories 63	Cholesterol 0mg 0%	Dietary Fiber 0.8g 3%
Total Fat 6g 8%	Sodium 2mg 0%	Total Sugars 0.3g
Saturated Fat 0.8g 4%	Total Carbs 1.8g 1%	Protein 1g

Crab and Avocado Duet

Serves: 4/Prep Time: 10 mins
Ingredients
- 3 tablespoons lemon juice
- 1 ripe avocado, chunked
- Salt and white pepper, to taste
- ½ pound lump crabmeat
- 2 teaspoons Dijon mustard

Directions
1. Mix the avocado chunks with half of lemon juice and some salt.
2. Mix together remaining lemon juice, Dijon mustard, white pepper and lump crabmeat in another bowl.
3. Put the avocado mixture on the plate and top with the crabmeat mixture.
4. Serve immediately.

Nutrition Amount per serving

Calories 165	Cholesterol 57mg 19%	Dietary Fiber 3.5g 13%
Total Fat 11g 14%	Sodium 192mg 8%	Total Sugars 0.5g
Saturated Fat 2.3g 11%	Total Carbs 4.7g 2%	Protein 12.6g

Bacon Wrapped Scallops

Serves: 4/Prep Time: 25 mins
Ingredients
- 1 lime, juiced and zested
- 8 slices center cut smoked bacon, cut in half
- 8 large sea scallops, trimmed and well drained
- 1 tablespoon sesame oil, toasted
- Salt, red pepper flakes and black pepper

Directions
1. Preheat the oven to 425°F and lightly grease a baking pan.
2. Mix together scallops, lime juice, sesame oil, salt, red pepper flakes and black pepper in a bowl.
3. Wrap the scallops with bacon slices and transfer to the baking pan.
4. Bake for about 15 minutes and remove from the oven to serve.

Nutrition Amount per serving

Calories 268	Cholesterol 50mg 17%	Dietary Fiber 0.5g 2%
Total Fat 17.9g 23%	Sodium 637mg 28%	Total Sugars 0.3g
Saturated Fat 5.5g 28%	Total Carbs 3.2g 1%	Protein 20.2g

Teriyaki Ginger Tuna Skewers

Serves: 8/Prep Time: 15 mins

Ingredients

- 3 ounces sesame oil
- 2 pounds fresh tuna steak, cut into 1 inch cubes
- 15 ounces teriyaki sauce
- 2 tablespoons ginger garlic paste
- 1 lemon, juiced

Directions

1. Preheat the grill to high heat.
2. Soak bamboo skewers in water for about 1 hour.
3. Mix together all the ingredients except tuna steak in a bowl.
4. Marinate tuna in this mixture for about 1 hour.
5. Thread the tuna on the skewers and transfer to the grill.
6. Grill for about 4 minutes and serve hot.

Nutrition Amount per serving

Calories 377	Cholesterol 56mg 19%	Dietary Fiber 0.3g 1%
Total Fat 20g 26%	Sodium 2094mg 91%	Total Sugars 7.7g
Saturated Fat 3.3g 17%	Total Carbs 10g 4%	Protein 37.3g

Strawberry Cheesecake Popsicles

Serves: 12/Prep Time: 15 mins

Ingredients

- 1 cup heavy cream
- 8 oz. cream cheese, softened
- 1 tablespoon Swerve, powdered
- 2 cups fresh strawberries chopped, divided
- ½ lemon, juice and zest

Directions

1. Put the all the ingredients in a food processor and process until smooth.
2. Pour this mixture into the popsicle molds and transfer to the freezer.
3. Freeze for at least 5 hours and remove from the molds to serve.

Nutrition Amount per serving

Calories 109	Cholesterol 34mg 11%	Dietary Fiber 0.6g 2%
Total Fat 10.4g 13%	Sodium 60mg 3%	Total Sugars 1.3g
Saturated Fat 6.5g 32%	Total Carbs 3g 1%	Protein 1.8g

Dark Chocolate Covered Walnuts

Serves: 8/Prep Time: 30 mins

Ingredients

- 2 cups walnuts, shelled
- 1 teaspoon Erythritol
- 5 oz. unsweetened chocolate, chopped
- ½ teaspoon vanilla extract
- 3 tablespoons walnut oil

Directions

1. Line a baking sheet with waxed paper and set aside.
2. Mix together chocolate, walnut oil, vanilla extract and Erythritol in a bowl and stir well.
3. Add walnuts and stir to coat well.
4. Transfer to the baking sheet and transfer put in the freezer for about 20 minutes.
5. Dish out and serve chilled.

Nutrition Amount per serving

Calories 328	Cholesterol 0mg 0%	Dietary Fiber 5.1g 18%
Total Fat 32.8g 42%	Sodium 5mg 0%	Total Sugars 1.2g
Saturated Fat 7.2g 36%	Total Carbs 9.1g 3%	Protein 9.8g

Cinnamon and Cardamom Fat Bombs

Serves: 5/Prep Time: 15 mins

Ingredients

- ½ cup unsweetened coconut, shredded
- 3 oz. unsalted butter
- ¼ teaspoon ground cardamom
- ¼ teaspoon ground cinnamon
- ½ teaspoon vanilla extract

Directions

1. Heat a nonstick pan and add shredded coconut.
2. Roast for about 3 minutes until brown and mix half of coconut with butter, cardamom, cinnamon and vanilla extract.
3. Form small balls out of this mixture and roll in the rest of the shredded coconut.
4. Transfer to the freezer for about 2 hours and serve chilled.

Nutrition Amount per serving

Calories 152	Cholesterol 37mg 12%	Dietary Fiber 0.8g 3%
Total Fat 16.5g 21%	Sodium 100mg 4%	Total Sugars 0.6g
Saturated Fat 11.1g 56%	Total Carbs 1.5g 1%	Protein 0.4g

Keto Pistachio Truffles

Serves: 3/Prep Time: 15 mins

Ingredients

- ¼ teaspoon vanilla extract
- 1 cup mascarpone cheese, softened
- 3 scoops Stevia
- 1 pinch cinnamon
- ¼ cup pistachios, chopped

Directions

1. Mix together mascarpone cheese, cinnamon, vanilla extract and Stevia in a bowl.
2. Mix thoroughly until well blended and form small balls out of this mixture.
3. Place pistachios in a plate and roll the balls in it.
4. Place in the freezer for about 3 hours and dish out to serve.

Nutrition Amount per serving

Calories 172	Cholesterol 42mg 14%	Dietary Fiber 0.6g 2%
Total Fat 13.1g 17%	Sodium 96mg 4%	Total Sugars 0.6g
Saturated Fat 7.1g 36%	Total Carbs 4g 1%	Protein 10.3g

Eggs and Dairy Recipes

Eggtastic Smoothie

Serves: 1/Prep Time: 10 mins

Ingredients

- 2 tablespoons cream cheese
- 2 raw eggs
- 1 tablespoon vanilla extract
- ¼ cup heavy cream
- 3 ice cubes

Directions

1. Put all the ingredients in a blender and blend until smooth.
2. Pour into 1 glass and immediately serve.

Nutrition Amount per serving

Calories 337	Cholesterol 390mg 130%	Dietary Fiber 0g 0%
Total Fat 26.8g 34%	Sodium 195mg 8%	Total Sugars 2.4g
Saturated Fat 14g 70%	Total Carbs 3.7g 1%	Protein 13.2g

Eggs and Bacon

Serves: 12/Prep Time: 35 mins

Ingredients

- ½ teaspoon dried organic thyme
- 7 oz full fat cream cheese
- ½ cup parmesan cheese, shredded
- 24 organic bacon slices
- 12 hard cooked organic large eggs, peeled, yolks removed and sliced lengthwise

Directions

1. Preheat the oven to 390°F and lightly grease a baking dish.
2. Mix together thyme and cream cheese in a bowl.
3. Fill the egg white halves with the thyme mixture and close with the other egg white halves.
4. Wrap each egg tightly with 2 bacon slices and arrange on the baking dish.
5. Transfer to the oven and bake for about 25 minutes.
6. Remove from the oven to serve warm.

Nutrition Amount per serving

Calories 340	Cholesterol 239mg 80%	Dietary Fiber 0.3g 1%
Total Fat 25.9g 33%	Sodium 1219mg 53%	Total Sugars 1.2g
Saturated Fat 10.5g 52%	Total Carbs 2.1g 1%	Protein 23.9g

Cheesy Ham Souffle

Serves: 4/Prep Time: 30 mins

Ingredients

- ½ cup heavy cream
- 1 cup cheddar cheese, shredded
- 6 large eggs
- Salt and black pepper, to taste
- 6 ounces ham, diced

Directions

1. Preheat the oven to 375°F and lightly grease ramekins.
2. Whisk together ham with all other ingredients in a bowl.
3. Mix well and pour the mixture into the ramekins.
4. Transfer to the oven and bake for about 20 minutes.
5. Remove from the oven and slightly cool before serving.

Nutrition Amount per serving

Calories 342	Cholesterol 353mg 118%	Dietary Fiber 0.6g 2%
Total Fat 26g 33%	Sodium 841mg 37%	Total Sugars 0.8g
Saturated Fat 13g 65%	Total Carbs 3g 1%	Protein 23.8g

Mushroom and Cheese Scrambled Eggs

Serves: 4/Prep Time: 20 mins

Ingredients

- 8 eggs
- 4 tablespoons butter
- 4 tablespoons parmesan cheese, shredded
- 1 cup fresh mushrooms, finely chopped
- Salt and black pepper, to taste

Directions

1. Whisk together eggs with salt and black pepper in a bowl until well combined.
2. Heat butter in a nonstick pan and stir in the whisked eggs.
3. Cook for about 4 minutes and add mushrooms and parmesan cheese.
4. Cook for about 6 minutes, occasionally stirring and dish out to serve.

Nutrition Amount per serving

Calories 265	Cholesterol 365mg 122%	Dietary Fiber 0.2g 1%
Total Fat 22.6g 29%	Sodium 304mg 13%	Total Sugars 1g
Saturated Fat 11.5g 58%	Total Carbs 1.7g 1%	Protein 15.1g

Red Pepper Frittata

Serves: 3/Prep Time: 15 mins
Ingredients
- 6 large eggs
- 2 red peppers, chopped
- Salt and black pepper, to taste
- 1¼ cups mozzarella cheese, shredded
- 3 tablespoons olive oil

Directions
1. Whisk together the eggs in a medium bowl and add red peppers, mozzarella cheese, salt and black pepper.
2. Heat olive oil over medium high heat in an ovenproof skillet and pour in the egg mixture.
3. Lift the mixture with a spatula to let the eggs run under.
4. Cook for about 5 minutes, stirring well and dish out onto a platter to serve.

Nutrition Amount per serving

Calories 308	Cholesterol 378mg 126%	Dietary Fiber 0.5g 2%
Total Fat 26.2g 34%	Sodium 214mg 9%	Total Sugars 2.4g
Saturated Fat 6.4g 32%	Total Carbs 3.9g 1%	Protein 16.5g

Cream Cheese Pancakes

Serves: 4/Prep Time: 25 mins
Ingredients
- ½ cup almond flour
- 2 scoops Stevia
- ½ teaspoon cinnamon
- 2 eggs
- 2 oz cream cheese

Directions
1. Put all the ingredients in a blender and blend until smooth.
2. Dish out the mixture to a medium bowl and set aside.
3. Heat butter in a skillet over medium heat and add one quarter of the mixture.
4. Spread the mixture and cook for about 4 minutes on both sides until golden brown.
5. Repeat with rest of the mixture in batches and serve warm.

Nutrition Amount per serving

Calories 166	Cholesterol 97mg 32%	Dietary Fiber 1.7g 6%
Total Fat 13.8g 18%	Sodium 78mg 3%	Total Sugars 0.2g
Saturated Fat 4.3g 21%	Total Carbs 3.8g 1%	Protein 6.9g

Spicy Chorizo Baked Eggs

Serves: 4/Prep Time: 40 mins
Ingredients
- 5 large eggs
- 3 ounces ground chorizo sausage
- ¾ cup pepper jack cheese, shredded
- Salt and paprika, to taste
- 1 small avocado, chopped

Directions
1. Preheat the oven to 400°F.
2. Heat a nonstick oven safe skillet and add chorizo.
3. Cook for about 8 minutes and dish into a bowl.
4. Break the eggs in the skillet and season with salt and paprika.
5. Add cooked chorizo and avocado and cook for about 2 minutes.
6. Top with pepper jack cheese and transfer to the oven.
7. Bake for about 20 minutes and remove from the oven to serve.

Nutrition Amount per serving

Calories 334	Cholesterol 269mg 90%	Dietary Fiber 3.6g 13%
Total Fat 28.3g 36%	Sodium 400mg 17%	Total Sugars 0.8g
Saturated Fat 10.3g 52%	Total Carbs 5.7g 2%	Protein 16.9g

Cheesy Taco Pie

Serves: 6/Prep Time: 45 mins
Ingredients
- 1 tablespoon garlic powder
- 1 pound ground beef
- 6 large eggs
- Salt and chili powder, to taste
- 1 cup cheddar cheese, shredded

Directions
1. Preheat the oven to 350°F and lightly grease a pie plate.
2. Heat a large nonstick skillet and add beef, garlic powder, salt and chili powder.
3. Cook for about 6 minutes over medium low heat and transfer to the pie plate.
4. Top with cheddar cheese and transfer to the oven.
5. Bake for about 30 minutes and remove from the oven to serve hot.

Nutrition Amount per serving

Calories 294	Cholesterol 273mg 91%	Dietary Fiber 0.3g 1%
Total Fat 16g 21%	Sodium 241mg 10%	Total Sugars 0.9g
Saturated Fat 7.3g 37%	Total Carbs 1.9g 1%	Protein 34.2g

Sausage Egg Casserole

Serves: 8/Prep Time: 40 mins
Ingredients
- 1 cup almond milk, unsweetened
- 6 large eggs
- Salt and black pepper, to taste
- 2 cups cheddar cheese, shredded
- 1 pound ground pork sausage, cooked

Directions
1. Preheat the oven to 350°F and lightly grease a casserole dish.
2. Whisk together eggs with almond milk, salt and black pepper in a bowl.
3. Put the cooked sausages in the casserole dish and top with the egg mixture and cheddar cheese. Transfer to the oven and bake for about 30 minutes.
4. Remove from the oven and serve hot.

Nutrition Amount per serving

Calories 429	Cholesterol 217mg 72%	Dietary Fiber 0.7g 2%
Total Fat 36.3g 47%	Sodium 657mg 29%	Total Sugars 1.4g
Saturated Fat 18.6g 93%	Total Carbs 2.3g 1%	Protein 23.5g

Egg Bites

Serves: 8/Prep Time: 25 mins
Ingredients
- 12 large eggs
- 1 (8 ounce) package cream cheese, softened
- 8 slices bacon, cooked and crumbled
- 1 cup gruyere cheese, shredded
- Salt and paprika, to taste

Directions
1. Put eggs, cream cheese, salt and paprika in a blender and blend until smooth.
2. Grease 8 egg poaching cups lightly with cooking spray and put half the gruyere cheese, bacon and egg mixture in them.
3. Put the cups in a large saucepan with boiling water and cover the lid.
4. Lower the heat and cook for about 10 minutes.
5. Dish out the eggs into a serving dish and slice to serve.

Nutrition Amount per serving

Calories 365	Cholesterol 346mg 115%	Dietary Fiber 0g 0%
Total Fat 29.7g 38%	Sodium 673mg 29%	Total Sugars 0.7g
Saturated Fat 13.7g 69%	Total Carbs 1.7g 1%	Protein 22.6g

Chorizo and Eggs

Serves: 2/Prep Time: 20 mins
Ingredients
- ½ small yellow onion, chopped
- 1 teaspoon olive oil
- 2 (3 ounce) chorizo sausages
- Salt and black pepper, to taste
- 4 eggs

Directions
1. Open the sausage casings and dish the meat into a bowl.
2. Heat olive oil over medium high heat in a large skillet and add onions.
3. Sauté for about 3 minutes and stir in the chorizo sausage.
4. Cook for about 4 minutes and add eggs, salt and black pepper.
5. Whisk well and cook for about 3 minutes. Dish into a bowl and serve warm.

Nutrition Amount per serving

Calories 270	Cholesterol 201mg 67%	Dietary Fiber 0.2g 1%
Total Fat 21.8g 28%	Sodium 587mg 26%	Total Sugars 0.7g
Saturated Fat 7.6g 38%	Total Carbs 2g 1%	Protein 15.9g

Egg in the Avocado

Serves: 6/Prep Time: 25 mins
Ingredients
- 3 medium avocados, cut in half, pitted, skin on
- 1 teaspoon garlic powder
- ¼ cup parmesan cheese, grated
- 6 medium eggs
- Sea salt and black pepper, to taste

Directions
1. Preheat the oven to 350°F and grease 6 muffin tins.
2. Put the avocado half in each muffin tin and season with garlic powder, sea salt, and black pepper.
3. Break 1 egg into each avocado and top with the parmesan cheese.
4. Transfer into the oven and bake for about 15 minutes.
5. Remove from the oven and serve warm.

Nutrition Amount per serving

Calories 107	Cholesterol 167mg 56%	Dietary Fiber 1.6g 6%
Total Fat 7.9g 10%	Sodium 105mg 5%	Total Sugars 0.5g
Saturated Fat 2.5g 13%	Total Carbs 2.4g 1%	Protein 7.6g

Egg, Bacon and Cheese Cups

Serves: 6/Prep Time: 30 mins
Ingredients
- ¼ cup frozen spinach, thawed and drained
- 6 large eggs
- 6 strips bacon
- Salt and black pepper, to taste
- ¼ cup sharp cheddar cheese

Directions
1. Preheat the oven to 400° and grease 6 muffin cups.
2. Whisk together eggs, spinach, salt and black pepper in a bowl.
3. Put the bacon slices in the muffin cups and pour in the egg spinach mixture.
4. Top with sharp cheddar cheese and transfer to the oven.
5. Bake for 15 minutes and remove from the oven to serve warm.

Nutrition Amount per serving

Calories 194	Cholesterol 212mg 71%	Dietary Fiber 0g 0%
Total Fat 14.5g 19%	Sodium 539mg 23%	Total Sugars 0.4g
Saturated Fat 5.2g 26%	Total Carbs 0.8g 0%	Protein 14.5g

Steak and Eggs

Serves: 4/Prep Time: 25 mins
Ingredients
- 6 eggs
- 2 tablespoons butter
- 8 oz. sirloin steak
- Salt and black pepper, to taste
- ½ avocado, sliced

Directions
1. Heat butter in a pan on medium heat and fry the eggs.
2. Season with salt and black pepper and dish out onto a plate.
3. Cook the sirloin steak in another pan until desired doneness and slice into bite sized strips.
4. Season with salt and black pepper and dish out alongside the eggs.
5. Put the avocados with the eggs and steaks and serve.

Nutrition Amount per serving

Calories 302	Cholesterol 311mg 104%	Dietary Fiber 1.7g 6%
Total Fat 20.8g 27%	Sodium 172mg 7%	Total Sugars 0.6g
Saturated Fat 8.1g 40%	Total Carbs 2.7g 1%	Protein 26g

Butter Coffee

Serves: 4/Prep Time: 20 mins
Ingredients
- ½ cup coconut milk
- ½ cup water
- 2 tablespoons coffee
- 1 tablespoon coconut oil
- 1 tablespoon grass fed butter

Directions
1. Heat water in a saucepan and add coffee.
2. Simmer for about 3 minutes and add coconut milk.
3. Simmer for another 3 minutes and allow to cool down.
4. Transfer to a blender along with coconut oil and butter.
5. Pour into a mug and serve immediately.

Nutrition Amount per serving

Calories 111	Cholesterol 4mg 1%	Dietary Fiber 0.7g 2%
Total Fat 11.9g 15%	Sodium 18mg 1%	Total Sugars 1g
Saturated Fat 10.3g 51%	Total Carbs 1.7g 1%	Protein 0.7g

California Chicken Omelet

Serves: 1/Prep Time: 20 mins
Ingredients
- 2 bacon slices, cooked and chopped
- 2 eggs
- 1 oz. deli cut chicken
- 3 tablespoons avocado mayonnaise
- 1 Campari tomato

Directions
1. Whisk together eggs in a bowl and pour into a nonstick pan.
2. Season with salt and black pepper and cook for about 5 minutes.
3. Add chicken, bacon, tomato and avocado mayonnaise and cover with lid.
4. Cook for 5 more minutes on medium low heat and dish out to serve hot.

Nutrition Amount per serving

Calories 208	Cholesterol 189mg 63%	Dietary Fiber 1.1g 4%
Total Fat 15g 19%	Sodium 658mg 29%	Total Sugars 0.9g
Saturated Fat 4.5g 23%	Total Carbs 3g 1%	Protein 15.3g

Eggs Oopsie Rolls

Serves: 3/Prep Time: 25 mins

Ingredients

- 3 oz cream cheese
- 3 large eggs, separated
- 1/8 teaspoon cream of tartar
- 1 scoop stevia
- 1/8 teaspoon salt

Directions

1. Preheat oven to 300°F and line a cookie sheet with parchment paper.
2. Beat the egg whites with cream of tartar until soft peaks form.
3. Mix together egg yolks, salt and cream cheese in a bowl.
4. Combine the egg yolk and egg white mixtures and spoon them onto the cookie sheet.
5. Transfer to the oven and bake for about 40 minutes.
6. Remove from the oven and serve warm.

Nutrition Amount per serving

Calories 171

Total Fat 14.9g   19%

Saturated Fat 7.8g   39%

Cholesterol 217mg   72%

Sodium 251mg   11%

Total Carbs 1.2g   0%

Dietary Fiber 0g   0%

Total Sugars 0.5g

Protein 8.4g

Easy Blender Pancakes

Serves: 2/Prep Time: 25 mins

Ingredients

- 2 eggs
- 2 oz. cream cheese
- 1 scoop Isopure Protein Powder
- 1 pinch salt
- 1 dash cinnamon

Directions

1. Mix together eggs with cream cheese, protein powder, salt and cinnamon in a bowl.
2. Transfer to a blender and blend until smooth.
3. Heat a nonstick pan and pour quarter of the mixture.
4. Cook for about 2 minutes on each side and dish out.
5. Repeat with the remaining mixture and dish out in a platter to serve warm.

Nutrition Amount per serving

Calories 215

Total Fat 14.5g   19%

Saturated Fat 7.7g   39%

Cholesterol 196mg   65%

Sodium 308mg   13%

Total Carbs 1.2g   0%

Dietary Fiber 0.1g   0%

Total Sugars 0.4g

Protein 20.2g

Shakshuka

Serves: 2/Prep Time: 25 mins

Ingredients

- 1 chili pepper, chopped
- 1 cup marinara sauce
- 4 eggs
- Salt and black pepper, to taste
- 1 oz. feta cheese

Directions

1. Preheat the oven to 390°F.
2. Heat a small oven proof skillet on medium heat and add marinara sauce and chili pepper.
3. Cook for about 5 minutes and stir in the eggs.
4. Season with salt and black pepper and top with feta cheese.
5. Transfer into the oven and bake for about 10 minutes.
6. Remove from the oven and serve hot shakshuka.

Nutrition Amount per serving

Calories 273

Total Fat 15.1g   19%

Saturated Fat 5.7g   29%

Cholesterol 342mg   114%

Sodium 794mg   35%

Total Carbs 18.7g   7%

Dietary Fiber 3.3g   12%

Total Sugars 12.4g

Protein 15.4g

Rooibos Tea Latte

Serves: 1/Prep Time: 20 mins

Ingredients

- 2 bags rooibos tea
- 1 cup water
- 1 tablespoon grass fed butter
- 1 scoop collagen peptides
- ¼ cup full fat canned coconut milk

Directions

1. Put the tea bags in boiling water and steep for about 5 minutes.
2. Discard the tea bags and stir in butter and coconut milk.
3. Pour this mixture into a blender and blend until smooth.
4. Add collagen to the blender and blend on low speed until incorporated.
5. Pour into a mug to serve hot or chilled as desired.

Nutrition Amount per serving

Calories 283	Cholesterol 31mg 10%	Dietary Fiber 0g 0%
Total Fat 23.5g 30%	Sodium 21mg 1%	Total Sugars 2.4g
Saturated Fat 18.3g 91%	Total Carbs 3.4g 1%	Protein 15g

Feta and Pesto Omelet

Serves: 3/Prep Time: 10 mins

Ingredients

- 3 eggs
- 2 tablespoons butter
- 1 oz. feta cheese
- Salt and black pepper, to taste
- 1 tablespoon pesto

Directions

1. Heat butter in a pan and allow it to melt.
2. Whisk together eggs in a bowl and pour into the pan.
3. Cook for about 3 minutes until done and add feta cheese and pesto.
4. Season with salt and black pepper and fold it over.
5. Cook for another 5 minutes until the feta cheese is melted and dish out onto a platter to serve.

Nutrition Amount per serving

Calories 178	Cholesterol 194mg 65%	Dietary Fiber 0.1g 0%
Total Fat 16.2g 21%	Sodium 253mg 11%	Total Sugars 1.1g
Saturated Fat 8.1g 40%	Total Carbs 1.1g 0%	Protein 7.5g

Eggs Benedict

Serves: 2/Prep Time: 25 mins

Ingredients

- 4 oopsie rolls
- 4 eggs
- 4 Canadian bacon slices, cooked and crisped
- 1 tablespoon white vinegar
- 1 teaspoon chives

Directions

1. Boil water with vinegar and create a whirlpool in it with a wooden spoon.
2. Break an egg in a cup and place in the boiling water for about 3 minutes.
3. Repeat with rest of the eggs and dish out onto a platter.
4. Place oopsie rolls on the plates and top with bacon slices.
5. Put the poached eggs onto bacon slices and garnish with chives to serve.

Nutrition Amount per serving

Calories 190	Cholesterol 275mg 92%	Dietary Fiber 0g 0%
Total Fat 13.5g 17%	Sodium 587mg 26%	Total Sugars 0.6g
Saturated Fat 5.8g 29%	Total Carbs 1.5g 1%	Protein 15.3g

Egg Clouds

Serves: 2/Prep Time: 25 mins
Ingredients
- 6 strips bacon
- ¼ teaspoon cayenne pepper
- 2 eggs, separated
- Salt and black pepper, to taste
- ½ teaspoon garlic powder

Directions
1. Preheat oven to 350°F and grease a baking sheet lightly.
2. Whisk the egg whites in a bowl until fluffy and add garlic powder and salt.
3. Make 2 bacon weaves and spoon the egg white mixture on to it to form a cloud.
4. Make a hole in the egg cloud and put the egg yolks in it.
5. Season with cayenne pepper and black pepper and transfer to the oven.
6. Bake for about 10 minutes and dish out on a platter to serve.

Nutrition Amount per serving

Calories 374
Total Fat 28.2g 36%
Saturated Fat 9.2g 46%
Cholesterol 226mg 75%
Sodium 1379mg 60%
Total Carbs 1.8g 1%
Dietary Fiber 0.1g 1%
Total Sugars 0.5g
Protein 26.8g

Spicy Shrimp Omelet

Serves: 6/Prep Time: 15 mins
Ingredients
- 6 eggs
- 10 large shrimp, boiled
- 4 grape tomatoes
- Sriracha salt and cayenne pepper, to taste
- 1 handful spinach

Directions
1. Whisk together eggs with all other ingredients in a bowl.
2. Heat a nonstick pan and pour the mixture in it.
3. Cook for about 5 minutes on medium low heat and flip the side.
4. Cook for another 5 minutes and dish out onto a platter to serve.

Nutrition Amount per serving

Calories 90
Total Fat 4.7g 6%
Saturated Fat 1.4g 7%
Cholesterol 183mg 61%
Sodium 93mg 4%
Total Carbs 3.9g 1%
Dietary Fiber 1.1g 4%
Total Sugars 2.5g
Protein 8.5g

Egg Pizza Crust

Serves: 4/Prep Time: 25 mins
Ingredients
- 4 eggs
- 2 tablespoons coconut flour
- 2 cups cauliflower, grated
- ½ teaspoon salt
- 1 tablespoon psyllium husk powder

Directions
1. Preheat the oven to 360°F and lightly grease a pizza tray.
2. Mix together all the ingredients in a bowl until well combined and set aside for about 10 minutes.
3. Pour this mixture into the pizza tray and place in the oven.
4. Bake for about 15 minutes until golden brown and remove from the oven.
5. Add your favorite toppings and serve.

Nutrition Amount per serving

Calories 98
Total Fat 4.8g 6%
Saturated Fat 1.6g 8%
Cholesterol 164mg 55%
Sodium 367mg 16%
Total Carbs 7.5g 3%
Dietary Fiber 4.5g 16%
Total Sugars 1.5g
Protein 7g

Coffee Egg Latte

Serves: 2/Prep Time: 15 mins
Ingredients
- 8 ounces black coffee
- 2 tablespoons grass fed butter
- 2 pasture   raised eggs
- 1 scoop vanilla collagen protein
- ¼ teaspoon Ceylon cinnamon

Directions
1. Put eggs, butter and coffee in a blender.
2. Blend until smooth and stir in the collagen protein.
3. Blend on low and pour into 2 mugs.
4. Sprinkle with cinnamon and serve hot or chilled as desired.

Nutrition Amount per serving

Calories 189	Cholesterol 246mg 82%	Dietary Fiber 0.2g 1%
Total Fat 16g 21%	Sodium 94mg 4%	Total Sugars 0g
Saturated Fat 8.8g 44%	Total Carbs 1.3g 0%	Protein 10.3g

Buttery Egg Waffles

Serves: 4/Prep Time: 30 mins
Ingredients
- 4 tablespoons coconut flour
- 5 eggs, whites separated
- 4 scoops Stevia
- 1 teaspoon baking powder
- ½ cup butter, melted

Directions
1. Mix together coconut flour, egg yolks, Stevia and baking powder in a bowl.
2. Add butter and mix well to form a smooth batter.
3. Whisk egg whites in another bowl until fluffy and pour into the flour mixture.
4. Put this mixture into a waffle maker and cook until golden in color.
5. Dish out on plates to serve.

Nutrition Amount per serving

Calories 313	Cholesterol 266mg 89%	Dietary Fiber 3g 11%
Total Fat 29.3g 38%	Sodium 242mg 11%	Total Sugars 0.4g
Saturated Fat 16.8g 84%	Total Carbs 6g 2%	Protein 8.2g

Egg and Bacon Breakfast Muffins

Serves: 4/Prep Time: 40 mins
Ingredients
- 4 large eggs
- 4 bacon slices, cooked and crisped
- 1/3 cup green onions, chopped green stem only
- Salt and black pepper, to taste
- ¼ teaspoon paprika

Directions
1. Preheat the oven to 350°F and lightly grease muffin tin cavities.
2. Whisk together eggs in a bowl and add green onions, bacon, paprika, salt and black pepper.
3. Pour this mixture into the muffin tin cavities and transfer to the oven.
4. Bake for about 25 minutes and remove from oven to serve.

Nutrition Amount per serving

Calories 177	Cholesterol 207mg 69%	Dietary Fiber 0.3g 1%
Total Fat 13g 17%	Sodium 510mg 22%	Total Sugars 0.6g
Saturated Fat 4.2g 21%	Total Carbs 1.4g 0%	Protein 13.5g

Egg Bacon Fat Bombs

Serves: 6/Prep Time: 15 mins

Ingredients
- ¼ cup butter, softened
- 4 large slices bacon, baked
- 2 large eggs, boiled
- 2 tablespoons mayonnaise
- Salt and black pepper, to taste

Directions
1. Preheat the oven to 375°F and lightly grease a baking tray.
2. Put the bacon on the baking tray and bake for about 15 minutes.
3. Remove from the oven, crumble it and set aside.
4. Mash together boiled eggs with butter, mayonnaise, salt and black pepper with a fork.
5. Refrigerate for about 1 hour and then form small balls out of this mixture.
6. Roll the balls into the bacon crumbles and refrigerate for an hour to serve.

Nutrition Amount per serving

Calories 180	Cholesterol 98mg 33%	Dietary Fiber 0g 0%
Total Fat 16.2g 21%	Sodium 406mg 18%	Total Sugars 0.5g
Saturated Fat 7.4g 37%	Total Carbs 1.5g 1%	

Soft Boiled Eggs with Butter and Thyme

Serves: 3/Prep Time: 20 mins

Ingredients
- 2 tablespoons butter, melted
- 3 large eggs
- ½ teaspoon black pepper
- 2 tablespoons thyme leaves
- ½ teaspoon Himalayan pink salt

Directions
1. Boil eggs in water for about 6 minutes and then put under cold water.
2. Peel the eggs and dip in the melted butter.
3. Top with thyme leaves and season with salt and black pepper to serve.

Nutrition Amount per serving

Calories 145	Cholesterol 206mg 69%	Dietary Fiber 0.8g 3%
Total Fat 12.8g 16%	Sodium 631mg 27%	Total Sugars 0.4g
Saturated Fat 6.5g 32%	Total Carbs 1.8g 1%	Protein 6.6g

Soups Recipes

Spicy Red Curry Roasted Cauliflower Soup

Serves: 6/Prep Time: 50 mins

Ingredients
- 4 tablespoons Thai red curry paste
- 1 large cauliflower, cut into florets
- 4 cups vegetable broth, low sodium
- ¼ teaspoon Himalayan pink salt
- 14 oz. can coconut milk, unsweetened

Directions
1. Preheat the oven to 400°F and grease a baking tray.
2. Arrange the cauliflower florets on the baking tray and bake for about 20 minutes.
3. Put the roasted cauliflower and vegetable broth in a blender and blend until smooth.
4. Pour this mixture in the pot and add Thai red curry paste, vegetable broth, coconut milk and pink salt. Mix well and allow to cook for about 20 minutes on low heat.
5. Dish out into a bowl and serve hot.

Nutrition Amount per serving

Calories 357	Cholesterol 0mg 0%	Dietary Fiber 3.5g 13%
Total Fat 29.7g 38%	Sodium 1220mg 53%	Total Sugars 3.8g
Saturated Fat 27g 135%	Total Carbs 12.4g 4%	Protein 8.3g

Cream of Mushroom Soup

Serves: 4/Prep Time: 40 mins

Ingredients

- 3 cups unsweetened almond milk
- 4 cups cauliflower florets
- Onion powder, salt and black pepper, to taste
- 3 cups diced white mushrooms
- 1 teaspoon extra-virgin olive oil

Directions

1. Put almond milk, cauliflower florets, onion powder, salt and black pepper in a saucepan.
2. Cover the lid and bring to a boil.
3. Lower the heat and allow to simmer for about 10 minutes.
4. Transfer into a food processor and process until smooth.
5. Meanwhile, heat olive oil in a saucepan and add mushrooms.
6. Cook for about 7 minutes and stir in the cauliflower puree.
7. Bring to a boil and allow to simmer, covered for about 10 minutes.
8. Dish out into a bowl and serve immediately.

Nutrition Amount per serving

Calories 76	Cholesterol 0mg 0%	Dietary Fiber 3.8g 14%
Total Fat 4.1g 5%	Sodium 168mg 7%	Total Sugars 3.3g
Saturated Fat 0.4g 2%	Total Carbs 8.6g 3%	Protein 4.4g

Broccoli Cheese Soup

Serves: 8/Prep Time: 30 mins

Ingredients

- 4 garlic cloves, minced
- 4 cups broccoli, cut into florets
- 1 cup heavy cream
- 3 cups cheddar cheese, shredded
- 3½ cups chicken broth

Directions

1. Sauté garlic in a nonstick saucepan for about 1 minute and add broccoli, heavy cream and chicken broth. Bring to a boil and cook on low heat for about 12 minutes.
2. Stir in the cheddar cheese and cook for about 8 minutes.
3. Dish out into a bowl and serve hot.

Nutrition Amount per serving

Calories 315	Cholesterol 65mg 22%	Dietary Fiber 1.2g 4%
Total Fat 22.4g 29%	Sodium 1763mg 77%	Total Sugars 2.4g
Saturated Fat 13.1g 66%	Total Carbs 6.3g 2%	Protein 21.6g

Keto Taco Soup

Serves: 4/Prep Time: 40 mins

Ingredients

- 2 tablespoons taco seasoning
- ½ pound ground beef
- 4 cups beef bone broth
- 4 tablespoons Ranch dressing
- ¼ cup tomatoes, diced

Directions

1. Brown the ground beef over medium high heat in the large pot for about 10 minutes.
2. Add taco seasoning and bone broth and cook on low heat for about 8 minutes.
3. Stir in the tomatoes and simmer for about 10 minutes.
4. Remove from heat and allow to cool. Add ranch dressing and mix well to serve.

Nutrition Amount per serving

Calories 136	Cholesterol 51mg 17%	Dietary Fiber 0.2g 1%
Total Fat 3.7g 5%	Sodium 738mg 32%	Total Sugars 1.7g
Saturated Fat 1.4g 7%	Total Carbs 5.3g 2%	Protein 18.2g

Tomato Soup

Serves: 6/Prep Time: 25 mins

Ingredients

- 1 medium white onion, chopped
- 3 (14 oz.) cans diced tomatoes, with their juices
- 3 garlic cloves, minced
- 3 cups heavy cream
- 1 handful basil leaves, julienned

Directions

1. Put onion, tomatoes, garlic and basil in a saucepan and stir well.
2. Cook over medium high heat for about 10 minutes and transfer into an immersion blender.
3. Puree until smooth and mix in the heavy cream.
4. Dish out into a bowl and serve hot.

Nutrition Amount per serving

Calories 252	Cholesterol 82mg 27%	Dietary Fiber 2.8g 10%
Total Fat 22.6g 29%	Sodium 33mg 1%	Total Sugars 6.1g
Saturated Fat 13.9g 69%	Total Carbs 11.6g 4%	Protein 3.3g

Cheesy Cauliflower Soup

Serves: 6/Prep Time: 30 mins

Ingredients

- 1 yellow onion
- 3 tablespoons butter
- 6 cups chicken broth
- 1½ cups cheddar cheese, shredded
- 6 cups cauliflower, cut into florets

Directions

1. Heat butter in a heavy pot and add onions.
2. Sauté for about 3 minutes and add chicken broth and cauliflower.
3. Allow to simmer for about 10 minutes and transfer into an immersion blender.
4. Blend until smooth and return to the pot.
5. Stir in the cheddar cheese and cook for about 3 minutes until the cheese is melted.
6. Dish out into a bowl and serve hot.

Nutrition Amount per serving

Calories 235	Cholesterol 45mg 15%	Dietary Fiber 2.9g 10%
Total Fat 16.6g 21%	Sodium 1010mg 44%	Total Sugars 4g
Saturated Fat 10g 50%	Total Carbs 8.3g 3%	Protein 14.1g

Hot Mushroom Clear Soup

Serves: 1/Prep Time: 10 mins

Ingredients

- ½ cup mushrooms, finely chopped
- 2 cups water
- 2 teaspoons butter
- Salt, to taste
- Black pepper, to taste

Directions

1. Heat butter in a heavy pot and add mushrooms.
2. Cook on low heat for about 5 minutes and add water.
3. Season with salt and black pepper and cook for about 6 minutes, stirring occasionally.
4. Ladle out into a bowl and serve hot.

Nutrition Amount per serving

Calories 75	Cholesterol 20mg 7%	Dietary Fiber 0.4g 1%
Total Fat 7.7g 10%	Sodium 225mg 10%	Total Sugars 0.6g
Saturated Fat 4.8g 24%	Total Carbs 1.2g 0%	Protein 1.2g

Mushrooms and Spinach Clear Soup

Serves: 3/Prep Time: 20 mins

Ingredients

- 3 cups clear vegetable stock
- 1 cup spinach, torn into small pieces
- ½ cup mushrooms, chopped
- Salt and black pepper, to taste
- 1 tablespoon olive oil

Directions

1. Heat olive oil on medium heat in a nonstick wok and add garlic.
2. Sauté for about 1 minute and add mushrooms and spinach.
3. Sauté for about 2 minutes and pour in clear vegetable stock.
4. Season with salt and black pepper and cook for about 4 minutes, stirring occasionally.
5. Ladle out in a bowl and serve hot.

Nutrition Amount per serving

Calories 51	Cholesterol 0mg 0%	Dietary Fiber 0.9g 3%
Total Fat 4.8g 6%	Sodium 59mg 3%	Total Sugars 0.9g
Saturated Fat 0.7g 3%	Total Carbs 1.7g 1%	Protein 1.1g

Creamy Garlic Chicken Soup

Serves: 4/Prep Time: 25 mins

Ingredients

- 1 large chicken breast, cooked and shredded
- 2 tablespoons salted butter
- 5 ounces cream cheese, cubed
- 2 tablespoons garlic seasoning
- 14.5 oz chicken broth

Directions

1. Heat butter in a saucepan over medium heat and add chicken.
2. Sauté for about 3 minutes and add garlic seasoning and cream cheese.
3. Cook for about 2 minutes and stir in the chicken broth.
4. Cook for about 7 minutes until boiled and reduce the heat to low.
5. Simmer on low heat for about 5 minutes and serve hot.

Nutrition Amount per serving

Calories 237	Cholesterol 72mg 24%	Dietary Fiber 0.4g 2%
Total Fat 19.4g 25%	Sodium 488mg 21%	Total Sugars 1.4g
Saturated Fat 11.6g 58%	Total Carbs 4.4g 2%	Protein 11.5g

Cream of Zucchini Soup

Serves: 4/Prep Time: 30 mins

Ingredients

- 1½ cups parmesan cheese, freshly grated
- 2 medium zucchinis, cut into large chunks
- 2 tablespoons sour cream
- Salt and black pepper, to taste
- 32 oz chicken broth

Directions

1. Mix together zucchini and chicken broth over medium heat in a pot and bring to a boil.
2. Lower the heat and simmer for about 18 minutes until tender.
3. Remove from heat and transfer into an immersion blender.
4. Stir in the sour cream and purée until smooth.
5. Add cheese and season with salt and black pepper to serve.

Nutrition Amount per serving

Calories 238	Cholesterol 45mg 15%	Dietary Fiber 1.1g 4%
Total Fat 16.2g 21%	Sodium 1162mg 51%	Total Sugars 2.4g
Saturated Fat 10.1g 50%	Total Carbs 5.7g 2%	Protein 19.3g

Cream of Asparagus Soup

Serves: 6/Prep Time: 30 mins

Ingredients
- 6 cups reduced sodium chicken broth
- 4 tablespoons unsalted butter
- 2 pounds asparagus, cut in half
- Salt and black pepper, to taste
- ½ cup sour cream

Directions
1. Heat butter in a large pot over medium low heat and add asparagus.
2. Sauté for about 3 minutes and stir in the chicken broth, salt and black pepper.
3. Bring to a boil, cover and cook for about 20 minutes on low heat.
4. Remove from heat and transfer into blender along with sour cream.
5. Pulse until smooth and ladle out in a bowl to serve.

Nutrition Amount per serving

Calories 154	Cholesterol 29mg 10%	Dietary Fiber 3.2g 11%
Total Fat 11.9g 15%	Sodium 638mg 28%	Total Sugars 3.9g
Saturated Fat 7.4g 37%	Total Carbs 7.7g 3%	Protein 7g

Cream of Brown Butter Mushroom Soup

Serves: 6/Prep Time: 25 mins

Ingredients
- ½ cup heavy cream
- 4 cups chicken stock
- 6 tablespoons butter
- Salt and black pepper, to taste
- 1 pound mushrooms, sliced

Directions
1. Heat butter in a large pot over medium heat and add mushrooms.
2. Sauté for about 4 minutes and stir in the chicken stock.
3. Allow it to simmer for about 10 minutes and transfer to food processor.
4. Blend until smooth and return to the pot.
5. Stir in the heavy cream and season with salt and black pepper to serve.

Nutrition Amount per serving

Calories 159	Cholesterol 44mg 15%	Dietary Fiber 0.8g 3%
Total Fat 15.8g 20%	Sodium 599mg 26%	Total Sugars 1.8g
Saturated Fat 9.7g 48%	Total Carbs 3.3g 1%	Protein 3.2g

Butternut Squash Soup

Serves: 4/Prep Time: 1 hour 30 mins

Ingredients
- 4 cups chicken broth
- 1 small onion, chopped
- 1 butternut squash
- Nutmeg, salt and black pepper, to taste
- 3 tablespoons coconut oil

Directions
1. Heat coconut oil in a large pot and add onion.
2. Sauté for about 3 minutes and stir in the chicken broth and butternut squash.
3. Let it simmer for about 45 minutes on medium low heat and transfer into an immersion blender.
4. Pulse until smooth and season with nutmeg, salt and black pepper.
5. Return to the pot and cook for about 35 minutes.
6. Dish out into a bowl and serve hot.

Nutrition Amount per serving

Calories 153	Cholesterol 0mg 0%	Dietary Fiber 1.3g 4%
Total Fat 11.7g 15%	Sodium 766mg 33%	Total Sugars 2.4g
Saturated Fat 9.2g 46%	Total Carbs 7.6g 3%	Protein 5.5g

Spring Soup

Serves: 4/Prep Time: 20 mins

Ingredients
- 4 tablespoons butter
- 4 eggs
- 8 cups chicken broth
- Salt, to taste
- 2 heads romaine lettuce, chopped

Directions
1. Boil the chicken broth over high heat and lower the flame.
2. Poach the eggs in the chicken broth for about 5 minutes and remove the eggs into a bowl.
3. Stir the chopped romaine lettuce into the broth and cook for about 10 minutes.
4. Ladle out into a bowl and season with salt and top with butter to serve.

Nutrition Amount per serving

Calories 264	Cholesterol 194mg 65%	Dietary Fiber 1g 4%
Total Fat 18.9g 24%	Sodium 1717mg 75%	Total Sugars 3.4g
Saturated Fat 9.4g 47%	Total Carbs 7g 3%	Protein 16.1g

Leek, Cauliflower and Bacon Soup

Serves: 4/Prep Time: 1 hour 30 mins

Ingredients
- ½ cauliflower head, chopped
- 4 cups chicken broth
- 1 leek, chopped
- 5 bacon strips, cooked and chopped
- Salt and black pepper, to taste

Directions
1. Put the leek, cauliflower and chicken broth into the pot and cook on medium heat for about 45 minutes.
2. Transfer into an immersion blender and puree until smooth.
3. Return the soup into the pot and add the bacon.
4. Season with salt and black pepper and cook for about 30 minutes on low heat.
5. Dish out into a bowl and serve hot.

Nutrition Amount per serving

Calories 185	Cholesterol 0mg 0%	Dietary Fiber 1.2g 4%
Total Fat 12.7g 16%	Sodium 1153mg 50%	Total Sugars 2.4g
Saturated Fat 4.1g 21%	Total Carbs 5.8g 2%	Protein 10.8g

French Onion Soup

Serves: 6/Prep Time: 40 mins

Ingredients
- 1 pound brown onions
- 5 tablespoons butter
- 4 drops liquid Stevia
- 3 cups beef stock
- 4 tablespoons olive oil

Directions
1. Heat butter and olive oil in a large pot over medium low heat and add onions.
2. Sauté for about 4 minutes and stir in beef stock and Stevia.
3. Cook for about 5 minutes and reduce the heat to low.
4. Allow to simmer for about 25 minutes and ladle out into soup bowls to serve hot.

Nutrition Amount per serving

Calories 203	Cholesterol 25mg 8%	Dietary Fiber 1.6g 6%
Total Fat 19.3g 25%	Sodium 462mg 20%	Total Sugars 3.2g
Saturated Fat 7.5g 38%	Total Carbs 7.1g 3%	Protein 2.3g

Homemade Thai Chicken Soup

Serves: 12/Prep Time: 7 hours 20 mins

Ingredients
- 1 whole chicken
- 5 ginger slices, fresh
- 20 fresh basil leaves
- 1 tablespoon salt
- 1 lime, juiced

Directions
1. Place the chicken, 10 basil leaves, ginger, salt and water into the crock pot.
2. Cover the lid and cook for about 7 hours on low.
3. Dish out into a bowl and stir in fresh lime juice and rest of the basil leaves to serve.

Nutrition Amount per serving

Calories 363	Cholesterol 128mg 43%	Dietary Fiber 0.1g 0%
Total Fat 27.1g 35%	Sodium 694mg 30%	Total Sugars 0g
Saturated Fat 7.5g 38%	Total Carbs 0.6g 0%	Protein 28.6g

Green Chicken Enchilada Soup

Serves: 5/Prep Time: 20 mins

Ingredients
- ½ cup salsa verde
- 4 oz. cream cheese, softened
- 1 cup cheddar cheese, shredded
- 2 cups chicken stock
- 2 cups cooked chicken, shredded

Directions
1. Put cheddar cheese, salsa verde, cream cheese and chicken stock in an immersion blender.
2. Blend until smooth and pour this mixture into a medium saucepan.
3. Cook for about 5 minutes on medium heat and add the shredded chicken.
4. Cook for another 5 minutes and dish out into a bowl to serve hot.

Nutrition Amount per serving

Calories 265	Cholesterol 92mg 31%	Dietary Fiber 0.1g 0%
Total Fat 17.4g 22%	Sodium 686mg 30%	Total Sugars 0.8g
Saturated Fat 10.3g 51%	Total Carbs 2.2g 1%	Protein 24.2g

Cheesy Mushroom Shrimp Soup

Serves: 8/Prep Time: 30 mins

Ingredients
- 24 oz. extra small shrimp
- 8 oz cheddar cheese, shredded
- 2 cups mushrooms, sliced
- 1 cup butter
- 32 oz. chicken broth

Directions
1. Put chicken broth and mushrooms in a large soup pot and bring to a boil.
2. Lower the heat and stir in butter and cheddar cheese.
3. Mix well and add shrimp to the soup pot.
4. Allow it to simmer for about 15 minutes and dish out into a bowl to serve hot.

Nutrition Amount per serving

Calories 445	Cholesterol 271mg 90%	Dietary Fiber 0.2g 1%
Total Fat 34.6g 44%	Sodium 1504mg 65%	Total Sugars 0.8g
Saturated Fat 21.1g 106%	Total Carbs 2.9g 1%	Protein 29.6g

Bacon and Pumpkin Soup

Serves: 6/Prep Time: 8 hours 15 mins

Ingredients

- 3 cups bacon hock, diced
- 400g pumpkin, diced
- Boiling water
- Salt, to taste
- 2 tablespoons butter

Directions

1. Pour some boiling water in the slow cooker.
2. Add pumpkin and bacon hock and cover the lid.
3. Cook on low for about 8 hours and pull the meat away from the bones.
4. Return the meat to the slow cooker along with salt and butter.
5. Allow it to simmer for about 5 minutes and ladle out into a bowl to serve hot.

Nutrition Amount per serving

Calories 327
Total Fat 24.9g 32%
Saturated Fat 9.4g 47%
Cholesterol 65mg 22%
Sodium 1213mg 53%
Total Carbs 6.1g 2%
Dietary Fiber 1.9g 7%
Total Sugars 2.2g
Protein 19.3g

Mint Avocado Chilled Soup

Serves: 2/Prep Time: 10 mins

Ingredients

- 1 medium ripe avocado
- 2 romaine lettuce leaves
- 1 cup coconut milk, chilled
- Salt, to taste
- 20 fresh mint leaves

Directions

1. Put mint leaves with the rest of the ingredients in a blender and blend until smooth.
2. Refrigerate for about 20 minutes and remove to serve chilled.

Nutrition Amount per serving

Calories 309
Total Fat 31.2g 40%
Saturated Fat 25.9g 129%
Cholesterol 0mg 0%
Sodium 99mg 4%
Total Carbs 9.1g 3%
Dietary Fiber 4.9g 17%
Total Sugars 4.1g
Protein 3.6g

Chilled Zucchini Soup

Serves: 5/Prep Time: 15 mins

Ingredients

- 4 cups chicken broth
- 1 medium zucchini, cut into ½ inch pieces
- 8 oz. cream cheese, cut into cubes
- Salt and black pepper, to taste
- ½ teaspoon ground cumin

Directions

1. Put chicken broth and zucchini in a large stockpot and bring to a boil.
2. Lower the heat and allow to simmer for about 10 minutes.
3. Stir in the cream cheese and transfer into an immersion blender.
4. Blend until smooth and season with cumin, salt and black pepper.
5. Refrigerate to chill for about 2 hours and remove from the fridge to serve chilled.

Nutrition Amount per serving

Calories 196
Total Fat 17g 22%
Saturated Fat 10.3g 51%
Cholesterol 50mg 17%
Sodium 749mg 33%
Total Carbs 3.4g 1%
Dietary Fiber 0.5g 2%
Total Sugars 1.3g
Protein 7.8g

Chilled Cantaloupe Soup

Serves: 8/Prep Time: 10 mins
Ingredients
- 6 tablespoons butter
- 2 cantaloupes, cut into chunks
- 2/3 cup plain, nonfat Greek yogurt
- 6 tablespoons fresh basil leaves, for garnish
- Pinch of kosher salt and nutmeg

Directions
1. Put all the ingredients except basil in a food processor and pulse until smooth.
2. Refrigerate for at least 3 hours and garnish with fresh basil leaves to serve.

Nutrition Amount per serving

Calories 100
Total Fat 8.8g 11%
Saturated Fat 5.5g 28%

Cholesterol 23mg 8%
Sodium 82mg 4%
Total Carbs 4.7g 2%

Dietary Fiber 0.6g 2%
Total Sugars 4.3g
Protein 1.4g

Turmeric Beef Broth Soup

Serves: 3/Prep Time: 10 mins
Ingredients
- 2 cups beef bone broth
- 2 tablespoons ginger, finely grated
- ½ teaspoon ground turmeric
- 1 cup coconut cream
- Himalayan salt and black pepper, to taste

Directions
1. Put all the ingredients except salt in a saucepan and allow it to simmer over medium heat.
2. Cook for about 5 minutes, stirring occasionally and season with salt and black pepper.
3. Dish out into a bowl and serve hot.

Nutrition Amount per serving

Calories 223
Total Fat 20g 26%
Saturated Fat 17.6g 88%

Cholesterol 6mg 2%
Sodium 193mg 8%
Total Carbs 10.4g 4%

Dietary Fiber 2.9g 11%
Total Sugars 3.4g
Protein 6g

Chicken Feet Soup

Serves: 8/Prep Time: 12 hours
Ingredients
- 1 teaspoon salt
- 12 chicken feet
- 2 tablespoons raw apple cider vinegar
- 1 (½ inch) piece of fresh ginger
- 1 sprig of rosemary

Directions
1. Put chicken feet with apple cider vinegar and water in a stock pot.
2. Bring to a boil and then reduce to a simmer for about 12 minutes.
3. Allow to cool by blanching the feet in cold water.
4. Return the chicken to the stock pot along with some water.
5. Bring to a boil and reduce the heat to low.
6. Simmer for about 5 minutes and add salt, rosemary and ginger.
7. Simmer for about 10 hours and allow to cool.
8. Dish out the liquid into glass jars through strainers and immediately serve.

Nutrition Amount per serving

Calories 324
Total Fat 21.9g 28%
Saturated Fat 5.9g 29%

Cholesterol 126mg 42%
Sodium 392mg 17%
Total Carbs 0.5g 0%

Dietary Fiber 0.1g 0%
Total Sugars 0g
Protein 29.1g

Savory Pumpkin Soup

Serves: 6/Prep Time: 30 mins

Ingredients

- 2 cups chicken bone broth
- 1 cup full fat coconut milk
- 6 cups pumpkin, baked
- Sea salt and black pepper, to taste
- ½ cup sour cream

Directions

1. Heat a soup pan over medium heat and add the chicken bone broth, coconut milk, pumpkin, sea salt and black pepper.
2. Stir well and allow the mixture to simmer for about 15 minutes.
3. Transfer into an immersion blender and blend until smooth.
4. Dish out into a bowl and stir in the sour cream to serve.

Nutrition Amount per serving

Calories 163	Cholesterol 8mg 3%	Dietary Fiber 0.6g 2%
Total Fat 12.1g 16%	Sodium 53mg 2%	Total Sugars 2.3g
Saturated Fat 9.9g 49%	Total Carbs 9.7g 4%	Protein 5.4g

Hearty Green Soup

Serves: 3/Prep Time: 20 mins

Ingredients

- 1 medium head broccoli
- 3 zucchinis, chopped
- ¾ cup butter, salted
- 3 leeks, chopped
- 1 cup chicken bone broth

Directions

1. Put broccoli, leeks and zucchinis in a large saucepan and mix well.
2. Stir in the butter and chicken broth and cook for about 10 minutes on medium low heat.
3. Transfer the mixture into a blender and blend until smooth.
4. Dish out into a bowl and serve hot.

Nutrition Amount per serving

Calories 259	Cholesterol 61mg 20%	Dietary Fiber 2.4g 8%
Total Fat 23.6g 30%	Sodium 316mg 14%	Total Sugars 3.9g
Saturated Fat 14.7g 74%	Total Carbs 11g 4%	Protein 3.4g

Keto Queso Chicken Soup

Serves: 4/Prep Time: 35 mins

Ingredients

- 3 cups chicken broth
- 1 pound chicken breast
- 10 ounces cream cheese
- 1 tablespoon taco seasoning
- Salt, to taste

Directions

1. Put all the ingredients in a wok over medium heat except cream cheese and cover with lid.
2. Simmer for about 25 minutes and transfer into an immersion blender.
3. Stir in the cream cheese and dish out into a bowl to serve.

Nutrition Amount per serving

Calories 413	Cholesterol 151mg 50%	Dietary Fiber 0g 0%
Total Fat 28.6g 37%	Sodium 1037mg 45%	Total Sugars 1g
Saturated Fat 15.9g 79%	Total Carbs 4.1g 1%	Protein 33g

Cheesy Sausage Soup

Serves: 10/Prep Time: 30 mins

Ingredients
- 1 yellow onion, chopped
- 6 cups chicken broth
- 1½ cups cheddar cheese, shredded
- 3 tablespoons butter
- 2 pounds Italian sausages

Directions
1. Heat butter in a heavy stock pot and add onion.
2. Sauté for about 5 minutes and add chicken broth and Italian sausages.
3. Simmer for about 10 minutes and transfer into an immersion blender.
4. Blend until smooth and stir in the cheese. Dish out into a bowl to serve.

Nutrition Amount per serving

Calories 440
Total Fat 38.3g 49%
Saturated Fat 16.2g 81%

Cholesterol 96mg 32%
Sodium 1251mg 54%
Total Carbs 2.4g 1%

Dietary Fiber 0.2g 1%
Total Sugars 1g
Protein 20.2g

Chilled Cucumber Soup

Serves: 5/Prep Time: 10 mins

Ingredients
- 4 cups chicken broth
- 2 cucumbers, cut into ½ inch pieces
- 8 oz cream cheese, cut into cubes
- Salt and black pepper, to taste
- 1/3 cup plain, nonfat Greek yogurt

Directions
1. Mix together chicken broth and zucchini in a large stockpot.
2. Bring to a boil and reduce the heat to low.
3. Allow to simmer for about 10 minutes and add cream cheese and yogurt.
4. Stir well and transfer to an immersion blender.
5. Blend until smooth and season with salt and black pepper.
6. Refrigerate to chill for about 3 hours and serve chilled.

Nutrition Amount per serving

Calories 216
Total Fat 17g 22%
Saturated Fat 10.3g 52%

Cholesterol 50mg 17%
Sodium 759mg 33%
Total Carbs 7.7g 3%

Dietary Fiber 0.8g 3%
Total Sugars 3.9g
Protein 8.9g

30-Day Breakfast Keto Meal Prep

Cauliflower Cheese Toast

Serves: 8/Prep Time: 45 mins

Ingredients
- 2 cups cheddar cheese, shredded
- 10 cups cauliflower florets, finely chopped
- 2 large eggs, beaten
- ¼ teaspoon salt
- ½ teaspoon black pepper

Directions
1. Preheat the oven to 425°F and grease a large baking sheet.
2. Microwave the cauliflower on high for about 3 minutes and allow to cool.
3. Dish out into a bowl and stir in rest of the ingredients.
4. Divide the mixture into 8 portions and arrange on the baking sheet.
5. Transfer to the oven and bake for about 25 minutes until the toasts are browned and crispy. Put the toasts between two layers of parchment paper and freeze for up to 3 months.

Nutrition Amount per serving   Calories 163 Total Fat 10.7g 14% Saturated Fat 6.4g 32% Cholesterol 76mg 25% Sodium 304mg 13% Total Carbs 7.2g 3% Dietary Fiber 3.2g 11% Total Sugars 3.3g Protein 11.1g

Vegetarian Keto Breakfast Casserole

Serves: 6/Prep Time: 50 mins

Ingredients

- 12 eggs
- 1/3 cup green olives
- 1 cup heavy whipping cream
- 3 oz. cherry tomatoes
- 8 oz. parmesan cheese, shredded

Directions

1. Preheat the oven to 400°F and lightly grease a casserole dish.
2. Whisk together eggs, cream and 6 oz. parmesan cheese in a bowl.
3. Arrange the olives on the casserole dish and top with the egg mixture.
4. Top with cherry tomatoes and remaining parmesan cheese.
5. Transfer to the oven and bake for about 40 minutes.
6. Remove from the oven and serve hot.
7. Refrigerate for up to 3 days and warm in microwave before serving.

Nutrition Amount per serving

Calories 323	Cholesterol 382mg 127%	Dietary Fiber 0.3g 1%
Total Fat 24.6g 32%	Sodium 527mg 23%	Total Sugars 1.1g
Saturated Fat 12.8g 64%	Total Carbs 3.4g 1%	Protein 23.8g

Orange Peel and Ginger Smoothie

Serves: 3/Prep Time: 10 mins

Ingredients

- 1 cup organic full fat Greek yogurt
- 2 cups ice cold water
- 1 tablespoon orange peel, freshly grated
- 2 packets Stevia
- 1 teaspoon organic ginger, freshly grated

Directions

1. Put all the ingredients in a blender and puree until smooth.
2. Pour into 3 glasses to serve immediately.
3. Refrigerate for up to 2 days.

Nutrition Amount per serving

Calories 74	Cholesterol 13mg 4%	Dietary Fiber 0.3g 1%
Total Fat 3.4g 4%	Sodium 34mg 1%	Total Sugars 2g
Saturated Fat 0g 0%	Total Carbs 5.6g 2%	Protein 6.4g

Cheese Crusted Omelet

Serves: 2/Prep Time: 20 mins

Ingredients

- 1 tablespoon butter
- 2 eggs
- 2 tablespoons heavy whipping cream
- Salt and black pepper, to taste
- 3 oz. cheddar cheese, sliced

Directions

1. Whisk together eggs, heavy whipping cream, salt and black pepper in a bowl.
2. Heat butter in a nonstick pan and add cheese slices.
3. Cook for about 3 minutes on medium low heat until bubbly and stir in the egg mixture.
4. Cook for about 5 minutes on low heat without stirring and dish out to serve hot.
5. Freeze for up to 3 days and warm in microwave before serving.

Nutrition Amount per serving

Calories 337	Cholesterol 244mg 81%	Dietary Fiber 0g 0%
Total Fat 29.8g 38%	Sodium 372mg 16%	Total Sugars 0.6g
Saturated Fat 17.4g 87%	Total Carbs 1.3g 0%	Protein 16.5g

Italian Breakfast Casserole

Serves: 8/Prep Time: 40 mins

Ingredients
- 2 oz. salted butter
- 8 oz. cheddar cheese, chopped
- 7 oz. cauliflower
- 12 oz. fresh Italian sausage
- 8 eggs

Directions
1. Preheat the oven to 375°F and lightly grease a baking dish.
2. Whisk together egg and cheddar cheese in a bowl and set aside.
3. Heat butter in a large skillet over medium high heat and add the cauliflower.
4. Cook for about 4 minutes and dish into the baking dish.
5. Put the sausage in the pan and fry until crumbled.
6. Transfer to the baking dish and top with the egg cheese mixture.
7. Transfer to the oven and bake for about 40 minutes. Dish out into a bowl and serve hot.
8. Refrigerate for up to 2 days or freeze for up to a week and heat before serving.

Nutrition Amount per serving

Calories 378

Total Fat 31.6g 41%

Saturated Fat 14.9g 74%

Cholesterol 244mg 81%

Sodium 604mg 26%

Total Carbs 2g 1%

Dietary Fiber 0.6g 2%

Total Sugars 1.1g

Protein 21.4g

Keto Bacon and Mushroom Breakfast Casserole

Serves: 8/Prep Time: 55 mins

Ingredients
- 10 oz. bacon
- 6 oz. mushrooms
- 2 oz. salted butter
- 1 cup heavy whipping cream
- 8 eggs

Directions
1. Preheat the oven to 400°F and lightly grease a casserole dish.
2. Heat butter in a skillet and add bacon and mushrooms.
3. Sauté for about 5 minutes until golden brown and place in the casserole dish.
4. Whisk together eggs and heavy whipping cream in a bowl.
5. Pour this mixture over the bacon and mushrooms and transfer to the oven.
6. Bake for about 40 minutes until golden brown and remove from the oven to serve.
7. Refrigerate for up to 3 days and warm in microwave before serving.

Nutrition Amount per serving

Calories 362

Total Fat 30.5g 39%

Saturated Fat 13.3g 67%

Cholesterol 238mg 79%

Sodium 928mg 40%

Total Carbs 2g 1%

Dietary Fiber 0.2g 1%

Total Sugars 0.7g

Protein 19.7g

Keto Egg Chorizo Muffins

Serves: 8/Prep Time: 20 mins

Ingredients
- 2 scallions, finely chopped
- 12 eggs
- 5 oz. air dried chorizo
- Salt and black pepper, to taste
- 6 oz. mozzarella cheese, shredded

Directions
1. Preheat the oven to 350°F and grease 8 muffin tins.
2. Put the chorizo and scallions in the muffin tins.
3. Whisk together eggs with salt and black pepper in a bowl.
4. Pour this mixture into the muffin tins and top with mozzarella cheese.
5. Transfer to the oven and bake for 20 minutes. Remove from the oven and serve warm.
6. Fold the muffins between parchment paper and freeze for up to 3 months.

Nutrition Amount per serving

Calories 236	Cholesterol 272mg 91%	Dietary Fiber 0.1g 0%
Total Fat 17.1g 22%	Sodium 439mg 19%	Total Sugars 0.6g
Saturated Fat 6.9g 34%	Total Carbs 1.9g 1%	Protein 18.6g

Keto Bacon Eggs Ham Muffin

Serves: 6/Prep Time: 25 mins

Ingredients

- 12 eggs
- 2 oz. ham, cooked
- 3 oz. mozzarella cheese, shredded
- Salt and black pepper, to taste
- 2 oz. bacon, cooked

Directions

1. Preheat the oven to 400°F and lightly grease 6 muffin tins.
2. Break 2 eggs in each muffin tin and season with salt and black pepper.
3. Top with ham, bacon and mozzarella cheese and place in the oven.
4. Bake for about 15 minutes and remove from the oven to serve warm.
5. Fold the muffins between parchment paper and freeze for up to 1 month.

Nutrition Amount per serving

Calories 232	Cholesterol 351mg 117%	Dietary Fiber 0.1g 0%
Total Fat 16g 21%	Sodium 550mg 24%	Total Sugars 0.7g
Saturated Fat 5.8g 29%	Total Carbs 1.7g 1%	Protein 20.1g

Low Carb Chia Pudding

Serves: 1/Prep Time: 15 mins

Ingredients

- 2 tablespoons chia seeds
- ¾ cup organic coconut milk
- ½ teaspoon vanilla extract
- 2 tablespoons almonds
- 2 scoops Stevia

Directions

1. Mix together all the ingredients in a glass jar and cover.
2. Refrigerate for at least 4 hours and remove from the fridge to serve chilled.
3. You can refrigerate this pudding for about 3 days.

Nutrition Amount per serving

Calories 192	Cholesterol 0mg 0%	Dietary Fiber 3.9g 14%
Total Fat 16.4g 21%	Sodium 9mg 0%	Total Sugars 0.8g
Saturated Fat 8.9g 45%	Total Carbs 6.6g 2%	Protein 4.4g

Low Carb Seedy Oatmeal

Serves: 2/Prep Time: 10 mins

Ingredients

- 2 tablespoons flaxseed, whole
- 2 cups organic coconut milk, full fat
- 2 tablespoons chia seeds
- 2 pinches salt
- 2 tablespoons sunflower seeds

Directions

1. Put all the ingredients in a small saucepan and bring to a boil.
2. Reduce the heat and allow it to simmer for about 20 minutes on low heat.
3. Dish out into a bowl and serve hot.
4. Let it cool down and refrigerate for about 3 days.

Nutrition Amount per serving

Calories 181	Cholesterol 0mg 0%	Dietary Fiber 3.4g 12%
Total Fat 15.8g 20%	Sodium 168mg 7%	Total Sugars 0.2g
Saturated Fat 11.6g 58%	Total Carbs 5.1g 2%	Protein 3.5g

Salad Sandwich

Serves: 2/Prep Time: 15 mins

Ingredients

- ½ oz. butter
- 2 oz. romaine lettuce
- 1 oz. edam cheese, shredded
- 1 cherry tomatoes
- ½ avocado

Directions

1. Spread butter on the lettuce leaves and top with avocado, cherry tomatoes and edam cheese.
2. Top with the remaining lettuce leaves and serve.
3. Wrap in the plastic food wrap and store in the freezer for about 3 days.

Nutrition Amount per serving

Calories 219	Cholesterol 28mg 9%	Dietary Fiber 4.3g 15%
Total Fat 19.7g 25%	Sodium 185mg 8%	Total Sugars 2.4g
Saturated Fat 8.2g 41%	Total Carbs 7.8g 3%	Protein 5.2g

Scrambled Eggs with Basil and Butter

Serves: 1/Prep Time: 15 mins

Ingredients

- 2 tablespoons sour cream
- 2 eggs
- Salt, to taste
- 2 tablespoons fresh basil
- 1 oz. butter

Directions

1. Whisk together eggs, sour cream and salt in a bowl.
2. Heat butter on low heat in a pan and stir in the egg mixture.
3. Cook for about 3 minutes on medium low heat and dish onto a platter.
4. Garnish with fresh basil and serve.
5. Store in the fridge for about 1 day and warm before serving.

Nutrition Amount per serving

Calories 382	Cholesterol 399mg 133%	Dietary Fiber 0.1g 0%
Total Fat 36.8g 47%	Sodium 454mg 20%	Total Sugars 0.8g
Saturated Fat 20.4g 102%	Total Carbs 1.9g 1%	Protein 12.2g

Coffee with Cream

Serves: 1/Prep Time: 10 mins

Ingredients

- ¾ cup water
- 1 tablespoon coffee
- 1 scoop Stevia
- 1 pinch cinnamon
- 4 tablespoons heavy whipping cream

Directions

1. Brew the coffee in water for about 5 minutes and add cinnamon and Stevia.
2. Heat heavy whipping cream in a saucepan until it is frothy.
3. Transfer into a large mug and top with the brewed coffee to serve.
4. Store in the fridge for about 1 day and warm before serving.

Nutrition Amount per serving

Calories 208	Cholesterol 82mg 27%	Dietary Fiber 0.2g 1%
Total Fat 22.2g 28%	Sodium 28mg 1%	Total Sugars 0.1g
Saturated Fat 13.8g 69%	Total Carbs 1.9g 1%	Protein 1.3g

Keto Cheese Roll Ups

Serves: 4/Prep Time: 10 mins

Ingredients

- 2 oz. butter
- 8 oz. provolone cheese, in slices
- 2 tablespoons sour cream
- Red chili flakes, to taste
- 2 tablespoons basil

Directions

1. Divide and spread the butter and sour cream onto the cheese slices.
2. Sprinkle with basil and red chili flakes.
3. Roll up the slices and serve.
4. Refrigerate for up to 2 days and freeze for up to 1 week.

Nutrition Amount per serving

Calories 314
Total Fat 27.9g 36%
Saturated Fat 17.7g 89%

Cholesterol 72mg 24%
Sodium 728mg 32%
Total Carbs 1.5g 1%

Dietary Fiber 0g 0%
Total Sugars 0.3g
Protein 14.9g

Dairy Free Keto Latte

Serves: 2/Prep Time: 5 mins

Ingredients

- 1½ cups boiling water
- 2 eggs
- 2 tablespoons coconut oil
- 1 pinch vanilla extract
- 1 teaspoon ground ginger

Directions

1. Put all the ingredients in a blender and blend until smooth.
2. Pour into 2 mugs and serve hot.
3. Refrigerate for up to 1 day and heat before serving.

Nutrition Amount per serving

Calories 184
Total Fat 18g 23%
Saturated Fat 13.1g 66%

Cholesterol 164mg 55%
Sodium 62mg 3%
Total Carbs 1g 0%

Dietary Fiber 0.1g 0%
Total Sugars 0.4g
Protein 5.6g

Creamed Green Cabbage Chorizo

Serves: 12/Prep Time: 20 mins

Ingredients

- 3 oz. butter
- 25 oz. chorizo
- 25 oz. green cabbage, shredded
- Salt and black pepper, to taste
- 1¼ cups heavy whipping cream

Directions

1. Heat half of butter over medium heat in a skillet and add chorizo.
2. Fry for about 3 minutes and dish out onto a platter.
3. Heat the remaining butter in the same skillet and add cabbage.
4. Sauté for about 3 minutes and stir in cream, salt and black pepper.
5. Lower the heat and allow to simmer for about 5 minutes.
6. Dish out onto a platter alongside the fried chorizo and serve warm.
7. Freeze for up to 3 days and warm in microwave before serving.

Nutrition Amount per serving

Calories 377
Total Fat 33g 42%
Saturated Fat 15g 75%

Cholesterol 84mg 28%
Sodium 786mg 34%
Total Carbs 4.9g 2%

Dietary Fiber 1.5g 5%
Total Sugars 1.9g
Protein 15.3g

Keto Chorizo and Spinach Frittata

Serves: 8/Prep Time: 50 mins
Ingredients
- 8 oz. fresh spinach, chopped
- 5 oz. chorizo, diced
- 4 tablespoons salted butter
- 8 eggs
- 8 oz. cheddar cheese, shredded

Directions
1. Preheat the oven to 350°F and lightly grease a baking dish.
2. Heat butter in a pan and add chorizo.
3. Cook for about 4 minutes and stir in the spinach.
4. Cook for about 3 minutes and add the eggs.
5. Mix well and cook for about 2 minutes.
6. Transfer into the baking dish and top with the cheddar cheese.
7. Bake for about 30 minutes until golden brown and remove from the oven to serve hot.
8. Put the frittata between two layers of parchment paper and freeze for up to 3 months.

Nutrition Amount per serving

Calories 315	Cholesterol 224mg 75%	Dietary Fiber 0.6g 2%
Total Fat 26.4g 34%	Sodium 520mg 23%	Total Sugars 0.6g
Saturated Fat 13.6g 68%	Total Carbs 2.1g 1%	Protein 17.7g

Keto Mushroom Omelet

Serves: 3/Prep Time: 15 mins
Ingredients
- 1 oz. butter, for frying
- 3 eggs
- 1 oz. mozzarella cheese, shredded
- Salt and black pepper, to taste
- 3 mushrooms, sliced

Directions
1. Whisk together eggs, salt and black pepper in a bowl until frothy.
2. Heat butter over medium heat in a frying pan and stir in the egg mixture.
3. Cook for about 2 minutes and add mushrooms and mozzarella cheese.
4. Cook for about 4 minutes and dish out into a bowl to serve.
5. Freeze for up to 1 week and warm in microwave before serving.

Nutrition Amount per serving

Calories 161	Cholesterol 189mg 63%	Dietary Fiber 0.2g 1%
Total Fat 13.8g 18%	Sodium 174mg 8%	Total Sugars 0.7g
Saturated Fat 7.2g 36%	Total Carbs 1.3g 0%	Protein 8.9g

Avocado Eggs with Bacon Sails

Serves: 4/Prep Time: 20 mins
Ingredients
- ½ avocado
- 1 teaspoon olive oil
- 2 hardboiled eggs, cut in halves lengthwise and yolks scooped out
- 2 oz. bacon
- Salt and black pepper, to taste

Directions
1. Preheat the oven to 350°F and lightly grease a baking dish.
2. Arrange the bacon on the baking sheet and transfer to the oven.
3. Bake for about 7 minutes and dish out onto a platter.
4. Mix the egg yolks with the avocado and olive oil.
5. Mash well and season with salt and black pepper.
6. Fill this mixture into the egg whites and place on the platter alongside bacon.
7. Serve immediately. You can freeze the egg yolks mixture for up to 3 days.

Nutrition Amount per serving

Calories 169	Cholesterol 97mg 32%	Dietary Fiber 1.7g 6%
Total Fat 14.2g 18%	Sodium 360mg 16%	Total Sugars 0.3g
Saturated Fat 3.8g 19%	Total Carbs 2.6g 1%	Protein 8.5g

Cauliflower Hash Browns

Serves: 4/Prep Time: 30 mins

Ingredients
- ½ yellow onion, grated
- 1 pound cauliflower, grated
- 3 eggs
- Salt and black pepper, to taste
- 4 oz. butter, for frying

Directions
1. Mix together cauliflower with the remaining ingredients except butter and stir well.
2. Heat butter in the nonstick pan and add some mixture.
3. Cook for about 10 minutes on both sides and repeat with the rest of the mixture.
4. Dish out onto a platter to serve. Put the hash browns between two layers of parchment paper and freeze for up to 3 months.

Nutrition Amount per serving

Calories 284	Cholesterol 184mg 61%	Dietary Fiber 3.1g 11%
Total Fat 26.4g 34%	Sodium 244mg 11%	Total Sugars 3.6g
Saturated Fat 15.6g 78%	Total Carbs 7.6g 3%	Protein 6.8g

Keto Western Omelet

Serves: 6/Prep Time: 15 mins

Ingredients
- 4 oz. cheddar cheese, shredded
- 6 eggs
- 2 oz. salted butter
- 5 oz. smoked deli ham, diced
- ½ green bell pepper, finely chopped

Directions
1. Whisk together eggs and cheddar cheese in a bowl until fluffy.
2. Heat butter on medium heat in a frying pan and add ham and bell pepper.
3. Sauté for about 5 minutes and stir in the egg cheese mixture.
4. Dish out onto a platter to serve.
5. Freeze for up to 3 days and warm in microwave before serving.

Nutrition Amount per serving

Calories 235	Cholesterol 214mg 71%	Dietary Fiber 0.1g 0%
Total Fat 19.2g 25%	Sodium 445mg 19%	Total Sugars 1.4g
Saturated Fat 10.6g 53%	Total Carbs 1.8g 1%	Protein 14.2g

Low Carb Baked Eggs

Serves: 3/Prep Time: 25 mins

Ingredients
- 3 tablespoons butter
- 3 oz. ground beef, cooked
- 2 eggs
- Salt and black pepper, to taste
- 2 oz. cheddar cheese, shredded

Directions
1. Preheat the oven to 400°F and lightly grease a baking dish.
2. Place the ground beef in the baking dish and create two holes with a spoon.
3. Crack the eggs into the holes and top with cheddar cheese.
4. Bake for about 15 minutes and remove from the oven to serve.
5. Put the baked eggs between two layers of parchment paper and freeze for up to 3 months.

Nutrition Amount per serving

Calories 273	Cholesterol 185mg 62%	Dietary Fiber 0g 0%
Total Fat 22.5g 29%	Sodium 259mg 11%	Total Sugars 0.3g
Saturated Fat 12.9g 64%	Total Carbs 0.5g 0%	Protein 17.1g

Boiled Eggs with Mayonnaise

Serves: 4/Prep Time: 15 mins

Ingredients
- 4 tablespoons mayonnaise
- 4 eggs, soft boiled
- 1 avocado, sliced
- Salt and black pepper, to taste
- 2 tablespoons fresh coriander

Directions
1. Place the boiled eggs on a plate and top with mayonnaise, avocado and fresh coriander.
2. Season with salt and black pepper to serve.
3. You can freeze the boiled eggs and defrost when required to make this dish.

Nutrition Amount per serving

Calories 223	Cholesterol 168mg 56%	Dietary Fiber 3.4g 12%
Total Fat 19.1g 24%	Sodium 169mg 7%	Total Sugars 1.5g
Saturated Fat 4.1g 21%	Total Carbs 8.2g 3%	Protein 6.6g

Scrambled Eggs with Halloumi Cheese

Serves: 3/Prep Time: 25 mins

Ingredients
- 2 tablespoons olive oil
- 3 oz. halloumi cheese, diced
- 4 eggs
- Salt and black pepper, to taste
- ½ cup olives, pitted

Directions
1. Whisk together eggs with salt and black pepper in a small bowl.
2. Heat olive oil in a frying pan over medium high heat and add halloumi.
3. Sauté for about 3 minutes until nicely browned and stir in the whisked eggs.
4. Reduce the heat and stir in the olives.
5. Cook for about 3 minutes and dish out into a bowl to serve.
6. Store in the fridge for about 1 day and warm before serving.

Nutrition Amount per serving

Calories 293	Cholesterol 241mg 80%	Dietary Fiber 0.7g 3%
Total Fat 26g 33%	Sodium 423mg 18%	Total Sugars 1.2g
Saturated Fat 9.3g 47%	Total Carbs 2.6g 1%	Protein 13.7g

Keto Deviled Eggs

Serves: 4/Prep Time: 15 mins

Ingredients
- 1 teaspoon tabasco
- 4 hardboiled eggs, cut in half lengthwise and yolks scooped out
- ¼ cup mayonnaise
- 8 shrimp, cooked and peeled
- 1 pinch herbal salt

Directions
1. Put the egg yolks with tabasco, mayonnaise and herbal salt in a bowl and mash with a fork. Arrange the egg whites on a plate and fill with the egg yolk mixture.
2. Top with shrimp and serve. You can freeze the egg yolks mixture for up to 3 days.

Nutrition Amount per serving

Calories 173	Cholesterol 260mg 87%	Dietary Fiber 0g 0%
Total Fat 10g 13%	Sodium 281mg 12%	Total Sugars 1.3g
Saturated Fat 2.3g 12%	Total Carbs 4.5g 2%	Protein 15.7g

Coconut Porridge

Serves: 1/Prep Time: 20 mins
Ingredients
- 1 egg
- 1 oz. butter
- 1 tablespoon coconut flour
- 4 tablespoons coconut cream
- 1 pinch ground psyllium husk powder

Directions
1. Heat all the ingredients over low heat in a nonstick saucepan and mix well.
2. Stir continuously for about 10 minutes and dish out ino a bowl to serve.
3. You can refrigerate this porridge for up to 3 days.

Nutrition Amount per serving

Calories 437	Cholesterol 225mg 75%	Dietary Fiber 4.9g 18%
Total Fat 42.4g 54%	Sodium 234mg 10%	Total Sugars 2.4g
Saturated Fat 29.1g 146%	Total Carbs 9.4g 3%	Protein 8.2g

Eggplant Hash with Eggs

Serves: 4/Prep Time: 20 mins
Ingredients
- 8 oz. halloumi cheese, diced
- 2 eggplants, diced
- 1 yellow onion, finely chopped
- 4 tablespoons butter
- 4 eggs

Directions
1. Heat butter on medium heat and add onions.
2. Sauté for about 3 minutes and stir in eggplants and halloumi cheese.
3. Cook for about 6 minutes until golden brown and dish out onto a platter.
4. Half fry the eggs and serve with the eggplant hash.
5. Store in the fridge for about 1 day and warm before serving.

Nutrition Amount per serving

Calories 314	Cholesterol 194mg 65%	Dietary Fiber 1.6g 6%
Total Fat 25.5g 33%	Sodium 144mg 6%	Total Sugars 4.2g
Saturated Fat 11.1g 55%	Total Carbs 6.6g 2%	Protein 15.7g

No Bread Keto Breakfast Sandwich

Serves: 2/Prep Time: 15 mins
Ingredients
- 4 eggs
- 2 tablespoons butter
- 1 oz. deli ham, smoked
- Salt and black pepper, to taste
- 2 oz. provolone cheese, cut in thick slices

Directions
1. Heat butter over medium heat in a pan and add eggs.
2. Season with salt and black pepper and sauté for about 2 minutes on each side.
3. Dish out onto a plate and place ham over fried egg.
4. Top with cheese and close with another fried egg to serve.
5. Store in the fridge for about 2 days and warm before serving.

Nutrition Amount per serving

Calories 350	Cholesterol 386mg 129%	Dietary Fiber 0.2g 1%
Total Fat 29g 37%	Sodium 638mg 28%	Total Sugars 0.9g
Saturated Fat 15.3g 76%	Total Carbs 1.9g 1%	Protein 20.8g

Coconut Cream with Berries

Serves: 1/Prep Time: 10 mins

Ingredients
- ¼ cup fresh strawberries
- ½ cup heavy cream
- ¼ cup fresh raspberries
- 1 tablespoon almonds
- 1 pinch vanilla extract

Directions
1. Put all the ingredients in an immersion blender and blend until smooth.
2. Dish out into a bowl and serve chilled.
3. You can refrigerate this for about 3 days and freeze for up to 1 month.

Nutrition Amount per serving

Calories 270	Cholesterol 82mg 27%	Dietary Fiber 3.5g 12%
Total Fat 25.5g 33%	Sodium 24mg 1%	Total Sugars 3.5g
Saturated Fat 14.1g 70%	Total Carbs 9.5g 3%	Protein 3.1g

Blueberry and Almond Smoothie

Serves: 4/Prep Time: 10 mins

Ingredients
- ½ cup frozen blueberries
- 8 oz heavy cream
- 4 tablespoons almond butter
- 3 scoops Stevia
- 28 oz almond milk, unsweetened

Directions
1. Put all the ingredients in an immersion blender and blend until smooth.
2. Pour into 4 glasses and immediately serve.
3. Refrigerate for up to 2 days and serve.

Nutrition Amount per serving

Calories 380	Cholesterol 39mg 13%	Dietary Fiber 3.2g 11%
Total Fat 38.7g 50%	Sodium 26mg 1%	Total Sugars 4.6g
Saturated Fat 27.9g 139%	Total Carbs 9.1g 3%	Protein 4.6g

30-Day Lunch Keto Meal Prep

Keto Salmon Filled Avocados

Serves: 2/Prep Time: 15 mins

Ingredients
- 2 avocados, halved and pits removed
- Salt and black pepper, to taste
- 2 tablespoons lemon juice
- 6 oz. salmon, smoked
- ¾ cup crème fraiche

Directions
1. Put a scoop of crème fraiche in the hole of the avocado and top with smoked salmon.
2. Sprinkle with lemon juice and season with salt and black pepper to serve.
3. You can freeze the salmon for up to 6 months and use the frozen salmon to make this keto dish.

Nutrition Amount per serving

Calories 309	Cholesterol 38mg 13%	Dietary Fiber 3.1g 11%
Total Fat 25.4g 33%	Sodium 41mg 2%	Total Sugars 0.3g
Saturated Fat 1.9g 9%	Total Carbs 3.4g 1%	Protein 18.4g

Keto Tex Mex Casserole

Serves: 6/Prep Time: 40 mins

Ingredients

- 2 oz. butter
- 1½ pounds ground beef
- 3 tablespoons Tex Mex seasoning
- 7 oz. Monterey Jack cheese, shredded
- 7 oz. tomatoes, crushed

Directions

1. Preheat the oven to 400°F and lightly grease a casserole dish.
2. Heat butter over medium heat and add ground beef.
3. Cook for about 5 minutes until brown and stir in tomatoes and Tex Mex seasoning.
4. Allow to simmer for about 6 minutes and transfer this mixture into the casserole dish.
5. Top with Monterey Jack cheese and place in the oven.
8. Bake for about 20 minutes until golden brown and remove from the oven to serve hot.
6. Refrigerate for up to 3 days and warm in microwave before serving.

Nutrition Amount per serving

Calories 408
Total Fat 24.8g 32%
Saturated Fat 13.8g 69%

Cholesterol 151mg 50%
Sodium 1118mg 49%
Total Carbs 1.5g 1%

Dietary Fiber 0.4g 1%
Total Sugars 1.1g
Protein 42.9g

Paprika Chicken with Rutabaga

Serves: 12/Prep Time: 50 mins

Ingredients

- 30 oz. rutabaga
- 30 oz. chicken thighs
- 4¼ oz. butter
- 1 cup mayonnaise
- Salt, black pepper and paprika powder, to taste

Directions

1. Preheat the oven to 400°F and lightly grease a baking dish.
2. Place chicken and rutabaga in the baking dish and season with salt, black pepper and paprika powder. Sprinkle with olive oil and transfer into the oven.
3. Bake for about 40 minutes and remove from the oven. Serve with mayonnaise and enjoy.
4. Store in the fridge for about 1 day and warm before serving.

Nutrition Amount per serving

Calories 309
Total Fat 20.1g 26%
Saturated Fat 7.6g 38%

Cholesterol 90mg 30%
Sodium 272mg 12%
Total Carbs 10.5g 4%

Dietary Fiber 1.8g 6%
Total Sugars 5.2g
Protein 21.6g

Cilantro Lime Cauliflower Rice

Serves: 4/Prep Time: 20 mins

Ingredients

- 3 tablespoons extra-virgin olive oil
- 1 medium lime, juiced
- 1 medium head cauliflower, coarsely chopped
- 2 green onions, chopped
- ¼ cup fresh cilantro, roughly chopped

Directions

1. Heat olive oil over medium heat in a pan and add green onions.
2. Sauté for about 2 minutes and add chopped cauliflower.
3. Cook for about 10 minutes on medium low heat and dish out into a bowl.
4. Sprinkle with the lime juice and garnish with cilantro to serve.
5. Refrigerate for up to 3 days and warm in microwave before serving.

Nutrition Amount per serving

Calories 132 Total Fat 10.7g 14% Saturated Fat 1.5g 8% Cholesterol 0mg 0% Sodium 45mg 2% Total Carbs 9.5g 3% Dietary Fiber 4.2g 15% Total Sugars 3.8g Protein 3.1g

Garlic Parmesan Roasted Cauliflower

Serves: 4/Prep Time: 40 mins

Ingredients

- Salt and black pepper, to taste
- 1 tablespoon extra-virgin olive oil
- d
- 2 tablespoons garlic, minced
- 1 large cauliflower head, cut into florets
- ½ cup parmesan cheese, grate

Directions

1. Preheat the oven to 400ºF and lightly grease a baking sheet.
2. Mix together cauliflower florets with olive oil, garlic, salt and black pepper in a bowl.
3. Transfer to the baking sheet and place in the oven.
4. Bake for about 15 minutes and flip the sides of the cauliflower.
5. Top with parmesan cheese and bake for about 15 more minutes.
6. Remove from the oven and serve hot. Serve in a casserole and garnish with parsley.
7. Freeze for up to 1 week and warm in microwave before serving.

Nutrition Amount per serving

Calories 167
Total Fat 10.6g 14%
Saturated Fat 4g 20%

Cholesterol 16mg 5%
Sodium 259mg 11%
Total Carbs 10.8g 4%

Dietary Fiber 4.3g 15%
Total Sugars 4.1g
Protein 10.7g

Mexican Street Broccoli Salad

Serves: 6/Prep Time: 20 mins

Ingredients

- 2 cups yellow squash, chopped
- 3 teaspoons chili and lime seasoning
- 30 oz. broccoli, riced
- ½ cup Mexican crema
- ½ cup cotija cheese

Directions

1. Mix together Mexican crema, cotija cheese and chili and lime seasoning in a small bowl.
2. Place yellow squash and broccoli in a bowl and top with the crema mixture.
3. You can use both the frozen and fresh yellow squash and broccoli for this salad.

Nutrition Amount per serving

Calories 128
Total Fat 7g 9%
Saturated Fat 4g 20%

Cholesterol 24mg 8%
Sodium 271mg 12%
Total Carbs 12g 4%

Dietary Fiber 4.1g 15%
Total Sugars 3.1g
Protein 7g

Parmesan Zucchini and Tomato Gratin

Serves: 6/Prep Time: 50 mins

Ingredients

- 3 medium zucchinis, sliced
- 2 medium tomatoes, sliced
- ½ cup parmesan cheese, shredded
- 2 tablespoons olive oil
- Salt and garlic powder, to taste

Directions

1. Preheat the oven to 350ºF and lightly grease a baking sheet.
2. Arrange the zucchini slices on the baking sheet and layer with tomato slices.
3. Layer again with zucchini slices and drizzle with olive oil.
4. Season with salt and garlic powder and top with parmesan cheese.
5. Transfer into the oven and bake for about 40 minutes.
6. Remove from the oven and serve warm.
7. You can use both the fresh and frozen zucchinis and tomatoes.

Nutrition Amount per serving

Calories 95 Total Fat 6.9g 9% Saturated Fat 2.1g 10% Cholesterol 7mg 2% Sodium 99mg 4% Total Carbs 5.5g 2% Dietary Fiber 1.6g 6% Total Sugars 2.9g Protein 4.6g

Roasted Brussels Sprouts with Parmesan

Serves: 4/Prep Time: 30 mins

Ingredients

- Salt and black pepper, to taste
- 1 tablespoon olive oil
- ½ cup parmesan cheese, shredded
- 13 oz. fresh Brussels sprouts, trimmed and halved
- ½ cup pork rinds, crushed

Directions

1. Preheat the oven to 400°F and lightly grease a baking dish.
2. Arrange the Brussels sprouts in a baking dish and drizzle with olive oil.
3. Season with salt and black pepper and top with crushed pork rinds.
4. Mix well and transfer, covered in the oven. Bake for about 15 minutes and uncover.
5. Top with the parmesan cheese and bake for 5 more minutes.
6. Remove from the oven and serve hot.
7. Freeze the Brussels sprouts and thaw before baking.

Nutrition Amount per serving

Calories 196	Cholesterol 30mg 10%	Dietary Fiber 3.5g 12%
Total Fat 11.9g 15%	Sodium 428mg 19%	Total Sugars 2g
Saturated Fat 4.7g 23%	Total Carbs 8.9g 3%	Protein 16.8g

Mixed Chicken and Veggies

Serves: 5/Prep Time: 25 mins

Ingredients

- 1 carrot, chopped
- 2 pounds chicken, boiled
- ½ cup mushrooms, chopped
- Salt and black pepper, to taste
- 1½ tablespoons olive oil

Directions

1. Heat olive oil in a skillet over medium heat and add carrots and mushrooms.
2. Sauté for about 5 minutes and add chicken.
3. Season with salt and black pepper and cover with lid.
4. Cook for about 7 minutes and dish out into a bowl to serve.
5. You can use the frozen as well as fresh chicken and veggies.

Nutrition Amount per serving

Calories 317	Cholesterol 140mg 47%	Dietary Fiber 0.4g 1%
Total Fat 9.7g 12%	Sodium 123mg 5%	Total Sugars 0.7g
Saturated Fat 2.1g 11%	Total Carbs 1.4g 1%	Protein 52.9g

Southwestern Grilled Spatchcock Turkey

Serves: 12/Prep Time: 2 hours 20 mins

Ingredients

- 1½ tablespoons chili powder
- Paprika, kosher salt and black pepper, to taste
- 1 (6 pound) turkey
- 1 scoop Stevia
- 1 teaspoon garlic powder

Directions

1. Preheat the grill to medium high heat.
2. Mix together garlic powder, chili powder, Stevia, paprika, salt and black pepper in a bowl.
3. Dredge the turkey in this mixture and place on the grill.
4. Grill for about 2 hours and remove from the oven to serve.
5. You can make this dish with turkey breasts or thighs too.

Nutrition Amount per serving

Calories 389	Cholesterol 172mg 57%	Dietary Fiber 0.4g 1%
Total Fat 11.5g 15%	Sodium 168mg 7%	Total Sugars 0.1g
Saturated Fat 3.8g 19%	Total Carbs 0.7g 0%	Protein 66.6g

Cheese Casserole

Serves: 12/Prep Time: 35 mins
Ingredients

- 10 ounce parmesan cheese, shredded
- 2 tablespoons olive oil
- 16 ounce mozzarella cheese, shredded
- 16 ounce marinara sauce
- 2 pounds sausage scramble

Directions

1. Preheat the oven to 375°F and grease a casserole dish.
2. Place half of the sausage scramble in the casserole dish and top with half of the marinara sauce. Sprinkle with half of the mozzarella and parmesan cheese and add remaining half of the sausage scramble.
3. Top with the remaining half of parmesan and mozzarella cheese and drizzle with the olive oil and remaining marinara sauce. Transfer to the oven and bake for about 23 minutes.
4. Remove from the oven and serve hot.
5. You can refrigerate this cheese casserole for about 3 months.

Nutrition Amount per serving

Calories 492
Total Fat 36.5g 47%
Saturated Fat 14.9g 74%
Cholesterol 101mg 34%
Sodium 1167mg 51%
Total Carbs 7.4g 3%
Dietary Fiber 1g 4%
Total Sugars 3.3g
Protein 33.6g

Oven Roasted Asparagus

Serves: 4/Prep Time: 35 mins
Ingredients

- 3 tablespoons extra-virgin olive oil
- 2 pounds asparagus, stalks trimmed
- ¼ cup Monterey Jack Cheese
- ½ teaspoon black pepper
- ½ teaspoon kosher salt

Directions

1. Preheat the oven to 400°F and lightly grease a baking dish.
2. Arrange asparagus on the baking sheet and drizzle with olive oil.
3. Season with salt and black pepper and top with Monterey Jack Cheese.
4. Transfer to the oven and bake for about 25 minutes until slightly charred.
5. Refrigerate for up to 2 days and warm before serving.

Nutrition Amount per serving

Calories 162
Total Fat 12.9g 17%
Saturated Fat 2.9g 15%
Cholesterol 6mg 2%
Sodium 333mg 14%
Total Carbs 9g 3%
Dietary Fiber 4.8g 17%
Total Sugars 4.3g
Protein 6.8g

Smashed Broccoli

Serves: 6/Prep Time: 15 mins
Ingredients

- Kosher salt and crushed red pepper, to taste
- 1 large head broccoli, cut into florets
- 2 tablespoons olive oil
- 1 cup parmesan cheese, grated
- 2 garlic cloves, smashed

Directions

1. Blanch the broccoli in salted water for about 2 minutes and smash it.
2. Heat olive oil over medium heat in a large skillet and add garlic and smashed broccoli.
3. Season with salt and crushed red pepper and cook for about 3 minutes on each side.
4. Dish out into a bowl and top with parmesan cheese to serve.
5. You can use both the frozen and fresh broccoli, but fresh broccoli works better.

Nutrition Amount per serving

Calories 108 Total Fat 8.8g 11% Saturated Fat 3.3g 17% Cholesterol 13mg 4% Sodium 374mg 16% Total Carbs 2.3g 1% Dietary Fiber 0.6g 2% Total Sugars 0.4g Protein 6.6g

Chicken Noodle Soup

Serves: 6/Prep Time: 30 mins

Ingredients

- 1 pound chicken, boiled and chopped
- ½ packet miracle noodles, boiled and rinsed
- 1 tablespoon olive oil
- Salt and black pepper, to taste
- ½ onion, chopped

Directions

1. Heat olive oil over medium heat in a pan and add onions.
2. Sauté for about 3 minutes and add chicken, salt and black pepper.
3. Cover with lid and cook for about 10 minutes.
4. Add miracle noodles with some water and cook for about 5 minutes.
5. Dish out into a bowl and serve hot.
6. You can refrigerate this soup for up to 3 days and warm before serving.

Nutrition Amount per serving

Calories 144	Cholesterol 58mg 19%	Dietary Fiber 0.2g 1%
Total Fat 4.6g 6%	Sodium 52mg 2%	Total Sugars 0.4g
Saturated Fat 1g 5%	Total Carbs 1.7g 1%	Protein 22.4g

Keto Bacon Sushi

Serves: 12/Prep Time: 30 mins

Ingredients

- 2 Persian cucumbers, thinly sliced
- 6 slices bacon, halved
- 2 medium carrots, thinly sliced
- 4 oz. cream cheese, softened
- 1 avocado, sliced

Directions

1. Preheat the oven to 400°F and grease a baking dish lightly.
2. Arrange bacon slices on the baking sheet and bake for about 12 minutes until crispy.
3. Spread cream cheese on each bacon slice and add cucumbers, carrots and avocado.
4. Roll up the bacon and serve.
5. Freeze for up to 3 days and warm before serving.

Nutrition Amount per serving

Calories 126	Cholesterol 21mg 7%	Dietary Fiber 1.7g 6%
Total Fat 10.5g 14%	Sodium 255mg 11%	Total Sugars 0.6g
Saturated Fat 4.1g 20%	Total Carbs 3.5g 1%	Protein 4.6g

Zoodle Alfredo with Bacon

Serves: 6/Prep Time: 20 mins

Ingredients

- 1½ cups heavy cream
- ½ pound bacon, crisped and chopped
- ½ cup parmesan cheese, grated
- Kosher salt and black pepper, to taste
- 16 oz. zucchini noodles

Directions

1. Heat a nonstick pan and add bacon, heavy cream, salt and black pepper.
2. Bring to a boil and reduce the heat to low.
3. Add parmesan cheese and cook for about 3 minutes.
4. Stir in the zucchini noodles and cook for about 2 minutes.
5. Dish out into a bowl and serve warm. Make the mixture without zucchini noodles and freeze for up to 1 month. Add zucchini noodles before serving.

Nutrition Amount per serving

Calories 350	Cholesterol 89mg 30%	Dietary Fiber 0.8g 3%
Total Fat 29g 37%	Sodium 979mg 43%	Total Sugars 1.3g
Saturated Fat 13.5g 67%	Total Carbs 4.3g 2%	Protein 18.5g

Broiled Salmon

ns

- Kosher salt and black pepper, to taste
- Juice of 1 lemon

. lightly grease a baking sheet.

..rd, thyme, lemon juice, salt and black pepper in a bowl.

..mon fillets on the baking sheet and top with this mixture.

..out 8 minutes and remove from the oven to serve hot.

..rate for up to 3 days and freeze for up to a week.

..ion Amount per serving

..ories 158	Cholesterol 50mg 17%	Dietary Fiber 0.7g 2%
Total Fat 7.2g 9%	Sodium 649mg 28%	Total Sugars 0.3g
Saturated Fat 1g 5%	Total Carbs 1.8g 1%	Protein 22.2g

Cajun Parmesan Salmon

Serves: 4/Prep Time: 25 mins

Ingredients

- Cajun seasoning and black pepper, to taste
- 4 (4 oz.) salmon fillets
- 4 tablespoons butter
- 2 tablespoons parmesan cheese, freshly grated
- 1/3 cup chicken broth, low sodium

Directions

1. Heat half of butter over medium high heat in a large skillet and add salmon fillets.
2. Season with Cajun seasoning and black pepper and cook for about 4 minutes on each side.
3. Dish out onto a plate and set aside.
4. Heat the remaining butter in the skillet and add broth and parmesan cheese.
5. Cook for about 5 minutes on high heat and return the salmon fillets.
6. Simmer for about 4 minutes and dish out to serve warm.
7. Refrigerate for up to 3 days and warm in microwave before serving.

Nutrition Amount per serving

Calories 266	Cholesterol 83mg 28%	Dietary Fiber 0g 0%
Total Fat 19.4g 25%	Sodium 240mg 10%	Total Sugars 0.1g
Saturated Fat 8.8g 44%	Total Carbs 0.2g 0%	Protein 23.7g

Cheesy Bacon Butternut Squash

Serves: 8/Prep Time: 40 mins

Ingredients

- 2 tablespoons olive oil
- 2 pounds butternut squash, peeled and cut into 1" pieces
- Kosher salt and black pepper, to taste
- 2 cups parmesan cheese, freshly grated
- ½ pound bacon, chopped

Directions

1. Preheat the oven to 425°F and lightly grease a baking dish.
2. Heat olive oil in a medium skillet and add butternut squash, bacon, salt and black pepper.
3. Sauté for about 2 minutes and then transfer into the baking dish.
4. Bake for about 25 minutes and remove from the oven.
5. Top with parmesan cheese and bake for another 10 minutes.
6. Remove the baking dish from the oven and serve warm.
7. Refrigerate for up to 3 days and warm in microwave before serving.

Nutrition Amount per serving

Calories 292

Total Fat 21.5g 28%

Saturated Fat 8.5g 42%

Cholesterol 51mg 17%

Sodium 917mg 40%

Total Carbs 5.2g 2%

Dietary Fiber 1.3g 4%

Total Sugars 2.5g

Protein 20.9g

Bacon Avocado Bombs

Serves: 6/Prep Time: 20 mins

Ingredients

- 1/3 cup cheddar cheese, shredded
- 2 avocados, halved and pits removed
- 8 bacon slices
- 2 tablespoons Dijon mustard
- 2 tablespoons butter

Directions

1. Preheat the broiler and lightly grease a baking sheet.
2. Put the cheddar cheese in the avocado halves and cover with the other halves.
3. Mix together butter and Dijon mustard and marinate stuffed avocados in it.
4. Wrap 4 slices of bacon around each avocado and transfer to the baking sheet.
5. Broil for about 10 minutes, flipping halfway through.
6. Remove from the oven, slice crosswise and serve immediately.
7. Refrigerate for up to 2 days and freeze for up to 1 week.

Nutrition Amount per serving

Calories 336

Total Fat 29.8g 38%

Saturated Fat 10g 50%

Cholesterol 45mg 15%

Sodium 715mg 31%

Total Carbs 6.5g 2%

Dietary Fiber 4.7g 17%

Total Sugars 0.4g

Protein 12.5g

Lemon Ginger Shrimp

Serves: 4/Prep Time: 15 mins

Ingredients

- 1 pound medium shrimp, peeled and deveined
- 3 tablespoons butter, divided
- 1 lemon, thinly sliced, plus juice of 1 lemon
- Kosher salt and crushed red pepper flakes, to taste
- 2 tablespoons ginger, minced

Directions

1. Heat butter over medium heat in a large skillet and add the rest of the ingredients.
2. Cook for about 3 minutes on each side and dish out into a bowl to serve.
3. You can freeze the shrimp for up to 6 months and use the frozen shrimp to make this dish.

Nutrition Amount per serving

Calories 199

Total Fat 10.3g 13%

Saturated Fat 5.5g 28%

Cholesterol 246mg 82%

Sodium 319mg 14%

Total Carbs 3.5g 1%

Dietary Fiber 0.9g 3%

Total Sugars 0.5g

Protein 24.9g

Jalapeño Popper Stuffed Zucchini

Serves: 6/Prep Time: 30 mins

Ingredients

- 6 oz. cream cheese, softened
- 3 medium zucchinis, ends removed and halved crosswise
- 1 cup mozzarella cheese, shredded and divided
- Garlic powder, kosher salt and black pepper
- 1 jalapeno, minced

Directions

1. Preheat the oven to 425°F and lightly grease a baking dish.
2. Arrange the zucchini on the baking sheet and bake for about 10 minutes.

3. Mix together cream cheese, ½ cup mozzarella cheese, jalapeño, garlic powder, kosher salt and black pepper in a bowl.
4. Remove zucchini from the oven and fill in the jalapeño mixture.
5. Bake again for about 8 minutes and remove from oven to serve.
6. Freeze up to 3 days but it is better to use fresh zucchini.

Nutrition Amount per serving

Calories 130	Cholesterol 34mg 11%	Dietary Fiber 1.2g 4%
Total Fat 10.9g 14%	Sodium 122mg 5%	Total Sugars 2g
Saturated Fat 6.8g 34%	Total Carbs 4.7g 2%	Protein 4.8g

Baked Cajun Salmon

Serves: 4/Prep Time: 30 mins

Ingredients
- 1 red bell pepper, thinly sliced
- ½ large white onion, thinly sliced
- Cajun seasoning, garlic powder, paprika, kosher salt and black pepper
- 4 (6 oz.) salmon fillets
- 4 tablespoons extra-virgin olive oil

Directions
1. Preheat the oven to 400°F and lightly grease a baking sheet.
2. Arrange onions and bell peppers on the baking sheet and season with salt and black pepper.
3. Whisk together Cajun seasoning, garlic powder and paprika in a bowl.
4. Put the salmon on the baking sheet and rub with seasoning blend.
5. Transfer to the oven and bake for about 20 minutes.
6. Refrigerate for up to 3 days and freeze for up to a week.

Nutrition Amount per serving

Calories 366	Cholesterol 75mg 25%	Dietary Fiber 1.1g 4%
Total Fat 24.7g 32%	Sodium 89mg 4%	Total Sugars 2.5g
Saturated Fat 3.5g 18%	Total Carbs 4.8g 2%	Protein 33.7g

Bacon Weave Pizza

Serves: 12/Prep Time: 45 mins

Ingredients
- ½ cup keto pizza sauce
- 12 slices thick cut bacon
- 1 cup green bell pepper, sliced
- 1¼ cup mozzarella cheese, grated
- ¼ cup black olives, sliced

Directions
1. Preheat the oven to 400°F and lightly grease a baking sheet.
2. Make the bacon weave with bacon slices and place on the baking sheet.
3. Transfer to the oven and bake for about 25 minutes until crispy.
4. Remove from the oven and spread keto sauce on it.
5. Top with green bell pepper, black olives and mozzarella cheese.
6. Bake for another 10 minutes and remove from oven to serve.
7. Refrigerate for up to 5 days and warm in microwave before serving.

Nutrition Amount per serving

Calories 105	Cholesterol 17mg 6%	Dietary Fiber 0.4g 2%
Total Fat 7.5g 10%	Sodium 365mg 16%	Total Sugars 0.7g
Saturated Fat 2.8g 14%	Total Carbs 2.3g 1%	Protein 7.7g

Cheesesteak Stuffed Portobellos

Serves: 4/Prep Time: 35 mins

Ingredients

- 3 tablespoons extra-virgin olive oil, divided
- 4 medium portobello mushrooms, stems and gills removed
- Italian seasoning, kosher salt and black pepper
- 4 slices provolone cheese
- 1 pound sirloin steak

Directions

1. Preheat the oven to 350°F and lightly grease a baking sheet.
2. Mix together half of olive oil, salt and black pepper in a bowl and marinate mushrooms in it. Heat the rest of the olive oil and add steak, salt and black pepper.
3. Cook for about 5 minutes on each side and stuff inside the portobello mushrooms.
4. Transfer onto the baking sheet and bake for about 20 minutes.
5. Remove from the oven and serve immediately. Freeze for about 5 days.

Nutrition Amount per serving

Calories 407	Cholesterol 121mg 40%	Dietary Fiber 0.2g 1%
Total Fat 25.4g 33%	Sodium 320mg 14%	Total Sugars 0.3g
Saturated Fat 9g 45%	Total Carbs 1.4g 0%	Protein 42.2g

Turkey Carrot Roll Up

Serves: 2/Prep Time: 15 mins

Ingredients

- 2 carrot sticks
- 2 thin slices of turkey breasts
- 2 teaspoons yellow mustard
- 2 cheddar cheese slices
- 2 tablespoons olive oil

Directions

1. Place turkey breast slices in a plate and spread mustard.
2. Put cheese slices in between and wrap around the carrot sticks.
3. Heat olive oil over medium heat in a skillet and add turkey carrot roll ups.
4. Sauté for about 3 minutes and dish out to serve.
5. Refrigerate for up to 3 days and warm in microwave before serving.

Nutrition Amount per serving

Calories 276	Cholesterol 44mg 15%	Dietary Fiber 0.2g 1%
Total Fat 23.5g 30%	Sodium 661mg 29%	Total Sugars 0.2g
Saturated Fat 7.9g 40%	Total Carbs 2.6g 1%	Protein 14.2g

Sweet and Savory Grilled Chicken

Serves: 4/Prep Time: 25 mins

Ingredients

- 2 teaspoons dry mustard
- 2 teaspoons light brown sugar
- 1 teaspoon onion powder
- 1¼ pounds boneless, skinless chicken breast
- Kosher salt and white pepper, to taste

Directions

1. Preheat the grill to medium high and grease the grill grate.
2. Mix together dry mustard, brown sugar, onion powder, kosher salt and white pepper in a small bowl. Dredge chicken breasts in this mixture and coat well.
3. Transfer to the grill and grill for about 6 minutes on each side.
4. Remove from the grill to serve hot.
5. You can use both the frozen and fresh chicken breasts. Frozen breasts need to be thawed.

Nutrition Amount per serving

Calories 177 Total Fat 4g 5% Saturated Fat 0g 0% Cholesterol 91mg 30% Sodium 73mg 3% Total Carbs 2.5g 1% Dietary Fiber 0.3g 1% Total Sugars 1.8g Protein 30.5g

Herb Roasted Turkey

Serves: 20/Prep Time: 55 mins

Ingredients
- ¾ cup mixed fresh herbs (thyme, rosemary, sage, oregano and marjoram)
- 1 (10 pound) turkey, giblets and neck removed
- 2 tablespoons olive oil
- 2 lemons, cut into 2 inch pieces
- Salt and black pepper, to taste

Directions
1. Preheat the oven to 475°F and lightly grease a large roasting pan.
2. Place the turkey on the roasting pan and drizzle with olive oil.
3. Season with mixed fresh herbs, salt and black pepper and top with lemons.
4. Add 3 cups water and transfer to the oven.
5. Roast for about 45 minutes until golden brown and remove onto a platter to serve.
6. You can store the leftovers in the freezer for up to 3 months.

Nutrition Amount per serving

Calories 539	Cholesterol 229mg 76%	Dietary Fiber 1.1g 4%
Total Fat 17.3g 22%	Sodium 213mg 9%	Total Sugars 0.2g
Saturated Fat 5.4g 27%	Total Carbs 2.2g 1%	Protein 88.8g

Cheesy Cauliflower Casserole

Serves: 6/Prep Time: 25 mins

Ingredients
- 4 oz. cream cheese
- 1 head cauliflower florets, boiled and drained
- 2 teaspoons Dijon mustard
- Garlic powder, salt and black pepper, to taste
- 2 cups cheddar cheese, shredded and divided

Directions
1. Preheat the oven to 375°F and grease glass baking dish.
2. Put cream cheese and Dijon mustard in a saucepan and cook for about 2 minutes.
3. Remove from the heat and stir in half of cheddar cheese, garlic powder, salt and black pepper. Mix well and stir in the boiled cauliflower.
4. Transfer into the baking dish and top with the remaining cheese.
5. Move into the oven and bake for about 15 minutes. Remove from the oven and serve hot.
6. If you are using frozen cauliflower, thaw it thoroughly and drain the water.

Nutrition Amount per serving

Calories 232	Cholesterol 60mg 20%	Dietary Fiber 1.2g 4%
Total Fat 19.2g 25%	Sodium 323mg 14%	Total Sugars 1.4g
Saturated Fat 12.1g 61%	Total Carbs 3.8g 1%	Protein 11.9g

Lemon Pepper Green Beans

Serves: 5/Prep Time: 20 mins

Ingredients
- 3 tablespoons butter
- Crushed red pepper flakes, sea salt and black pepper, to taste
- 1½ pounds fresh green beans, trimmed and boiled
- 2 garlic cloves, minced
- 1½ teaspoons lemon pepper seasoning

Directions
1. Heat butter in a large skillet over medium high heat and add garlic, red pepper flakes and lemon pepper seasoning. Sauté for about 1 minute and add green beans.
2. Season with sea salt and black pepper and cook for about 5 minutes.
3. Dish out into a bowl and serve hot. You can store the green beans in the freezer for up to 3 months and they can be thawed before using.

Nutrition Amount per serving

Calories   106
Total Fat 7.1g   9%
Saturated Fat 4.4g   22%

Cholesterol 18mg   6%
Sodium 61mg   3%
Total Carbs 10.3g   4%

Dietary Fiber 4.8g   17%
Total Sugars 2g
Protein 2.7g

30-Day Dinner Keto Meal Prep

Spatchcock Turkey with Sage and Thyme

Serves: 24/Prep Time: 2 hours

Ingredients

- 3 tablespoons extra-virgin olive oil
- Salt and black pepper, to taste
- 2 tablespoons fresh thyme, chopped
- 1 tablespoon fresh sage, chopped
- 1 (12 pound) turkey, giblets removed

Directions

1. Preheat the oven to 45 F and grease a large roasting pan.
2. Mix together oil, thyme, sage, salt and black pepper in a bowl.
3. Dredge the turkey in this mixture and place in the roasting pan.
4. Bake for about 1 hours 45 minutes and remove from the oven to serve.
5. You can make this dish with turkey breasts or thighs too.

Nutrition Amount per serving

Calories   402
Total Fat 13.1g   17%
Saturated Fat 4g   20%

Cholesterol 172mg   57%
Sodium 159mg   7%
Total Carbs 0.3g   0%

Dietary Fiber 0.1g   1%
Total Sugars 0g
Protein 66.5g

Fried Cabbage with Kielbasa

Serves: 5/Prep Time: 20 mins

Ingredients

- 2 tablespoons red wine vinegar
- 6 tablespoons butter, divided
- 14 oz. kielbasa, thinly sliced
- Paprika, sea salt and black pepper, to taste
- 1 large head green cabbage, cored and sliced

Directions

1. Heat half of butter over medium heat in a large skillet and add kielbasa.
2. Sauté for about 3 minutes and add red wine vinegar.
3. Cook for about 2 minutes and stir in the green cabbage, paprika, sea salt and black pepper. Cook for about 5 minutes and dish out into a bowl to serve.
4. You can prepare the kielbasa mixture but do not add cabbage. Add cabbage when you reheat it.

Nutrition Amount per serving

Calories   308
Total Fat 27.8g   36%
Saturated Fat 13.7g   69%

Cholesterol 92mg   31%
Sodium 1055mg   46%
Total Carbs 4.2g   2%

Dietary Fiber 0.4g   2%
Total Sugars 0.6g
Protein 10.8g

Garlic Butter Beef Sirloin Steak

Serves: 6/Prep Time: 10 mins

Ingredients

- 1 teaspoon garlic powder
- Salt and black pepper, to taste
- 2 pounds beef top sirloin steaks
- 2 garlic cloves, minced
- ¼ cup butter

Directions

1. Heat butter in a wok and add beef top sirloin steaks.
2. Sauté for about 3 minutes and stir in the rest of the ingredients.

3. Cover the lid and cook on medium low heat for about 25 minutes.
4. Dish out into a bowl and serve hot.
5. Thaw properly if you are using frozen beef steaks.

Nutrition Amount per serving

Calories 352	Cholesterol 155mg 52%	Dietary Fiber 0.1g 0%
Total Fat 17.1g 22%	Sodium 154mg 7%	Total Sugars 0.1g
Saturated Fat 8.4g 42%	Total Carbs 0.7g 0%	Protein 46.1g

Garlic Prime Rib

Serves: 20/Prep Time: 9 hours 20 mins

Ingredients
- 2 tablespoons olive oil
- 1 (10 pound) prime rib roast
- Salt and black pepper, to taste
- 2 teaspoons dried thyme
- 10 garlic cloves, minced

Directions
1. Mix together olive oil, garlic, thyme, salt and black pepper in a small bowl.
2. Marinate the beef in the mixture for about 10 minutes.
3. Put the marinated beef in a slow cooker and cover with lid.
4. Cook on low for about 9 hours and dish out into a bowl to serve.

Nutrition Amount per serving

Calories 555	Cholesterol 135mg 45%	Dietary Fiber 0.1g 0%
Total Fat 41.9g 54%	Sodium 1269mg 55%	Total Sugars 0g
Saturated Fat 16.4g 82%	Total Carbs 3.3g 1%	Protein 37.9g

Keto Beef Pot Roast

Serves: 6/Prep Time: 45 mins

Ingredients
- ½ teaspoon garlic powder
- 2 pounds beef
- ½ teaspoon ginger powder
- Salt and black pepper, to taste
- 1 tablespoon avocado oil

Directions
1. Season the beef with ginger powder, garlic powder, salt and black pepper.
2. Heat avocado oil in a nonstick skillet and add beef.
3. Sauté for about 6 minutes on each side and close the lid.
4. Cook on medium low heat for about 30 minutes and dish out into a bowl to serve hot.
5. You can store the leftovers in the freezer for up to 3 months.

Nutrition Amount per serving

Calories 285	Cholesterol 135mg 45%	Dietary Fiber 0.2g 1%
Total Fat 9.7g 12%	Sodium 100mg 4%	Total Sugars 0.1g
Saturated Fat 3.6g 18%	Total Carbs 0.4g 0%	Protein 46g

Green Chile Pork Taco Bowl

Serves: 8/Prep Time: 35 mins

Ingredients
- 4 tablespoons olive oil
- Garlic powder, salt and black pepper
- 2 pounds pork sirloin roast, thickly sliced
- 20 oz. green chile tomatillo salsa, without added sugar
- 2 teaspoons cumin powder

Directions
1. Mix together cumin powder, garlic powder, salt and black pepper in a bowl.
2. Coat this mixture on both the sides of pork.
3. Heat olive oil in a pressure cooker and add pork with green chile tomatillo salsa.
4. Lock the lid and cook on High Pressure for about 25 minutes.

5. Naturally release the pressure and dish out into a bowl.
6. You can freeze the pork and defrost when required to make this dish.

Nutrition Amount per serving

Calories 324
Total Fat 17.8g 23%
Saturated Fat 4.9g 24%

Cholesterol 98mg 33%
Sodium 290mg 13%
Total Carbs 5.8g 2%

Dietary Fiber 2.6g 9%
Total Sugars 2.7g
Protein 32.5g

Keto Corned Beef

Serves: 4/Prep Time: 45 mins

Ingredients

- 4 whole peppercorns
- 2 pounds corned beef, flat cut
- ½ small onion, quartered

- 1 cup low sodium chicken broth
- 2 large bay leaves

Directions

1. Put all the ingredients along with the beef in a pressure cooker.
2. Lock the lid and cook on High Pressure for about 35 minutes.
3. Naturally release the pressure and dish out into a bowl.
4. You can freeze this dish for up to 3 months.

Nutrition Amount per serving

Calories 398
Total Fat 28.4g 36%
Saturated Fat 12.2g 61%

Cholesterol 142mg 47%
Sodium 2023mg 88%
Total Carbs 2.3g 1%

Dietary Fiber 0.3g 1%
Total Sugars 0.4g
Protein 31g

Thai Curry Insta Pork

Serves: 4/Prep Time: 55 mins

Ingredients

- 1 cup coconut milk, canned
- 1 pound pork tenderloin
- 2 tablespoons Thai curry paste

- ½ cup water
- 1 tablespoon butter

Directions

1. Mix together coconut milk, butter, Thai curry paste and water in a bowl.
2. Put the pork meat in a nonstick skillet and pour the Thai curry sauce over it.
3. Cover with lid and cook on medium low heat for 40 minutes.
4. Naturally release the pressure and dish out to serve hot.
5. Wrap in the plastic food wrap and store in the freezer for about 3 months.

Nutrition Amount per serving

Calories 333
Total Fat 21.2g 27%
Saturated Fat 15.9g 79%

Cholesterol 90mg 30%
Sodium 290mg 13%
Total Carbs 4.8g 2%

Dietary Fiber 1.3g 5%
Total Sugars 2.5g
Protein 31.1g

Lamb Roast

Serves: 6/Prep Time: 8 hours 10 mins

Ingredients

- ¼ cup carrots
- 1 cup beef broth
- 2 pounds lamb roasted Wegman's

- 1 cup onion soup
- ¼ cup potatoes

Directions

1. Put all the ingredients in a slow cooker and mix well.
2. Cover the lid and cook on Low for about 8 hours. Dish out into a bowl and serve hot.
3. You can use both the frozen and fresh lamb. Frozen lamb meat needs to be thawed.

Nutrition Amount per serving   Calories 355 Total Fat 18.8g 24% Saturated Fat 0.2g 1% Cholesterol 122mg 41% Sodium 483mg 21% Total Carbs 4.3g 2% Dietary Fiber 0.6g 2% Total Sugars 1.5g Protein 40g

Green Chili Adobo Turkey

Serves: 7/Prep Time: 40 mins

Ingredients
- 1 tablespoon Goya adobo all-purpose seasoning with pepper
- 2 pounds turkey breasts
- 1 cup green chilies, diced
- 2 cups tomatoes, diced
- 2 tablespoons butter

Directions
1. Season the turkey breasts with adobo seasoning on both sides.
2. Heat butter in a wok and add seasoned turkey breasts.
3. Cook for about 5 minutes per side and stir in the green chilies and tomatoes.
4. Cover the lid and cook on medium low heat for about 25 minutes.
5. Dish out into a bowl and serve hot.
6. You can store the leftovers in the freezer for up to 3 months.

Nutrition Amount per serving

Calories 190	Cholesterol 64mg 21%	Dietary Fiber 2.8g 10%
Total Fat 5.9g 8%	Sodium 1395mg 61%	Total Sugars 8.1g
Saturated Fat 2.6g 13%	Total Carbs 11.2g 4%	Protein 23.2g

Mediterranean Turkey Cutlets

Serves: 4/Prep Time: 25 mins

Ingredients
- 2 tablespoons olive oil
- 1 pound turkey cutlets
- ½ cup low carb flour mix
- 1 teaspoon Greek seasoning
- 1 teaspoon turmeric powder

Directions
1. Mix together turkey cutlets with low carb flour mix, turmeric powder and Greek seasoning in a bowl. Heat oil in a frying pan and add cutlets.
2. Cook on medium low heat for about 5 minutes on each side and dish out onto a platter to serve. Store these cutlets in the freezer for about 3 months.

Nutrition Amount per serving

Calories 284	Cholesterol 86mg 29%	Dietary Fiber 1.7g 6%
Total Fat 13.2g 17%	Sodium 482mg 21%	Total Sugars 2.6g
Saturated Fat 3g 15%	Total Carbs 5.5g 2%	Protein 34.9g

Keto Mustard Lemon Chicken

Serves: 6/Prep Time: 30 mins

Ingredients
- 1 cup chicken broth
- 2 pounds chicken thighs, boneless
- Italian seasoning, salt and black pepper, to taste
- 3 tablespoons Dijon mustard
- ¼ cup lemon juice

Directions
1. Season the chicken thighs with salt and black pepper.
2. Mix together chicken broth, lemon juice and Dijon mustard in a bowl.
3. Transfer this mixture to a skillet and add seasoned chicken thighs.
4. Cover with lid and cook on medium low heat for about 20 minutes.
5. Dish out onto a platter and serve hot.
6. Store in the fridge for about 1 day and warm before serving.

Nutrition Amount per serving

Calories 302	Cholesterol 135mg 45%	Dietary Fiber 0.3g 1%
Total Fat 11.9g 15%	Sodium 348mg 15%	Total Sugars 0.4g
Saturated Fat 3.2g 16%	Total Carbs 0.8g 0%	Protein 45g

Keto Citrus Turkey

Serves: 7/Prep Time: 35 mins

Ingredients

- 1 cup scallions, thinly sliced
- 2 pounds turkey breasts
- 9 ounces mandarin oranges, canned and drained
- Poultry seasoning and crushed red pepper flakes, to taste
- 4 tablespoons butter

Directions

1. Mix together mandarin oranges, scallions, poultry seasoning and crushed red pepper flakes in a bowl. Place turkey breasts in the pressure cooker and top with orange mixture.
2. Cover with lid and cook on High Pressure for about 25 minutes.
3. Dish out into a bowl and serve hot.
4. You can store the leftovers in the freezer for up to 3 months.

Nutrition Amount per serving

Calories 212	Cholesterol 73mg 24%	Dietary Fiber 1.4g 5%
Total Fat 8.8g 11%	Sodium 1366mg 59%	Total Sugars 8.2g
Saturated Fat 4.6g 23%	Total Carbs 10.3g 4%	Protein 22.7g

Special Salsa Beef Steak

Serves: 6/Prep Time: 45 mins

Ingredients

- 2 pounds beef steak
- 2 cups salsa
- 1 cup Monterey Jack cheese, shredded
- Garlic powder, salt and pepper, to taste
- ½ teaspoon hot pepper sauce

Directions

1. Season beef steak with garlic powder, salt and black pepper.
2. Mix together salsa and hot pepper sauce in a bowl.
3. Heat a nonstick skillet and add seasoned beef steak.
4. Cook for about 6 minutes on each side and stir in the salsa mixture.
5. Cook covered for about 20 minutes and dish out to serve warm.
6. You can store the leftovers in the freezer for up to 3 months.

Nutrition Amount per serving

Calories 375	Cholesterol 152mg 51%	Dietary Fiber 1.4g 5%
Total Fat 15.3g 20%	Sodium 721mg 31%	Total Sugars 2.8g
Saturated Fat 7.2g 36%	Total Carbs 5.6g 2%	Protein 51.8g

Keto Enticing Chicken

Serves: 8/Prep Time: 40 mins

Ingredients

- 1 tablespoon unsalted butter, melted
- 8 ounces fresh mushrooms, sliced
- 3 pounds boneless halved chicken breasts
- ¼ cup dry white wine
- Salt and black pepper, to taste

Directions

1. Mix together dry white wine, salt and black pepper in a bowl.
2. Heat butter in a skillet over medium heat and add chicken.
3. Sauté for about 6 minutes on both sides and stir in the mushrooms.
4. Cover with lid and cook for about 20 minutes. Dish out into a bowl and serve warm.
5. Refrigerate for up to 5 days and warm in microwave before serving.

Nutrition Amount per serving

Calories 207 Total Fat 3.8g 5% Saturated Fat 0.9g 5% Cholesterol 103mg 34% Sodium 116mg 5% Total Carbs 1.1g 0% Dietary Fiber 0.3g 1% Total Sugars 0.6g Protein 40.4g

Quick Beef

Serves: 6/Prep Time: 8 hours 10 mins

Ingredients
- 2 pounds grass fed beef
- ¾ cup homemade beef broth
- 1 tablespoon olive oil
- ½ cup cilantro, chopped
- Salt, to taste

Directions
1. Put beef along with rest of the ingredients in a slow cooker and cover with lid.
2. Cook on low for about 8 hours.
3. Dish out into a bowl and serve hot.
4. You can use both the frozen and fresh beef. Frozen beef meat needs to be thawed.

Nutrition Amount per serving

Calories 290	Cholesterol 100mg 33%	Dietary Fiber 0g 0%
Total Fat 17.1g 22%	Sodium 226mg 10%	Total Sugars 0g
Saturated Fat 6.4g 32%	Total Carbs 0.1g 0%	Protein 31.2g

Chicken Leg Quarters

Serves: 4/Prep Time: 30 mins

Ingredients
- 1 cup homemade chicken broth
- 2 tablespoons olive oil
- 4 skinless chicken leg quarters
- Salt and black pepper, to taste
- 1 teaspoon turmeric powder

Directions
1. Heat olive oil in a skillet over medium heat and add chicken.
2. Sauté for about 4 minutes on each side and add chicken broth, turmeric powder, salt and black pepper.
3. Cover the lid and cook on medium low heat for about 20 minutes.
4. Dish out into a bowl and serve hot.
5. You can store the leftovers in the freezer for up to 3 months.

Nutrition Amount per serving

Calories 262	Cholesterol 85mg 28%	Dietary Fiber 0.1g 0%
Total Fat 20.4g 26%	Sodium 371mg 16%	Total Sugars 0.2g
Saturated Fat 4.6g 23%	Total Carbs 0.6g 0%	Protein 20.3g

Keto Whole Chicken

Serves: 8/Prep Time: 40 mins

Ingredients
- 2 cups homemade chicken broth
- 3 pounds whole chicken, neck and giblet removed
- Salt and black pepper, to taste
- 2 tablespoons olive oil
- 1 tablespoon cayenne pepper

Directions
1. Season the chicken with cayenne pepper, salt and black pepper.
2. Heat olive oil in a skillet over medium heat and add chicken.
3. Sauté for about 4 minutes per side and stir in the chicken broth.
4. Cover with lid and cook on medium low heat for about 30 minutes.
5. Dish out into a bowl and serve hot.
6. Refrigerate for up to 5 days and warm in microwave before serving.

Nutrition Amount per serving

Calories 361	Cholesterol 137mg 46%	Dietary Fiber 0.2g 1%
Total Fat 25.2g 32%	Sodium 313mg 14%	Total Sugars 0.2g
Saturated Fat 6.7g 33%	Total Carbs 0.6g 0%	Protein 33.2g

Moroccan Fish

Serves: 8/Prep Time: 10 mins
Ingredients
- 3 pounds salmon fillets
- 1 pound cherry tomatoes, crushed slightly
- 1 tablespoon fresh basil leaves, torn
- 1 tablespoon butter
- Salt and crushed red pepper flakes, to taste

Directions
1. Heat butter in a skillet and add salmon fillets.
2. Sauté for about 4 minutes and stir in the rest of the ingredients.
3. Cover and cook for about 30 minutes.
4. Dish out onto a platter and serve hot.
5. You can store the leftovers in the freezer for up to 3 months.

Nutrition Amount per serving

Calories 249
Total Fat 12.1g 16%
Saturated Fat 2.4g 12%

Cholesterol 79mg 26%
Sodium 107mg 5%
Total Carbs 2.4g 1%

Dietary Fiber 0.8g 3%
Total Sugars 1.5g
Protein 33.6g

Quick Cod

Serves: 6/Prep Time: 25 mins
Ingredients
- 3 lemon slices
- 2 pounds salmon fillets
- 3 teaspoons fresh lemon juice
- Salt and black pepper, to taste
- 1 tablespoon tamari

Directions
1. Preheat the oven to 350°F and lightly grease a baking sheet.
2. Season the salmon fillets with salt and black pepper and transfer onto the baking sheet.
3. Squeeze the lemon juice and tamari over the salmon fillets and top with lemon slices.
4. Bake for about 15 minutes and dish out onto a platter to serve.
5. Wrap in plastic food wrap and store in the freezer for about 3 months.

Nutrition Amount per serving

Calories 203
Total Fat 9.4g 12%
Saturated Fat 1.4g 7%

Cholesterol 67mg 22%
Sodium 235mg 10%
Total Carbs 0.6g 0%

Dietary Fiber 0.1g 1%
Total Sugars 0.2g
Protein 29.7g

Keto Easy Mahi Mahi Fillets

Serves: 5/Prep Time: 25 mins
Ingredients
- 5 garlic cloves, minced
- 5 (8 ounce) mahi mahi fillets
- 5 tablespoons feta cheese
- Red pepper flakes, salt and black pepper, to taste
- 5 tablespoons fresh lime juice

Directions
1. Preheat the oven to 350°F and lightly grease a baking sheet.
2. Season mahi mahi fillets with salt and black pepper and arrange on the baking sheet.
3. Mix together garlic, red pepper flakes and lime juice in a bowl.
4. Pour this mixture over the fillets and place in the oven.
5. Bake for about 15 minutes and dish out to serve.
6. You can store the leftovers in the freezer for up to 4 months.

Nutrition Amount per serving

Calories 215
Total Fat 2.1g 3%
Saturated Fat 1.4g 7%

Cholesterol 89mg 30%
Sodium 296mg 13%
Total Carbs 3.1g 1%

Dietary Fiber 0.3g 1%
Total Sugars 0.8g
Protein 43.8g

Foolproof Cod Fillets

Serves: 6/Prep Time: 20 mins

Ingredients
- 6 lemon slices
- 2 pounds cod fillets
- 2 tablespoons butter
- Garlic powder, salt and black pepper, to taste
- 3 fresh dill sprigs

Directions
1. Preheat the oven to 350°F and lightly grease a baking sheet.
2. Season the cod fillets with garlic powder, salt and black pepper.
3. Arrange on the baking sheet and top with lemon slices, dill and butter.
4. Transfer to the oven and bake for about 18 minutes.
5. Dish out onto a platter and serve hot.
6. Wrap in the plastic food wrap and store in the freezer for about 3 months.

Nutrition Amount per serving

Calories 160	Cholesterol 84mg 28%	Dietary Fiber 0.3g 1%
Total Fat 5.2g 7%	Sodium 123mg 5%	Total Sugars 0.3g
Saturated Fat 2.4g 12%	Total Carbs 1.3g 0%	Protein 27.3g

Low Carb Flavored Pork

Serves: 4/Prep Time: 5 mins

Ingredients
- 4 (4 ounce) pork chops
- 2 tablespoons butter
- 1 (14 ounce) can sugar free diced tomatoes
- 2 tablespoons fresh lemon juice
- Salt and black pepper, to taste

Directions
1. Heat butter in a skillet and add pork chops.
2. Sauté for about 3 minutes per side and season with salt and black pepper.
3. Mix well and add tomatoes, lemon juice, salt and black pepper.
4. Cover the lid and cook for about 35 minutes. Dish out into a bowl and serve hot.
5. Store in the fridge for about 3 days and warm before serving.

Nutrition Amount per serving

Calories 451	Cholesterol 113mg 38%	Dietary Fiber 0g 0%
Total Fat 34g 44%	Sodium 157mg 7%	Total Sugars 0.2g
Saturated Fat 14.3g 71%	Total Carbs 0.2g 0%	Protein 29.1g

Stuffed Chicken with Asparagus and Bacon

Serves: 8/Prep Time: 50 mins

Ingredients
- ½ teaspoon salt
- 8 chicken tenders
- ¼ teaspoon black pepper
- 8 bacon slices
- 12 asparagus spears

Directions
1. Preheat the oven to 400°F and lightly grease a baking sheet.
2. Put 2 bacon slices on a baking sheet and top with 2 chicken tenders.
3. Season with salt and black pepper and drop in 3 spears of asparagus.
4. Wrap asparagus and chicken inside the bacon slices and make 3 more.
5. Transfer to the oven and bake for about 40 minutes.
6. You can store the leftovers in the freezer for up to 3 months.

Nutrition Amount per serving   Calories 300 Total Fat 15.4g 20% Saturated Fat 4.7g 23% Cholesterol 110mg 37% Sodium 673mg 29% Total Carbs 1.7g 1% Dietary Fiber 0.8g 3% Total Sugars 0.7g Protein 36.8g

Baked Sausage with Creamy Basil Sauce

Serves: 6/Prep Time: 45 mins

Ingredients

- 1½ cups cream cheese
- 2 pounds Italian sausage
- 4 tablespoons basil pesto
- 1½ cups mozzarella cheese, shredded
- 4 tablespoons heavy cream

Directions

1. Preheat the oven to 400°F and lightly grease a casserole dish.
2. Arrange sausage in the casserole dish and transfer to the oven.
3. Bake for about 30 minutes and dish out into a bowl.
4. Whisk together cream cheese, heavy cream and basil pesto in a bowl.
5. Pour this cheese sauce over the sausages and transfer to the oven.
6. Bake for about 10 minutes and remove from the oven to serve.
7. You can store the leftovers in the freezer for up to 4 months

Nutrition Amount per serving

Calories 545
Total Fat 46.1g 59%
Saturated Fat 19g 95%
Cholesterol 140mg 47%
Sodium 1043mg 45%
Total Carbs 1.6g 1%
Dietary Fiber 0g 0%
Total Sugars 0.1g
Protein 29.8g

Low Carb Pork Medallions

Serves: 3/Prep Time: 30 mins

Ingredients

- 3 medium shallots, finely chopped
- 1 pound pork tenderloin, cut into ½ inch thick slices
- ¼ cup olive oil
- Salt and black pepper, to taste
- 3 tablespoons basil

Directions

1. Press shallots on both sides of the pork.
2. Heat oil over medium heat in a skillet and add pork and shallots.
3. Season with salt and black pepper and cook for about 8 minutes on both sides.
4. Dish out onto a platter and top with basils to serve.
5. Wrap in the plastic food wrap and store in the freezer for about 3 months.

Nutrition Amount per serving

Calories 397
Total Fat 22.2g 28%
Saturated Fat 4.2g 21%
Cholesterol 110mg 37%
Sodium 92mg 4%
Total Carbs 8.5g 3%
Dietary Fiber 0.1g 0%
Total Sugars 0g
Protein 40.9g

Mozzarella and Pesto Chicken Casserole

Serves: 8/Prep Time: 40 mins

Ingredients

- 2 cups cream cheese, softened
- ¼ cup pesto
- ½ cup heavy cream
- 2 pounds chicken breasts, cooked and cubed
- 2 cups mozzarella cheese, cubed

Directions

1. Preheat the oven to 400°F and lightly grease a large casserole dish.
2. Mix together cream cheese, pesto and heavy cream in a bowl.
3. Stir in the chicken cubes and mozzarella cheese.
4. Move to the casserole dish and place in the oven.
5. Bake for about 30 minutes and remove from the oven to serve warm.
6. Refrigerate for up to 3 days and warm in microwave before serving

Nutrition Amount per serving Calories 454 Total Fat 29.3g 38% Saturated Fat 13.9g 70% Cholesterol 159mg 53% Sodium 402mg 17% Total Carbs 2.5g 1% Dietary Fiber 0.1g 0% Total Sugars 0.6g Protein 43.9g

Spinach and Bacon Salad

Serves: 8/Prep Time: 10 mins

Ingredients
- 2 eggs, boiled and sliced
- 8 pieces thick sliced bacon, cooked and chopped
- ½ medium red onion, thinly sliced
- 10 oz. organic baby spinach
- ½ cup mayonnaise

Directions
1. Mix together baby spinach and mayonnaise in a bowl.
2. Fold in the rest of the ingredients and serve.
3. Store in the fridge for about 2 days and warm before serving

Nutrition Amount per serving

Calories 219	Cholesterol 67mg 22%	Dietary Fiber 0.9g 3%
Total Fat 19.2g 25%	Sodium 563mg 24%	Total Sugars 0.5g
Saturated Fat 4.5g 22%	Total Carbs 2.3g 1%	Protein 9.5g

Spicy Baked Chicken

Serves: 3/Prep Time: 55 mins

Ingredients
- ½ cup salsa
- 1 pound boneless, skinless chicken breasts
- 4 ounces cream cheese, cut into large chunks
- Salt and black pepper, to taste
- 1 teaspoon parsley, finely chopped

Directions
1. Preheat the oven to 350°F and lightly grease a baking dish.
2. Heat salsa, cream cheese, salt and black pepper in a saucepan, stirring constantly.
3. Place chicken in the baking dish and pour in the cream cheese sauce.
4. Transfer to the oven and bake for about 45 minutes.
5. Remove from the oven and garnish with parsley to serve.
6. You can store the leftovers in the freezer for up to 5 months.

Nutrition Amount per serving

Calories 431	Cholesterol 176mg 59%	Dietary Fiber 0.7g 3%
Total Fat 24.5g 31%	Sodium 502mg 22%	Total Sugars 1.4g
Saturated Fat 11.4g 57%	Total Carbs 3.8g 1%	Protein 47.3g

Tortilla Pork Rind Wraps

Serves: 4/Prep Time: 40 mins

Ingredients
- 3 ounces pork rinds, crushed
- 4 large eggs
- ½ teaspoon garlic powder
- ¼ cup coconut oil
- ¼ cup water

Directions
1. Put pork rinds, eggs, garlic powder and water in a food processor and process until smooth.
2. Heat a little oil over medium low heat in a nonstick skillet and add 3 tablespoons of the batter.
3. Cook for about 5 minutes on both sides and repeat with the remaining batter.
4. Dish out onto a platter and serve hot.
5. Store in the fridge for about 2 days and warm before serving.

Nutrition Amount per serving

Calories 312	Cholesterol 216mg 72%	Dietary Fiber 0g 0%
Total Fat 26.2g 34%	Sodium 480mg 21%	Total Sugars 0.5g
Saturated Fat 16.4g 82%	Total Carbs 0.6g 0%	Protein 20g

Bottom Line

The keto diet plan by far has been the most befitting weight loss plan with numerous health benefits. Switching from carbs to ketones can literally change your life in ways enabling you to have a healthy and sound life without any hindrance.

Made in the USA
San Bernardino, CA
21 July 2019